Good Housekeeping
HOME MAKEOVER

Good Housekeeping
Institute
TRIED·TESTED·TRUSTED

Good Housekeeping

HOME
MAKEOVER

Emma Callery
and the GOOD HOUSEKEEPING INSTITUTE

TED SMART

A TED SMART Publication 2000

First published in 1999

1 3 5 7 9 10 8 6 4 2

First published in the United Kingdom in 1999 by Ebury Press
Random House, 20 Vauxhall Bridge Road, London SW1V 2SA

Random House Australia (Pty) Limited
20 Alfred Street, Milsons Point Sydney,
New South Wales 2061, Australia

Random House New Zealand Limited
18 Poland Road, Glenfield, Auckland 10 New Zealand

Random House South Africa (Pty) Limited
Endulini, 5a Jubilee Road, Parktown 2193, South Africa

Random House UK Limited Reg. No. 954009

A CIP catalogue record for this book is available from the British
Library.

Project Editor Emma Callery
Designed and Art Directed by Ruth Prentice
Text for Part 2 by Trisha Schofield
Illustations by Kate Simunek
Styling for all new photography by Tessa Evelegh

Printed and bound in Slovenia by Delo Tiskarna, d.d.
by arrangement with Korotan – Ljubljana d.o.o.

CONTENTS

INTRODUCTION

Your home is as individual as your fingerprint. Architecturally, it may well be the same as the whole street but the interior will be unique because home is a personal space where we can express our own personality and style.

But what we all need are ideas, inspiration and information so we can turn thoughts and dreams into reality. This book will provide all you need to make the most of your home, whatever your chosen style. These pages can partner your plans for anything from transforming the whole house to simply changing the curtains. Use it to fuel your imagination and as a reference book for projects large and small.

Good Housekeeping is Britain's best known monthly magazine and our experts at the Good Housekeeping Institute are well used to giving impartial advice on consumer choices and practical projects to homemakers. Their guidance in our *Home Makeover* book is based on years of experience and the understanding that wherever you live is a very special place indeed.

Pat Roberts Cairns
Editor-in-chief

RIGHT: The well-planned living room. Neutral shades predominate in the decor with splashes of green and terracotta to give a subtle lift. It is the small details that make the space look so complete. The rope tieback with chunky tassel, the bobbly edging around the cushions, and the ultra-tall lily in the corner have each been carefully chosen with this room in mind.

Assessing the situation

Whatever changes you make to your home – whether it's on the scale that involves hiring builders, electricians and plumbers or adding a few decorative touches here and there – you will always need to stand back and take an objective view of the rooms before going any further. If it is a major overhaul that you are planning, take this opportunity to get right down to basics. Once the room is decorated, it is unlikely that you will want to think about changing the lighting, installing a fireplace or adding a built-in shelving unit. Look to the check list opposite and consider each aspect fully. These are pointers aimed at guiding you in the right direction.

BELOW: Before building bookshelves and choosing soft furnishing materials, assess the fabric of the room and plan alterations to suit your current requirements.

It can be very difficult to visualise what a room could look like, especially when it is filled with furniture and if there are pictures hanging on the walls, ornaments ranged on shelves and rugs scattered around the floor. If you have difficulty imagining how to change the room, experiment by removing as much as possible and then move the furniture about. The proportions of a room can look quite different if you move that two-seater sofa from one wall to another and turn a rectangular rug through ninety degrees.

Of course, this type of experimentation is all very well if you just have a few pieces of furniture but if there is a piano, dining table or heavy display cabinet to lug about, the matter is quite different. Buy some squared paper and draw a scaled plan of the room onto it – don't forget to add the doors (and which way they open), windows and any other permanent fixtures such as radiators and sockets (although these could always be moved if you found the ideal furniture arrangement that blocked these items). Also make scaled templates of your larger pieces of furniture and then have fun playing around with them to see what you can come up with. For an especially thorough job, you should ideally draw a scale drawing of each wall of the room, too – called an elevation – and you can then double check that your ideas fit together heightwise too.

Once you have firmed up your plans for arranging the major elements in the room, sketch in potential lighting and decor ideas. Think about whether you prefer to have a wallpaper, perhaps with a co-ordinating or contrasting border, or paint finish and what sort of soft furnishings you like. Do you enjoy traditional styling or want a more contemporary, clean finish? To a certain extent the direction that the room faces will help you determine your colours for finishing so read the sections overleaf on colour, pattern and texture before going any further.

Determining your style

Some people just seem to know instinctively what decor suits them and their surroundings, but it isn't always straightforward. With the myriad styles featured in magazines, books and television programmes it can be difficult to stand back and decide what you want for your home.

To help focus your ideas, get hold of as many magazines and interiors catalogues as possible and tear out any pages with rooms and colours that appeal. You will very quickly start to see a pattern emerging. Maybe you find that you predominantly like traditional shades with classic furnishings or all those pale shades of aqua, pink and grey leap out at you. Whatever your taste, keep these tear sheets together to act as a reminder. Cut out a few or your favourite photographs and pin them to a board or large piece of card – this will be the beginning of your sample board and is something to be treasured as you will be adding to it as you continue to read on.

MAKING CHANGES

Work through this list and then after you have read the text overleaf on colour, pattern and texture you can begin to make your plans, as outlined on pages 14-15.

◆ Do you want to add any major features, such as:
– a fireplace
– built-in shelving
– lights that will need to be traced into the wall
– radiators
– electricity points
– television point?

◆ Do you want to change or add architectural details, such as:
– windows
– door frames
– mouldings (eg cornice, picture rail, dado rail)
– skirting boards
– flooring finish?

◆ Which direction does the room face? Is it light and airy or dark and atmospheric? Do you want to enhance these features or disguise them?

◆ Are you happy with the rooms' proportions? Do you want to enhance these features or disguise them?

Colour

When it comes to decorating a room, colour is the current buzz-word. With leading paint manufacturers producing almost any shade you desire and a profusion of paint specialists developing traditional colour ranges and increasingly flexible paints, there is huge scope for creativity. But where to begin? You already have the beginnings of your sample board so you know which colours naturally appeal to you – but are they right for the room that you are decorating? Do you need to add an extra colour to give it a lift? Do you need to use colour in one part of the room for a specific job?

To assess this, look first to the direction that your room faces. The amount of daylight that comes into the room will affect its atmosphere and this may or may not be what you aspire to for the setting you are intent on creating. So use colour to enhance or disguise the room's natural properties (see the box, opposite). To help you finalise your decisions as to the colour or colours that you would like to use, buy some tester pots in your favoured shades and paint them onto your sample board. It is extraordinary how two shades of cream can look so different when next to each other and/or another colour. Depending on what colours the creams are mixed with, the overall effect can be warming or cooling, and reflections from adjacent colours come into play too.

Consider whether you will use colour as a backdrop to your room combining it with patterned and textural elements (see overleaf) or whether you will make play of colour alone. Decide whether you want one colour or two and how you will combine them and in what ratio. If you have existing furnishings that you want to keep, you will need to find colours to complement them so work with these items very much in the forefront of your mind. If there is one colour that you especially like but can't find it in any of the paint brochures, consider having it mixed – almost any colour you like can be achieved in this way.

BELOW & RIGHT: By painting the same room in two strongly opposed colours the power of light and dark becomes obvious. The white kitchen appears to recede, whereas the blue jumps out of the page. The wall looks so much nearer. In reality this would make a small kitchen look yet smaller – but could be very dramatic in a larger one.

Colour effects

Much has been written about the colour wheel but it is well worth bearing in mind its basic principles when planning the contents of your room.

• Divided into the primary colours red, yellow and blue, secondary colours are then achieved by mixing together two of the colours in different quantities. More subtle colours are achieved by further mixes.

• As a result, harmonious colours have the same base – red, yellow or blue – and are found next or near to each other on the colour wheel. By using various shades of one colour or different colours derived from the same base, harmonious colour schemes are achieved.

• Contrasting colours have different bases and the further away they are from each other on the colour wheel, the more obvious the colour change. Subtle use can be made of this to give the room a lift by decorating it mainly in one colour but adding highlights in a colour from the opposite side of the wheel as an occasional accent. Skirting boards and window and door frames, a rug or even a coloured vase are perfect ways to do this.

• One half of the wheel contains warm shades and the other half is cool. Use them to your advantage. Remember, too, that dark and warm colours advance, pale and cool colours recede.

USING COLOUR TO IMPROVE THE SPACE

✦ For a dark, north-facing room or a room with small windows look to white, creams and pastel colours so that the space will look as large and light as possible. Pale colours reflect light.

✦ A room that has big windows and is very sunny can be decorated with any colour depending on whether you would like to retain its brightness or develop something a bit more muted. Cool colours will tone down the room, warm colours enhance its sunny properties.

✦ For a high-ceilinged room, look to warm colours for painting the ceiling. Warm colours advance so will make the ceiling look lower.

✦ To develop this theme still further, use a colour that is darker than the walls, which will make the ceiling appear even lower. For yet more effect – and this is especially good if you have a picture rail – paint the top of the walls the same colour as the ceiling. Alternatively, paint a ceiling in a paler colour than the walls to heighten it.

✦ A long narrow corridor benefits from pale colours on the walls, ceiling and floor (even more if the colour is from the cool side of the colour wheel); to shorten it, paint a dark or warm colour at the end.

✦ A narrow corridor with high walls would definitely benefit from colours on the ceiling and floor that are quite a bit darker than those used on the walls.

Pattern and texture

Traditional or contemporary, striped or flowery, large or small, abstract or specific, subtle or bold: these are just a few of the decisions that need to be taken before venturing into the world of pattern. Look to pattern in the form of wallpapers, borders, soft furnishing fabrics or paint effects. You may prefer to wallpaper an entire room or just one or two walls; you may like to paint a wall and then add pattern with a border running at dado height (conventionally one-third of the way up the wall) or along the top of the wall; or add stencilled or stamped patterns wherever you please.

One way to decorate a room – and probably the most obvious – is to use plain colours as a backdrop. Paint is the easiest finish, but there are some wonderfully subtle wallpapers that incorporate a slight pattern. Then you can add pattern to the room through curtains and cushions and throws. In this way, the finished effect is not too overpowering and you can also ring the changes more easily by, say, swapping around cushions and making lightweight, unlined curtains for the summer and heavier, lined ones for the winter months.

But don't feel constrained to this way of thinking. It is perfectly viable to combine different patterns and if you don't feel especially confident about doing this, there are many co-ordinated ranges produced by textile and wallpaper manufacturers to do the work for you. Papers, borders and fabrics are designed to work well together and can be helpful if you aren't quite sure about what would look good together.

One word of warning though – when it comes to mixing different patterns, ensure that they are at least taken from a similar range of colours. Or if you want to mix colours, use variations of the same design. If you have too many colours and patterns, the end result will be a rather confusing jumble of images.

When texture also comes into play the combination of effects that can be created in your home becomes endless. Over the last few years many new textured fabrics have been developed and with the neutral setting so much in vogue these textures have come into their own as a way to create visual variety or give a focus to a room. Fake fur, leather, slubby cottons and silks, mohair and wool all have their place in the soft furnishing department of stores. Mix and match and add some tactile pleasures to your living and sleeping spaces.

Right: The patterns and textures used in this room may be varied but basing them on a simple checked pattern and only mixing shades of blue means that they are not too disparate. The furnishings look great and have a tremendous tactile quality.

SAMPLE BOARD

By now, you will have room styles and paint colours that you like attached to your sample board.

✦ Pin wallpaper and fabric swatches to it, too. If you plan on mixing different patterns, this is a good place to experiment.

✦ If you want to use large patterns it helps to get hold of as big a sample as possible as it is almost impossible to determine what it will look like from a small scrap.

✦ Bear in mind the sketches that you made of the room when assessing it and the ideas you have for window furnishings, in particular. The scale of these will have a bearing on the types of patterns you would like to use.

✦ Attach textured swatches and any trimming and other accessories you wish to incorporate into the room's decor. Whereas swatches for patterned fabrics and papers can be too small, there is no problem with textured accessories. You can still tell how smooth or rough something is from a small quantity.

✦ Once you have amassed all this material you will need to narrow it down to a workable size. So go ahead and choose the main decorating colour and whatever patterns and textures you like.

✦ Do all this in daylight so that you can determine the true colour of items and check that they complement each other well.

Making plans

The sequence of events for decorating a room is crucial – particularly if you are hiring people to do a lot of the nitty gritty for you. Lists are the order of the day and plenty of time spent in the planning process should enable the transformation to take place as smoothly as possible. Discovering that you would like some light fittings traced into the wall after you have painted the surface would, after all, represent quite a considerable waste of time. Read through the order of events in the box opposite and write down your own requirements in the same sequence.

Hiring help

If you have several jobs for, say, a joiner to do, list these separately so that you will then be able to compile a brief for getting quotations. Ideally, you should get two or three quotations so that you can really compare prices, but this can all too often be easier said than done. Even getting hold of one tradesperson can mean numerous phone calls, so if you use somebody regularly and know you can trust that person it is worth a lot more than saving a few pounds to get the cheapest work. However, get a quotation in advance nevertheless so that you know what to budget for.

If you haven't employed anyone before, ask around for recommendations. If you see some work that has been done especially well or whose style you like, ask who did it. Word of mouth really is the best way to achieve good results; a name out of a telephone directory tells you nothing about workmanship, reliability or value for money. Having said that, a professional will always be able to tell you of other jobs he or she has done and if you are planning on hiring an interior designer, there should be a portfolio available to show you style and previous work.

When you are briefing other people, it is best to get as much of the detail you require down in writing. For example, how many electrical points you would like and where, what type of wood you would like used for your shelves, what pelmet ideas you have. These may well change in the course of discussions but at least you have an outline to base your meeting on. Once you have settled on what you want, revise the brief if necessary – again in writing – and then sit back and wait for the quotation. In this way, both you and the person you are hiring know what is required.

RIGHT: All those lists and plans will have been well worth the trouble when you reach the end. You can then sit down and put up your feet while you survey the room and marvel at all that has been achieved.

THE ORDER OF EVENTS

✦ Get right back to the basics. Strip any existing wallpaper, lift up carpets.

✦ If necessary, put in a damp course.

✦ Plan lighting and electricity points and employ an electrician.

✦ Plan plumbing and heating requirements and employ a plumber and heating engineer.

✦ Plan flooring. If floor to be tiled, consider employing a tiler.

✦ Plan woodwork and employ a joiner. Install flooring if new floorboards.

✦ Make good walls and ceiling, with new plastering if necessary, and prepare any previously painted surfaces.

✦ Decorate ceiling, walls and then woodwork.

✦ Install soft or semi-hard flooring.

✦ Finish off with the soft furnishings.

1

Designs for Living

LIVING ROOMS

ABOVE: *Shades of blue and aqua combine to create a restrained setting. Collections of family photographs and some special pieces of glass give the room those final personal touches.*

Today's living room is a versatile space. It is a place for sitting quietly to read in; it is somewhere that you share with friends and family for conversation or a game or two; the television and perhaps a computer will be situated in it, and you may also need to make space for a small work area or your dining table. So, before you even begin to think of your decorating plans, sit down with anyone else who lives with you and decide exactly how you will be using the room. You will then be able to allocate space as necessary and plan your colour schemes accordingly.

Start with those things you can't see: don't treat the electrics as an afterthought. Think about ways of hiding the cabling and flexes for media equipment, such as inside walls and under floorboards, and at the same time, maybe look at installing speakers in the ceiling, walls or floor. Today's choice of light fittings are also likely to include some re-plastering when they are installed so you need to think of your requirements now too.

When planning your lighting scheme, bear in mind your discussed activities – and have a potential furniture arrangement in mind, too. Essentially, you will need to

RIGHT: *This living room is large enough to have two seating areas and the furniture has been arranged so the fireplace is the focal point in one side and a desk in the other.*

combine atmospheric lighting with some more specific task lighting. For a warm evening light, you may want to provide general light from wall-mounted or free-standing uplighters, which throw a wash of light up to the ceiling. Introduce a standard lamp or two and you have a very versatile lighting scheme. Alternatively, if you have a gloomy, north-facing room and want to create a realistic daytime effect, set a series of halogen downlighters into the ceiling. But ensure that you also have dimmer switches for the lights; halogen is so white when turned on to full brightness, it can be difficult to achieve a more subtle light for the evening.

Focal points

Now consider your furniture and its layout. 'Where can we put this?' is not a good starting point for furnishing a room. Instead, begin by deciding which part of the room you want to make into the focal point. If you have a fireplace, for example, this would most naturally form the focus for your seating arrangements. Or you may have a fine view from large windows that you like to look at. If your living room is a large space, there could be an opportunity for you to have two seating areas – one for relaxing in, grouped around a low coffee table, for example, and the other for watching television.

Most people don't want to have a television as a focal point in a room, but you need to think through how you are going to watch it and/or conceal it, so that you can get at it easily and enjoy it from a comfortable chair. To prevent modern technology from getting in the way of the finished look – or appearing as though it has been dropped into the scheme by some passing bird – it is much easier and more effective to have the television in the place you want to watch it, but installed in a cupboard, together with your sound system if you have one. The doors can then be closed in seconds, shutting everything away.

When building or adapting cupboards for televisions and other technology think about ergonomics – make sure the television sits on a shelf at a comfortable height for viewing, and allow for space above and below for storage or music systems. Also, electrical appliances

choosing light bulbs 182-183   choosing fireplaces 188-189

LEFT: *When shelves are filled with books they can form a very heavy backdrop to a room. Here, the living room shelves are being used for display purposes with rows of family photographs and favourite pieces of china.*

ABOVE & OPPOSITE: *Here are two very different styles of living room. One is restrained and makes great play of natural materials and the other is filled with personal mementoes. Each says a lot about the people who live in them.*

◀ planning colour 10-11   ◀ planning pattern & texture 12-13

generate heat so ensure there are holes in the back or sides to allow for a good circulation of air.

Furniture choices

It is more likely than not that you already own some pieces of living room furniture – a sofa and armchair or two, say. But if you are completely re-decorating a living room take this opportunity to take stock of your furniture and decide if there is anything else you need, or if you would be better served by selling one or two of your pieces, replacing them with something more suitable.

Anyone with a loft or storage space can also ring the changes: regularly moving furniture in and out of a room can mean that you don't have to make difficult choices between, say, two tables, and finish up cluttering the room with both. 'Inherited' pieces of furniture often cause the most problems in decorating. Emotional attachment or mere habit means that all too easily they sit there for year after year. Consider putting all such pieces into auction, and spend the result on one item of furniture that you really want or need.

Changing the backdrop

Now that you have established the basic outline of your living room and installed any messy light fittings, the fun can really begin with choosing decorating colours, patterns and textures. You may already own a much-loved rug, brightly coloured curtains or a piece of furniture that will be the starting point for your colour scheme, or be starting totally fresh. Whatever your situation, you will first need to decide on the overall style of the end result. Do you want a light, airy living room; a jewel-bright interior featuring splashes of bright colour, or a dark, mysterious space ripe for intimate evenings? Do you want a spare, minimal effect; have you travelled widely and brought back with you great collections from afar that you want to display to best effect; do contemporary shades of citrus green and orange appeal? Does your room demand a traditional treatment to enhance a period property or would you prefer a contemporary setting? These may be extreme ends of the decorating

spectrum but by considering them you will focus your thoughts on what you like and feel you can live with.

If you have plain painted walls, say, you might choose to go for patterned fabrics that tone in with the backgrounds or look at plain fabrics, perhaps with a roughly hewn texture but in a contrasting colour to the background. Likewise, walls that have been wallpapered or painted with patterns, colourwashed, stippled or some other paint effect benefit from plainer dressings at windows and on seating. By creating a sample board, you will arrive at a workable scheme for background

colours and soft furnishings, and you can then set to work to apply your choices as time and money dictate

Tread carefully

After walls and ceilings, the floor is the next largest surface area in a room and whatever you choose will have a dramatic effect on the end result. Neutral, no-fashion, safe floors work very well in most environments: a dark or strong coloured floor can make a room look smaller, and also ties you to one colour range. There is no doubt that fitting, say, a burgundy red carpet, however magnificent, throughout the house will limit your scope for making changes later on, whereas all the natural hues, such as wood, terracotta and sisal (or carpeting in those shades) will go with more or less anything. Add a rug or two for extra cosiness under foot with flashes of colour to tone in or contrast with the main decorative colour in the room.

Soft furnishing fabrics

And so onto soft furnishings – all those finishing touches that can make or break a living room. Whether deciding on fabric for small extras like cushions and throws or for larger areas like the window treatments and upholstery, the soft furnishing fabric represents one of the main considerations in a living room and they can be an expensive one, too. Reupholstering a sofa and buying curtain materials are major purchases. The temptation is often to play safe and choose fabrics that you hope you won't tire of, or which won't go out of fashion because they weren't in fashion to start with. This approach can work well, but can sometimes be rather depressing.

To create long-lasting, pleasing interiors look at texture rather than pattern. Knobbly tweeds, smooth silk and varied weaves create depth without making too big a statement. Having said that, a really glorious curtain treatment in stunning fabric will always provide a striking focus, particularly if the room is otherwise featureless. Perhaps the most important thing is to keep looking and trying out swatches until you can be confident that whether a fabric is a restrained neutral or a blaze of colour, it's the one you like the best.

A cheaper way to change your furnishings is to disguise them with throws and piles of cushions. A large piece of fabric casually draped over the back of an armchair or sofa will add whatever style you desire. You can easily and quickly brighten or cool down the rest of the decor and with cushions you can experiment with colours in a comparatively cheap way. As the amount of

LEFT: By combining fabrics that are similar in colour it is possible to use various patterns in the same room. Here different checks and stripes sit side by side for an overall effect that is warm and fiery.

RIGHT: *Soft rose pink, pale mauve and powdery blue combine in the foreground against yellow walls. These are enriched by the subtle marbelled veins running across the surface.*

OPPOSITE: *To echo the simplicity of the room's furnishings, the window has been dressed with a plain canvas roller blind. It can be pulled down during the day to tone down the sunlight that floods in, or at night for privacy.*

fabric needed to cover a pad is small there is plenty of scope to be had with your choices. Mix textures, patterns or colours; mix textures and patterns, colours and patterns, or textures and colours; but don't mix all three. If there is too much variety, the effect will be overkill. When choosing several different patterns for cushion covers, go for patterns that use a similar colour palette. To unify the cushions further, surround them with piping covered with the same, plain fabric; or add the same tassels to the corners of each.

Wonderful windows

Living rooms provide the most scope for stunning curtain treatments, and if you have a featureless room with modern windows, curtain effects are a good way of adding the kind of decorative detail that is usually supplied by architecture. However, there are many factors to be taken into account before deciding on the final shape and fabric of the curtains such as how much nat-

ural light you want or whether there is a strong architectural or decorative style in the room that needs a complementary curtain treatment. A low ceiling, for example, makes an elaborate pelmet treatment difficult to carry off, and a dark room will be made even gloomier with thick, heavy curtains hanging sumptuously over a small window area. Conversely, a too low window can be made to seem higher with a tall pelmet, or a narrow window can look wider with a lavish curtain treatment taken across the wall on either side.

If light is important, ensure that when the curtains are drawn back they do not obscure too much of the window, or use a delicate fabric that lets in plenty of light (assuming you don't need curtains to retain warmth in the cooler months). The sun's rays can be especially damaging to curtain fabric hanging at windows in south-facing rooms, causing it to fade and eventually rot. To help counteract this, hang a lightweight roman blind behind the curtains, which can be pulled down during the day.

choosing curtains 207-211

creating soft furnishings 268-273

creating finishing touches 274-275

Added extras

RIGHT: A screen is both a decorative and practical object. Buy one ready-decorated or do-it-yourself and then use the end result to create space within a space, to keep out draughts, or to divide two areas of a room.

ABOVE: Family photographs in attractive frames are very decorative. Favourite paintings and drawings are just as effective and can bring valuable spots of colour to your living room.

LEFT: *Make a small space look larger by continuing the flooring and perhaps also the decorating colours from one room to another.*

ABOVE: *Interest need not only be added through colour – texture too has an important role to play. The sheen on this beautifully soft velvet throw adds depth and a sense of luxury to this curvy armchair.*

RIGHT: *Make use of wide window sills for displaying a collection or two. If they are breakable make sure the window treatment is suitable: a roman blind might not be such a good idea.*

OPPOSITE, LEFT & ABOVE: *Cushions have to be the easiest way to add interest to chairs and sofas. Bobbly trimmings, textural contrast and piping are small but significant details.*

Living room makeover

When Peter and Jane Harris moved into this Victorian town house they were faced with a building that was structurally sound but the decor hadn't been touched since the 1970s. It was quite a feat of imagination to transform it into the home of their dreams. Before deciding on what they would like to do with the living room, however, they removed all the existing wallpaper and curtains and brought in their main pieces of furniture. Use your furniture as the starting point for colour and styling as it is unlikely that you will want to change or re-cover them immediately. Similarly, by stripping the room like this you can think much more clearly about what decorating options you would like to explore in your home.

When this room was emptied and stripped, the result was bare walls, some slatted blinds at the window, an ageing pelmet board and fireplace surround plus a very comfortable two-seater sofa and deep arm chair. The fabrics on the seating were warm shades of red and as the room is south-facing and beautifully light and airy,

ABOVE: *The stained glass details on the windows led Jane to decide that she would not want to detract from their eye-catching qualities by hanging more ornate curtains than those seen here.*

BELOW *The cushion covers incorporate the green that is the third colour used in the decorating scheme.*

Jane and Peter plumped for a cooler colour for the walls to offset the warmth of the central area – a lovely, fresh spring yellow. The rest of the soft furnishings and the rug thrown over the stripped floorboards were then chosen to unite the colourscheme. The fabric for the cushion and stool covers has been chosen for the similarity of colours and pattern rather than using just one of the materials throughout the room.

The sage green of the woodwork and ceiling complements everything and is further picked out in the rug and cushion covers. As you can see from the 'before' photograph on the previous page, there was originally a picture rail in this room. But the owners decided not to replace it because they preferred to decorate the walls in as understated a way as possible. The heavily patterned rug and the mixture of soft furnishing fabrics definitely benefit from a simple backdrop – add more pattern, and the whole room would feel smaller.

Jane and Peter thought long and hard about the tiles in the fireplace. While they could have replaced them with a colour that would tone with the rest of the decor – or paint over them – they decided that retaining the blue would bring a greater sense of focus to the fireplace. This has been further enhanced by the large bunch of hydrangeas in their striped pot and the arrangement of the furniture.

LEFT: *Attention to detail is important when adding the finishing touches to a room. The lampshade and bowls enhance the red/pink of the soft furnishings.*

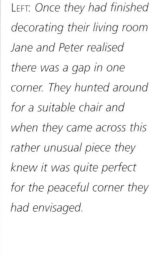

LEFT: *Once they had finished decorating their living room Jane and Peter realised there was a gap in one corner. They hunted around for a suitable chair and when they came across this rather unusual piece they knew it was quite perfect for the peaceful corner they had envisaged.*

ORDER OF EVENTS

1 Damp proofing: when they acquired the house there was a guarantee for a damp proof course installed within the last 10 years.

2 Back to basics: Peter and Jane stripped the wallpaper and removed the carpet from the basically sound floorboards.

3 Electricity: there were sufficient points in this room and Peter and Jane planned to light the room with standard lamps so there was no need to call in an electrician.

4 Plumbing and heating: this was in good order with a large radiator on the wall opposite the fireplace.

5 Flooring I: they decided to strip this back to its original colour and then seal with a clear varnish. As so much dust is created with this job they did this early, varnishing the floor before progressing any further in case it was stained once stripped.

6 Woodwork: again, the cornice, skirting boards and fireplace surround were in place and all were to stay. They decided to also remove the existing pelmet boards from above the window.

7 Surface preparation: the walls were sound but cracks needed filling and all the woodwork had to be stripped right back so the mouldings would be more prominent once painted.

8 Decorating: the room was painted all over so this was a comparatively fast makeover. First the ceiling and cornice, then the walls, and finally the skirtings and window frames.

9 Flooring II: for softness under foot in the sitting area, Jane's large rug was laid in the centre of the room.

10 Soft furnishings: first the curtains were made using fabric that echoed the colours in the carpet and upholstery. Cushion covers followed slowly as remnants were collected that contained the similar colours.

Adapting the makeover

A guide to alternative decorative details

Ceiling: dark-coloured surfaces advance towards the eye. If your living room has a high ceiling and you want to create something more intimate, go for darker tones.

◄ planning colour 10-11

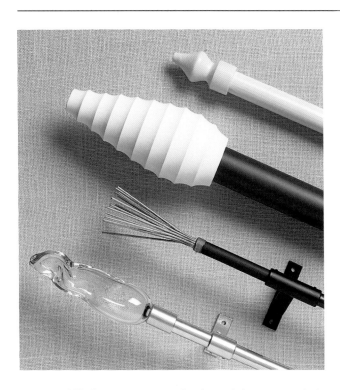

Window treatments: in place of the comparatively unadorned cast iron curtain pole, consider one of the more decorative finials on a cast iron or wooden pole. A traditional style of wooden poles and finials would also be suitable, or cover the heading of the window treatment with a pelmet.

choosing poles, rails and holdbacks 212-213
choosing pelmet boards 214-215

Mouldings: pick out in contrasting colour, and if injecting more of a period feel, consider reinstating picture rail and dado.

Walls: for a more muted effect that will glow with the amount of sunlight that floods into a south-facing room, use pastel shades that are based on blue. Although cooler in tone, these subtle colours will nevertheless be comfortable to live with by day and night.

◀ planning colour 10-11

Flooring: If insulation (both heat and sound) is a concern, look at fitted carpets or natural matting that cover the whole floor and throw a rug over this. Natural matting is available in many different finishes some of which are softer underfoot than others.

choosing flooring 172-179

Fire surround: leave as plain wood, stripping if necessary. More unusual surrounds can be created from wood found at salvage yards.

KITCHENS

ABOVE: *Pots and pans don't have to be hidden away in cupboards. With open shelves they can be pulled out quickly and also enjoyed as decorative items in their own right.*

The kitchen is so often the heart of the home that it needs to be a warm, stylish and individualistic room. It is the place where family and friends naturally gravitate on entering the home. Big, friendly tables, sofas and books add to the feeling of a real 'living' room. The changing role of the kitchen also reflects the growing emphasis on cooking as an essential part of today's lifestyle, rather than a behind-the-scenes activity, with chefs becoming celebrities and people in all walks of life avidly prepared to discuss food and its ingredients.

Planning the perfect layout

The core of the perfect kitchen is a well-planned layout. More than any other room in the house, the kitchen represents a big investment, so you will want something you can live with for a long time. Equally, however, tastes change, and there will be times when you feel tempted to rip it all out and start again. Fortunately, you can, in a sense, do both.

Well-designed kitchens have the flexibility to look completely different without having to replace any of

RIGHT: *With island workstations there is less walking around the kitchen. Meal preparation is easier and quicker and there is the opportunity to face the rest of the room too.*

the major items, simply by painting woodwork and changing accessories such as blinds, curtains and collections. And if you have moved into a house where the kitchen is fundamentally sound, but not to your taste, it's worth thinking carefully about what really needs changing and how you could make the rest more visually attractive before spending thousands on a completely new set-up. For a half-way-house compromise, look into changing the doors of the cupboards. There are several companies who specialise in doing this, and for a comparatively small amount of money, the whole feel of your kitchen can be changed.

For sound planning advice look to the many excellent kitchen designers and companies making stylish units. Alternatively, if you prefer to work on the design yourself, the essentials of a layout are very logical. The key elements – the ones you will use constantly, such as the fridge, cooker and sink – need to be within easy reach of each other so that you are not dashing round or moving everything twice. Everything else follows.

The dishwasher should preferably be close to both sink and china storage so you can unload and put away in one motion. You will frequently be taking ingredients in and out of the fridge for preparation or cooking with,

so you need a work surface with easy access to both cooker and fridge. And you will need to drain cooked food at almost every meal, so the sink needs to be no more than a step or so away from the cooker or you will be lugging around potentially dangerous pots of boiling water. This is especially bad news with children around.

The other factor to consider is sociability. The style of kitchen where all the work is done facing the wall, with your back to the room, can be frustrating if you want to keep an eye on children or enter into the conversation, and this is why the central island has become so popular in recent years. Some people fit sinks or hobs onto central islands, and most have a chopping area, which means that chopping, cooking or washing-up can go on while the cook is facing the room. In a traditional kitchen, there would always have been a large table in the centre for food preparation. So now, where there isn't space for a table, a small central island can provide a valuable staging post. It is also always useful for extra storage, both under the surface or above.

Making work surfaces work

At one point in kitchen design the fact that work surfaces are essential to good planning turned into a belief that the more the better. The result was metre upon metre of Formica or steel. Now everyone has realised that you only need sufficient, say, to serve food onto four to six plates, somewhere to place the food you are serving, and space for permanent kitchen accessories, such as the electric kettle, toaster, blender, scales and possibly a coffee maker. (All these items are a bore to put away when you have finished using them, so they are usually better permanently plugged in somewhere convenient.) You also need a surface on which to rest hot pans from the oven, and, as carrying hot food around is dangerous, this should be within arm's length

LEFT: *A kitchen of textural contrasts: wood, granite and stone flooring create a backdrop for ceramic tiles and colourful rugs.*

RIGHT: *For a light and airy feel to your kitchen, look for a reflective finish for the worktops such as the granite shown here.*

choosing kitchen appliances 190-195

ABOVE & OPPOSITE: *In place of plain wood for kitchen units, think about painting them. For the best effect, install simply designed doors and drawer fronts and then dress up with interesting handles or knobs.*

of the cooker. And, of course, you will need space on either side of the sink in order to stack dirty and clean dishes, and you will also want to chop food, roll out pastry and so on.

But remember that you are never going to be doing all this at once. You are extremely unlikely to be rolling out pastry, washing-up and serving food at the same time, for example, so many of these surfaces will do double duty. Even kitchens where there are several people working and different activities going on all the time, such as those in hotels or restaurants, often have surprisingly little work surface for the amount of elaborately prepared food that comes out of them.

Small or awkwardly shaped rooms may feel even smaller if there is an unbroken line of units around three walls, so before installing them, you may find it more rewarding to think in terms of activity areas: wet area, food preparation space, cooking and serving zone, and give each the amount of work surface it really needs. It is also worth remembering that you may find it more comfortable to have some of these surfaces at different levels – a convenient height for carving a joint is not quite the same as one for washing dishes. Act out the cooking of a typical meal and see how you move around. At the same time you can ensure that everything you use regularly (such as plates, pans, cups, and utensils) are within an arm's reach of where they are most likely to be used.

Storage

Storage is key in today's kitchens, particularly now that we work with so many more ingredients than in the past. Most kitchens work well with a combination of cupboards, shelves, racks and drawers, as well as a certain number of implements, such as wooden spoons, kept permanently to hand where they will be used, either in jars or hanging from a wall. The walk-in larder, beloved of Victorian cooks, has now become sought-after again, and if you don't have one, you may be able to have a larder – basically a large cupboard – built. It can often make a better use of space than two parallel rows of cupboards above and beneath the workspace,

as you can use all three walls and the door to their full length for shelves and hooks.

Think about the depth of shelving. Narrow shelves can be easier to live with than wide ones, as scrabbling around in the back of a deep cupboard or shelf to find a particular spice is infuriating – or you can vary the depth of shelves to maximise space while minimising inconvenience. Putting small spice shelves on the backs of cupboard doors is a useful trick, or semi-circular shelves that attach to a corner door make potentially lost space at the back of a corner much easier to access.

Open shelves will make a small space look less closed-in and display china and glass well, but they do attract grime and dust. Glass doors on some cupboards may be a good compromise. Pull-out drawers, too, help with organisation: big drawers for pans, for example, make grubbing around in the back of cupboards a thing of the past. Wire racks on walls, kitchen crowns and rows of pegs all have their part to play in storing useful cooking implements, and you can even hang pans from such arrangements, but don't forget to have somewhere to keep pan lids conveniently to hand. Finally,

choosing storage 184-187

OPPOSITE: *Keep a close eye on what you really need when installing shelves and cupboards. If you are hanging wall cupboards over counter units, don't forget the height of anything you want to keep on the counter, such as a microwave. Cupboards over the sink will probably feel claustrophobic as they will be at face level. Certain household items, such as cereal packets and tall bottles don't fit in standard shelves, so include some high ones.*

don't forget that tall items, such as brooms and ironing boards, need somewhere to slot in.

Farmhouse wood or city steel?

The most important visual thing about installing your kitchen is, of course, the material and design of the kitchen units, but it is worth thinking about all the above first, as what you need will probably affect your choice. It also stops you from being talked into having units you don't really want, and may mean that you can spend more on a few high-quality fittings rather than buying a complete off-the-peg kitchen that looks just like everybody else's. Once you've decided what you want, the choice is almost unlimited so talk to as many kitchen companies as you feel able. You can then decide on what would most suit you and your kitchen backed with practical expertise.

The finish of the worktops is a matter of considerable debate. Cheap and hygienic, Formica and other laminates have been the most popular worktops for the past thirty years. Fortunately, these now simulate the look and feel of various natural materials, including stone and granite. More expensive man-made finishes are also available which are extremely hard and versatile and they can be moulded to fit your exact specifications so that work surfaces that turn corners do so without the need for a join. Other finishes include ceramic tiles, granite, stainless steel and wood, each of which has its pros and cons.

Creating two areas

If your kitchen is large enough for eating in as well as cooking, consider artificially dividing it into two areas through, say, flooring or lighting or by the arrangement of the furniture. The chapter on dining areas (pages 58-69) shows how to successfully achieve this.

Decoration

First comes the flooring of which practicality is the primary consideration. Few people would even consider

RIGHT: *Stainless steel appliances give a kitchen an especially automated feel. When combined with good planning – here the close juxtaposition of cooker, fridge and island unit – a kitchen is a great place to work in.*

OPPOSITE: *For a less expensive but nevertheless smart finish, install kitchen units fashioned in the popular Shaker style. They can be painted as neutrally or colourfully as you like.*

carpet, sisal and seagrass as by the sink and cooker areas, in particular, they suffer from too much wear and soil damage. Linoleum and vinyl are warm and relatively soft underfoot, as is the more recently developed rubber flooring; and terracotta, slate, stone and quarry tiles are harder but are good at acting like heat bricks, picking up warmth from stoves and radiators and holding it for several hours.

If you have run out of money and want a temporary kitchen floor for a few years, the two cheapest options are to paint the concrete screed floor and varnish it, or to install MDF flooring, and paint and varnish that. Chequerboard designs look very smart or you can experiment with unusual ideas like brightly coloured stripes or paint effects to recreate the Mediterranean stone floor of your dreams.

Decorate the kitchen with the same principles you use in any room, working from the ceiling down to the floor and then move onto any soft furnishings you have

in mind. Don't feel that you have to have cheap curtains. Unless they are directly over the sink, there is no reason why they should become any dirtier than anywhere else in the house. More practical window treatments, however, are roman or roller blinds which can be housed within the recesses of the window by night and pulled or rolled up neatly out of the way by day.

It is worth remembering, too, that in the kitchen there is more work surface and woodwork than anywhere else in the house, and the colours of these will dominate in any colour scheme. Light reflects off work surfaces, so a dark surface can be an unsuccessful choice in smaller, darker rooms, for example. This is why historic colours – which look elegant in large kitchens – can look dismal in smaller ones. If it is stronger or brighter colours that you favour, design your kitchen so that it has lots of shelves, wall-cupboards, and hanging items. In such a kitchen, the colour will be broken up and not too over-powering.

planning colour 10-11   choosing blinds 212-213

Added extras

RIGHT: *Storage in the kitchen need not only be concerned with hiding away unsightly utensils and other kitchen paraphernalia. Display storage is just as important – you will invariably have favourite plates and glassware to show off.*

ABOVE: *Wine bottles are not objects of beauty and they can be space-consuming to store. Search for an attractive wine rack which will make the bottles look more attractive and prevent them from rolling all over the place when laid down. They then need not necessarily eat up valuable cupboard space.*

LEFT: *A set of small drawers in the kitchen is invaluable for all those small items that make their way into this room.*

ABOVE: *If a free-standing wine rack isn't for you, consider installing one beneath a worktop. This one has been painted in a contrasting colour to the rest of the kitchen for added interest.*

RIGHT: *Kitchen units attached high up on a wall can be difficult to reach. Here is a happy compromise: cupboards below and a long, deep shelf above.*

ABOVE: *Wooden storage boxes on wheels glide easily from beneath a table or from inside a ground level cupboard.*

LEFT: *Kitchen crowns are made in various finishes and look very smart hanging above a cooker or worktop, especially if it is an island unit. On smaller crowns such as this, hang lightweight items to prevent distorting the shape.*

ABOVE: *Fruit and vegetables make colourful displays in the kitchen and when they are stored in baskets like this, the air can circulate, allowing the produce to stay fresher longer.*

Kitchen makeover

The cook's kitchen. Moyra's career is developing and testing recipes so when she was planning this room, she needed to ensure that everything was readily to hand and yet safe as she has a young family.

This kitchen is in a basement so light was always in short supply. In order to keep it as airy as possible, Moyra knew that she needed a light finish to her units and also not have them along every wall. The result was this mixture of cupboards and deep shelves where her favourite pieces of china can be displayed. The free-standing workstation in the centre of the room contains the oven and mircrowave and consequently makes meal preparation very straightforward without lots of walking around the kitchen.

Before: *Early in the planning, Moyra new that she would have to block-up a doorway so that she would have a sizeable area to use. The door is now at the other side of the room. Recessed downlights were also installed for their good white light properties.* BELOW

After: *After much careful planning and re-allocation of the space, here is a kitchen that is easy and enjoyable to work in.* RIGHT

LEFT: *Although there is a solid-fuel range installed in this kitchen, Moyra felt that she needed the flexibility of a microwave and electric oven for her recipe testing. These have been built into the central island with a sliding drawer beneath the microwave for storing pots and pans.*

First and foremost, work surfaces do need to be practical and easy to keep clean. The beech wood counter top is heat resistant and has only to be oiled monthly to maintain its sheen and resistance to heat. Moyra particularly likes the brushed stainless steel surface around the sink area. It is excellent for preparing vegetables and very easy to keep clean as water can be swept directly into the adjacent double sink. This last is also a piece of practical planning because it allows dirty and clean tasks to be done simultaneously. The surface has been moulded in one piece so there are no nooks to harbour dirt. In addition, the reflective qualities of stainless steel, which has also been chosen as the finish for the fridge/freezer, enhance what daylight there is.

A practical floor that would be warm underfoot and easy to clean was also a great concern to Moyra, especially with her young daughter padding about. The laminated flooring has proved successful as it is easy to sweep and wash. It also looks wonderful as it leads the eye along the room to the comfortable dining area.

ABOVE: Wicker baskets that slide out on runners are a feature of many designed kitchens and can be successfully used for cutlery and tableware. Moyra uses them as filing trays.

The finishing touches in this practical and smart kitchen include the simple handles on the doors that nevertheless have a good grip. This is a useful design tip: always think about the use of the handles before buying them as they might well look great but end up being too lightweight. Moyra admits that her initial decision would have caused just this problem: it was the kitchen design company who pointed her in the right direction. The fretwork in the long doors on each side of the fridge also show an attention to detail (see the main photograph on page 53). It successfully breaks up a large and plain expanse of white painted wood.

A sense of space and airiness could have been lost as this room is in the basement. But by keeping all the decorating colours pale, including the floor and woodwork, the finished kitchen is stylish and practical.

ORDER OF EVENTS

1 **Damp proofing:** this was the first thing that needed to be done together with insulation so that the room would stay as warm as possible and for as long as possible.

2 **Electricity:** great thought was needed to ensure there was sufficient light and sockets.

3 **Plumbing and heating:** as with the damp proofing, this needed to be carefully thought through because basements can be cold. However, Moyra knew there would eventually be a solid-fuel range which keeps a room beautifully warm. The plumbing also needed to be installed for the sink.

4 **Flooring I:** the laminated floorboards needed to be installed early so that units and appliances could progress.

5 **Woodwork:** as Moyra was starting from scratch in this room she needed to choose her skirting boards and new door frames. They were installed at the same time as the kitchen units.

6 **Surface preparation:** once the lights were installed, the ceiling and all the walls were re-plastered leaving a smooth surface ready for painting once the plaster had dried out sufficiently.

7 **Decorating:** with the emphasis on pale colours, the room was swiftly decorated and painted from ceiling to floor.

8 **Soft furnishings:** Moyra's choice of wooden slatted roller blind over the sink tones with her beech wood work surfaces. To differentiate between the practical, working part of the kitchen and the comfortable dining area at the other end she chose fabric blinds for the french doors with matching covers for cushions on the chairs.

Adapting the makeover

A guide to alternative decorative details

Walls: these are best treated with a washable surface such as one of the specialised paints or ceramic tiles.

    choosing paints 166-167

    choosing wall tiles 170-171

Ceiling: directional lighting is needed. In place of recessed downlighters, look to strips of halogen spots with a pendulum light centred over the kitchen or dining table.

    choosing lighting 180-183

Flooring: as a change from bare floorboards, there is a huge range of vinyl, linoleum and rubber flooring that can be laid as squares, sheeting or cut-up for more elaborate designs. Warm underfoot, colour, texture or pattern can be combined in whatever mix suits you and your kitchen.

    choosing semi-hard flooring 172-173

Door handles: changing these is a comparatively cheap way of injecting a different feel to your kitchen if you don't want to completely re-fit the cupboards. Available in a wide range of finishes, shapes and colours, decide on whether you would like, say, contemporary, Shaker, traditional, big and bold or small and neat, and then simply screw them in place to replace the old handles.

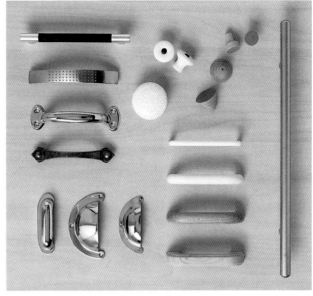

Splashbacks: continue the work surface up and onto the wall or use a different finish altogether as a splashback. Smooth stainless steel can run into a textured finish; use lengths of granite or ceramic tiles for something more colourful; or look to perspex as a protective coating for your paintwork.

choosing wall tiles 170-171

choosing kitchen work surfaces 196-197

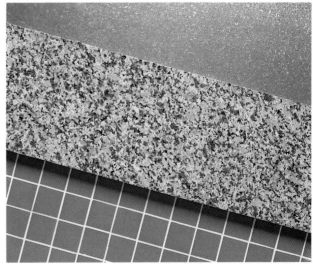

DINING AREAS

ABOVE: *Use a tablecloth, colourful napkins and a floral arrangement to dress your dining table for even the most informal of meals.*

The demise of the dining room has been one of the most hotly debated issues on the home front, but reports of its death have possibly been greatly exaggerated. It is true, however, that when space is short, it doesn't make sense to have a separate room only for formal dining. When a small kitchen is knocked through into a dining room, the loss of it may be compensated for by the chance to have a big, family kitchen that everyone enjoys all the time. Even where dining rooms are not open-plan, it usually makes sense to allocate them a dual purpose, such as a home office, nursery or hall. Lived-in rooms have so much more personality than ones that are opened only once or twice a week.

In an open-plan kitchen-diner, for example, there are many ways of dividing the eating and cooking areas with half-walls, island units, lighting or decorative detail marking the division. Even if all you have is a central table surrounded by kitchen working areas, you can still disguise the paraphernalia of meal preparation by setting and lighting the table to make it the focus of the room, while dimming the lights over the pile of washing-up. Create this by several separate light circuits for, say,

RIGHT: *The dining table has been positioned to make the best possible use of the large windows that dominate this room.*

choosing lighting 180-181

a pull-down ceiling light over the table along with other lights for the working part of the room. Dimmer switches make a huge difference, too – if your kitchen is lit by halogen downlighters in the ceiling, for instance, put them on two or three circuits so that some can be turned very low while others train pinpoints of light on the table. More simply, you can light the room entirely by candlelight, concentrating mainly on the table.

Other ways of marking out dining areas include using different types of flooring; introducing soft areas, such as a sofa or armchairs or comfortably cushioned window seats, and curtains.

Decorative devices

If you are lucky enough to have the space for a purpose-designed dining room, remember that it will mainly be used in the evening and decorate it accordingly. Rich, warm reds are classic dining room colours, as are golden yellows – a room that you only eat in a few times a week can take a little experimentation. Colourwashes in dark shades are very subtle and to give added depth to a paint effect such as this don't limit yourself to two colours – add a third, slightly deeper, shade and then varnish the whole surface with a matt coat to seal it. If you have unsightly radiators on the wall, don't forget that you can paint these to tone in as well.

You can also go to town with your window treatments because it won't be so essential to allow daylight in at all times. Fixed curtain heads can be very dramatic and the sweep of a floor-length curtain that is held open with tiebacks is very elegant. A puffball or smocked heading allows you to hang curtains without having to worry about pelmets; or for a slightly softer top make a self-pelmet, perhaps with a dramatic bullion fringe hanging from its lower edge. Self-covered buttons, fringes and tassels are perfect accessories for curtains with a little extra, so don't hold back when you are planning an extravaganza like this. For added detail you might like to line the curtains with a coloured fabric instead of the more usual beige or cream lining. Tie the whole creation together by, say, piping the tieback with the same fabric that you use for the lining; and make a

RIGHT: *The rustic dresser forms a colourful painted backdrop. It has been filled with plenty of equally colourful china.*

roman blind to match so that you don't need to rearrange the curtains each time you close them. Instead, just pull down the blind of an evening.

Finding the right flooring

On the flooring front, one word of warning. While natural matting is a relatively cheap form of carpeting a room, it is not a great surface beneath a dining table as it is so difficult to extract bits of food. Matting rugs are available, however, so if this surface appeals to you – and it can undeniably look extremely smart in a dining room – then it would be worth investing in one of these because it can be removed slightly more readily than a fitted carpet and periodically taken outside for a good shake. There are various binding materials that are used to edge these rugs so why not echo one of your decorating colours; or go for something that contrasts quite dramatically as an accent?

This form of flooring looks especially good in a dining room that is decorated in essentially neutral tones. Shades of cream and beige combine in a cool and restrained setting where texture comes to the fore. Look for knobbly fabrics for window and table dressings and cover the walls with a tinted and textured plaster finish. The many wrought-iron accessories that are now available for curtain rods and holdbacks, wall sconces, chandeliers and candlesticks are perfect for a room such as this. The stark contrast of black with cream is dramatic and yet can be warmed by candlelight and dimmed bulbs to create the perfect dinner party setting.

If you are planning a more exotic piece of decor, kelims and oriental rugs look especially handsome either over carpeting or a hard flooring – particularly stripped and varnished floorboards. Beautifully patterned and richly coloured, a rug such as this cannot fail to add rich visual interest to a room. They are only made to a few

planning colour 10-11   choosing flooring 172-177   choosing light bulbs 182-183

choosing curtains 207-211   choosing tracks & poles 214-215   creating paint effects 244-249

OPPOSITE: *The furniture in the dining area of this kitchen-dining room helps to differentiate between the two spaces. It contrasts strongly with the pale wood of the kitchen units.*

LEFT: *The furniture here has been chosen for its similarity to the kitchen units. However, the glass-fronted doors behind the table help to make this area slightly more formal and the overhead lighting has been wired to separate circuits so that the kitchen can be plunged into darkness during a meal.*

standard sizes, however, so measure your available space before rushing off to buy one.

The dining table

The dining table will undoubtedly be the focal point of your dining area. If space is a problem, purchase a table that can be extended as necessary. In this way, the table can be made smaller and pushed to one side by day if the room is being used for needs other than dining. The size can also be varied according to how many people are sitting down at it of an evening. There is nothing worse than four people being ranged around a table designed for eight – having to shout to be heard isn't

exactly the requirement for a relaxed supper party.

Ensure, too, that the chairs are comfortable for a few hours at a time. While metal chairs can look great they aren't a joy to sit on after more than half an hour. However, padded seat and back cushions can go a long way towards alleviating this discomfort. If you like to ring the changes of your dining table decor, make the cushions with different fabrics on the front and back so they can be reversed as your mood takes you.

Decorating the table

Perhaps the greatest advance in recent years has been the injection of a sense of fun and celebration into table

creating soft furnishings 268-273   creating finishing touches 274-275

RIGHT: *On a hot summer's day, decorate the table with crsip cool whites and enjoy the sun as it shines through the window and muslin drapes.*

RIGHT: *Sometimes the simplest of combinations are the most effective. Glass glistens in candlelight; when combined with white and gold it looks still better.*

style, and shops have coined a new merchandising phrase – tabletop – to cover all the things you can buy to dress up your table. This is a quick, relatively inexpensive way of ringing the changes in the home, and turns a simple meal into a real occasion as well as focusing the eye on the table and away from the domestic detail behind. White linen, crystal and fine porcelain, with carefully constructed floral arrangements, are only one way of making a table look special. Keeping a wide range of tablecloths (many can be off-cuts from market stalls), and collecting candlesticks or napkin rings gives you lots of options that you can have fun playing with. Remember, too, that there is also an enormous amount that can be borrowed from the pantry or garden for spur-of-the-moment transformations. Terracotta pots filled with candles pushed into florist's foam disguised with fine gravel and napkin rings made from twists of ivy – or sweet peas – are just as effective as any purchase made from a shop.

There is no longer any need to have a smart set of dinner party china porcelain – a simple mixture of white china is often all you need and you can build the atmosphere around it. Having said that, it's never been easier or cheaper to buy fun, stylish china and many more people now have two or three sets: brightly coloured dayware, simple white china and a smart dinner party set, for example. Or you may want to build on a theme of, say, blue-and-white, rose patterns, or yellow, collecting different styles and mixing them.

Improvise napkin rings – anything that ties will do, from ivy and ribbon to scraps of shot taffeta and raffia. If you have time, thread beads or shells onto the raffia. You could collect napkin rings with a theme – farm animals, for example, or natural wood. Place cards don't have to be formally printed by top stationers – instead, craft paper with loosely torn edges can look charming, especially if you spray the edges with gold. Or you could stencil designs on card. All these ideas quickly change the atmosphere from a sophisticated setting to something rural, such as a harvest festival dinner.

Flowers, of course, are a wonderful way of decorating a table, and you don't have to have a huge stock of vases. Milk bottles and jam jars can be quickly covered in fabric – gingham for a country event, gold taffeta or net for a formal one, for example – and tied at the neck with cord. It's also a good way of covering up flower pots. A quick way to decorate a long table or a large number of tables is to buy a tray of bright pot plants and tie fabric over the plastic containers.

These ideas do take time, so don't set yourself impossible standards. If you're so exhausted at the prospect of laying the table that you won't have the energy to enjoy your guests, then just buy a couple of tablecloths with matching napkins and forget about it.

Added extras

RIGHT: *A dining table laden with goodies for teatime is a tempting sight, made even more so when the china is a special collection gathered over the years.*

ABOVE: *For a casual tea-party, mix and match similar colours. A collection like this also looks good when on display between occasions.*

ABOVE & LEFT: *Never before has china been so accessible and the choice so wide. Whether you favour bright colours or plenty of white you will have no trouble finding something to suit you.*

RIGHT: *A dining area benefits from a display of some sort, whether on shelves or in a cupboard with glass doors. Paint the interior a pale colour to enhance your collections.*

ABOVE: *If your dining area is in the kitchen, china and glass can still be displayed on open shelves – even if they are directly above the kitchen sink.*

LEFT: *Pick up an old cupboard from an auction or reclamation yard and give it a coat of paint. You will end up with a unique cupboard and an excellent shelf as well.*

ABOVE: *A dresser is the ultimate storage unit with plenty of room on top for displaying all your best crockery. A piece like this look great in a kitchen or dining room.*

HALLWAYS AND STAIRWAYS

ABOVE: *To make an entrance hall more welcoming try to make space for a table featuring some flowers or other display. But don't have too large a table or it will all too quickly become a repository for unwanted post, hats and gloves.*

The first room that anyone will see when visiting you is the hall, so make it as inviting and welcoming as possible. Choose warm colours for the decor and make sure the lighting is sufficiently bright – and yet warm – to enable your visitors to see everything well. There is nothing worse than arriving at a home on a dark and stormy night, to walk into a murky, gloomy entrance hall. Equally, if you have a porch or standing area outside the front door, make sure that this is well lit, too. Lights with infra-red sensors are especially useful here as you can leave them turned on when you go out so that on your return they immediately light your way home.

Sadly, all too often the hallway is merely a narrow passageway with the staircase leading from it and it can be very difficult to make sense of the space. If you have a hall like this, one option you may want to consider before doing anything else, is knocking it through to another room to create a living-room hall, or even a dining-room hall. Rooms are becoming increasingly multifunctional and if you look at your space laterally like this, you can often bring to mind some excellent solutions for making the most of what you have.

RIGHT: *A generously proportioned entrance hall is a fine thing and if there is provision for hanging coats and storing shoes and boots, so much the better. Stone flagged floors are the ultimate in practical flooring for a room such as this.*

choosing lighting 180-181

If possible, though, it is worth trying to retain a small lobby, especially if there is nowhere else for coats, boots and buggies to go. If there is no space, at least make sure there is a sufficiently large cupboard to hand where coats can be hung, boots neatly installed and buggies flung. With hooks, racks and containers, a small space can be used to its maximum potential.

Making the most of the decor

Halls, or even hall-dining rooms, tend to be places where you pass through all too quickly, and so are good candidates for strong colours or exciting decorations. Research by a paint company has shown that many people choose to decorate their hallway in shades of green – a subconscious desire to bring the outdoors in, perhaps. If this is your natural inclination, remember that greens can be either warm shades, if there is a higher proportion of yellow in the mix, or cooler, if the blue element of green predominates.

When you are choosing your shade, experiment with tester pots first. The expanse of wall in a hall is usually so large – by far the greatest surface area in this space – and awkward to decorate, that it would be disastrous to find you have the wrong colour when you have finished. Look at the colour in natural and electric lighting, too. Depending on the sort of bulb that you use to light the hallway, the colour will be greatly affected. A yellow tungsten bulb or the white of halogen lighting, for example, will dramatically change the overall effect in the evening.

Of course, if your hallway doubles as another room, you may find green a little too difficult to live with for long periods of time. Dining with such a colour in the background is not particularly comfortable so bear this in mind when looking at colour schemes: warm shades of terracotta are especially lovely in the evenings. Put your lights onto dimmer switches, too.

Enhancing proportion

As the proportions of a hall are frequently rather uncomfortable – a long and narrow room, or high walls

ABOVE: *By painting a stairwell wall a different colour above and below a dado rail and hanging pictures at eye level the upward sweep of the wall is relieved.*

RIGHT: *By using the same curtain fabric for the blinds in the hall and the curtains at the half-landing the eye is led onwards rather than upwards.*

leading up to the stairwell – this area is a prime candidate for playing with colour and lighting to enhance the good points, and detract from the bad. To make the space seem wider and the back of a long, narrow corridor appear closer, paint the ceiling and back wall in a dark shade, but keep the side walls as pale as possible. Shiny surfaces will also reflect light making them appear to recede so you might want to consider a paint with a slight sheen for the walls.

If you live in a period property, there may already be mouldings on the walls of your rooms and the hallway

is a prime candidate for them as they add decorative details and enhance proportion. The large expanses of wall can also be well served by adding a dado rail and being decorated with different colours or finishes above and below. Authentic mouldings are available in plaster or wood, or you may just prefer to paste on a wallpaper border. Getting the proportions right for positioning the top of the dado can be difficult, but the best place to aim for is about a third of the way up the wall. Experiment by drawing chalk lines along the wall.

For a high stairwell, it would be worth installing wall-mounted downlighters at just above head height so that when the lights are switched on, the lower half of the wall is bathed in light, or starry halogen bulbs inset into the ceiling. With either of these ideas, the eye is discouraged from sweeping up to the ceiling above. Pictures hung at eye level as you walk up the stairs will also help to break up the sheer quantity of walls that are the feature of staircases, as will a continuation of a dado from the hallway below.

Flooring

Flooring for halls need to be extremely hard-wearing as people traipse in and out all day – hence the popularity of stone, quarry tiles and bare floorboards. Hard surfaces like this need minimal upkeep and can be easily cleaned; but the downside is that they are cold underfoot and anything dropped on them will break all too easily. If you are lucky enough to have inherited such a flooring you will no doubt want to show it off, but installing stone and quarry tiles in particular can be very expensive. To add warmth, lay down a rug or two. But as these surfaces tend to be slippery, put an underlay beneath the rug to make it safer to walk over – especially if you have children or older people in the home.

Carpeting is a cheaper option but before installing, check how tough it is (the greater the density of tufts per square centimetre, the stronger the carpet) and remember that this is the one room in the house where leaves and dust will blow in from the outside. A dark coloured carpet will show every speck of dirt, as will a plain pale cream. Natural matting is another alternative

LEFT: *With a hall this large, big pieces of furniture such as the grandfather clock and piano look perfect. Make sure that the scale of furniture in your hall is equally compatible: nothing too big or too small.*

choosing light bulbs 182-183   choosing flooring 172-177

RIGHT: *To prevent a hall from becoming wasted space see if you can double it up with another use, whether it be as a dining area or somewhere to keep a desk – as here.*

you may want to consider here as it is less expensive yet hard-wearing. However, the problems with both carpets and natural matting is keeping them clean. To help, make sure that you have a large area by the front door where feet can be wiped and treat the carpet or matting with stain inhibitor early in its life. Small remnants of carpet off-cuts can also be bound so that for most of the time you can have a second layer of carpet near entrance doors in case of excess dirt. Such small carpets can be more easily cleaned and, indeed, removed for formal occasions.

Finishing touches

It is not often that hallways have windows, but if you wish to add some softness with furnishings you may decide to cover the door with a full-length curtain or blind – a great boon if you also suffer from a draughty entrance. Special curtain poles (portière rods) are available that lift as you open the door so that the curtain won't drag on the floor or get caught as the door opens; or you may find it useful to have a curtain on a hinged pole that will swing back against the wall when you would like the curtain open.

For added interest in the hall and up the stairs display favourite pictures and paintings; have a low but long bookshelf along one wall which will also serve as a handy shelf; and hang a mirror for the last – or first – adjustments on the way out or in. This last is an especially valuable addition to a hallway. If the space is long and narrow, a mirror hanging on one wall will enhance the width by reflecting whatever is on the opposite wall (a light, for example, would become doubly strong) and if it can be positioned to reflect some outside light, so much the better.

A hallway, then, need not be the place where people come and go at speed. Turn it into a place to linger, somewhere where greetings and departures need not be hurried. Even a small space can be interesting.

choosing curtains 207–211   choosing blinds 212–213

LEFT: *A small standard lamp and bunches of flowers create a friendly welcome – especially on a cold and dusky evening.*

ABOVE: *By painting the underside of this staircase white to differentiate from the yellow, its beautiful curves are highlighted.*

Added extras

LEFT: *A chair, small table and mirror are the perfect accessories in a hallway, as long as the space is not too small. They are each useful in their own way.*

RIGHT & BELOW RIGHT: *Small pieces of fabric hung simply at the window or over the door disguise what might otherwise not be especially lovely fittings. They are also effective ways of affording the occupiers of the home greater privacy from the world at large.*

ABOVE: *For the most effective of flower displays, group together bunches of the same flowers or seed heads. To keep them fresh, change the water daily.*

BEDROOMS

Bedrooms are becoming more and more like private living rooms – not only do they have a bed, but often a television, books, music, a telephone and even a personal computer, as well as chairs, tables and storage. Many people come home in the evening, spend some time in the kitchen eating and socialising, before moving upstairs to spend what is left of the day in their bedroom, by-passing the more conventional living room. Our most personal possessions – clothes, well-loved ornaments, photographs and pictures – are mainly kept in the bedroom. Consequently, its decoration can be a matter of dispute between couples, although many men concede that it is largely female territory. However, whether shared by one or two people, the bedroom is nevertheless the most private room in the house, and decorating it affords indulgences and fantasies that are rarely possible elsewhere.

The first decision is which room to pick as your bedroom, and it might be worth avoiding the obvious choices. The best bedrooms were often built at the front of the house, but now that streets are so much noisier, it may be more restful for adults to change this. Large, light,

front rooms may be perfect bedrooms-cum-playrooms for children, who wake early anyway and will make the most of the space for play. Some people believe that an east-facing bedroom is healthier – the theory is that being woken by the sun's rays provides a natural sleep pattern, and you will leap out of bed alert and refreshed, while being dragged from a deep sleep in darkness, especially by the sudden, loud noise of the alarm clock, will leave you feeling groggy for hours.

Certainly, it is well worth thinking about the patterns of living in the house before allocating rooms. For example, parents will have a better night's rest if they are next door to babies' and toddlers' rooms for a quick sort-out in the middle of the night. Conversely, teenagers will prefer to be as far away as possible so that they can begin to establish their independence and their own lifestyle. And anyone who regularly does night work will need the quietest room in daytime.

Fitting everything in

Apart from the bed, furniture has shrunk as bedrooms grow smaller, and now most secondary bedrooms have room only for a chest of drawers, a small bedside table and a fitted wardrobe. The result is that in many homes, storage is a major problem. When most nineteenth- and early twentieth-century housing stock was built, only the very wealthiest people had more than a couple of regular outfits plus something for 'best'. Now a dozen pairs of shoes, several coats and a big selection of clothing for the office, sport, parties and casual wear would be considered unremarkable. Accessories need to be stored in quantity, and even magazines, toys and books need somewhere to go. Lines of floor-to-ceiling fitted wardrobes were the original response to this, but many people now find them unaesthetic and impersonal.

The answer is sometimes to be clever about storage in the rest of the house. One of the best space-saving ideas is a walk-in wardrobe, carved out of space from a big bathroom or corridor, or even by cutting an adjacent bedroom in half. Because there are no doors, the space can be maximised for hanging, shelves or drawers, and storage can run from floor to ceiling. If you can manage

choosing storage 184-187

LEFT: *If you are able to create a separate dressing room elsewhere it leaves your bedroom free of all the bits and pieces of daily life. Freeing up space in this way in your bedroom means you can indulge yourself by bringing in your favourite artefacts.*

Left: *Make the bed as comfortable and inviting as possible. Large pillows and colourful bedding enhance the room's focal point.*

a walk-in cupboard, you won't have to have a wardrobe in your bed-room, or you can buy a small one, and adapt it to hold a television set and a row of drawers.

Borrow ideas from industry or offices: 'file' colour-coded socks and jumpers in drawers, stack smart boxes on open shelves or use dress rails behind a curtain in spaces that are too narrow for cupboard doors to open into. Dual-function furni-ture is also useful, such as beds with storage built into them, and odd-shaped spaces – under the stairs or the eaves of a roof – are ideal for built-in drawers and cupboards. It is most important to give yourself plenty of options from the start. Decide where to keep all your clothes so your beautifully designed bedroom doesn't simply become a hell-hole of mess once you live in it.

The focal point

The bed is most likely to be the dominant feature, so your choice will probably determine the way you deco-rate the rest of the room. There are hundreds of options in bed and bedhead design, from historic bateau lits and Victorian wrought iron to traditional fabric and four-postered beds or sleek contemporary divans.

If you watch television in the bedroom, both head-board and footboard will be affected: headboards need to be easy to clean as heads propped against them will

Above: *For something more restrained, use white and other netural tones to decorate the bedroom. The long table at the bottom of the bed is the practical equivalent of a footboard.*

make them grubby quickly – wood or iron is ideal. If, however, you intend to have a fabric cover, make sure that it is easy to remove for cleaning. Covers that are slipped over the top or tied at the top and sides are the best options. If you have an iron bedhead you may also prefer to make a padded cover to slip over the top as a softer surface on which to rest your head. Footboards should be low enough so that you can see the television comfortably, and it is also worth remembering that tall people will find footboards restricting.

Bed dressing

Having chosen your bed, the next important question is how you dress it, and because new bed linen usually has

choosing bedroom furnishings 224-227

to be purchased every few years, you may want to opt for a single theme, such as stripes, checks, roses, or a colour like blue or plain white so that the linen cupboard doesn't turn into a ragbag of impulse buys that don't team and tone too successfully. Imposing a broad discipline means that you won't be left with a bed covered with the handsome black and cream duvet cover from a modernist period that clashes violently with the cottage roses on the romantic, spur-of-the-moment-purchase pillow case.

However, new bed linen is fun, and is a quick way of transforming a room. So a successful way to plan the decor is to keep the bedroom itself very plain and allow the design and colour of sheets, quilt covers, blankets and bedcovers to make the style statements. Piles of blankets, eiderdowns and collections of cushions can add to comfort and cosiness, and make your bed a real refuge. They can also be swapped around quickly and easily so that you can ring the changes in your bedroom.

Bed dressings, too, are becoming increasingly fun – especially once a four-poster is brought into play. The frame can be left bare to great effect, particularly if the bed itself is dressed stylishly. Or any combination of curtain and even tenting can be employed to create a room within a room. You may just prefer fabric to hang down the back of the bed, feeling that to be totally surrounded would be too claustrophobic. Alternatively, by suspending a metal ring from the ceiling above the centre of the bed, create a tented canopy with fabric running in swathes from the ring to the top of the frame. Continue this exotic treatment by winding the rest of the fabric strips down the poles, or curtain all four sides, holding back the sides with tiebacks.

For something a little more restrained, empty your bedroom of everything other than the bare essentials and try to keep it that way. A wrought iron bed frame simply dressed with a monotone duvet cover, stripped floorboards, creamy canvas roman blinds and a single, well-chosen picture on the wall, would be the perfect, restful haven. In these days of frenetic living, computers at every office desk, and all those opportunities to rush hither and thither, what could be better than sleeping in such an environment where all possible distractions

have been removed – a space designed for restoring and recharging the batteries. If there are items that you feel you really must have in your bedroom, store them in cupboards or stacked storage boxes. Whatever else you do, keep all clutter hidden away – and definitely not under the bed. In feng shui practice, a cleared space in the bedroom gives restful sleep and restorative energy.

Lovely lighting

The two kinds of lighting most commonly used in bedrooms are general lighting and task lighting – few people bother to use lighting to highlight special features. However, if you have an attractive old ceiling cornice or decide to install your own, you could think of using uplighters throwing a wash of light over the ceiling as general light. Having decided on this form of lighting, you then need to be quite specific about the task lighting, such as bedside lamps and light in which to apply make-up or brush hair.

Dressing-table light is an almost forgotten ingredient of the bedroom. In the past, dressing tables were always positioned facing the window to maximise light – now they are placed where they fit best according to the rest of the furniture in the room. This means trying extra hard with the lighting, experimenting with different lights and lamps until you find one that illuminates both sides of your face equally without glare or shadow. Don't light the mirror from above or with strip lighting as neither of these options are flattering, especially first thing in the morning.

Dressing up the windows

Bedrooms can differ quite dramatically from the rest of the house in their window treatments because there is often a real need for privacy or control of light. If either of these matter to you, they will dominate your choice of curtains or blinds. The other factor that influences

RIGHT: *The collection of blue and white china that the owner of this bedroom had collected over the years formed the starting point for the rest of the room's decor.*

treating floorboards 258-259 creating soft furnishings 268-273

window treatments is the architecture. While appropriateness for the house is an important factor to consider – a very grand window treatment, perfect in a big country house, can be stifling or pretentious in a tiny cottage – it is also possible to use window treatments in very boxy, modern rooms as a substitute for architectural detail.

Certainly it's important to think about light and lighting before choosing colour schemes and fabric, because if you are someone who loves the morning sun streaming in through the window, then heavy draped and swagged curtain treatments will spoil the effect. Instead, lightweight curtains simply hung from tabs, ties or café clips from the finest of wrought iron poles will be what you are after. If, on the other hand, keeping the room dark is important, then filmy voiles and light, summery fabrics will play havoc with your sleeping patterns. Shutters, too, are a possibility as they let through maximum light when open, and are completely private and dark when closed.

Small points

Bedrooms are good places for painted-up junk furniture such as a chest of drawers rescued from the back of an old shop, given new handles and a paint treatment or side tables renovated with a favourite paint effect. Bedside tables can also be created with a simple circle of MDF placed on a trestle and covered by a favourite fabric, or a non-matching pair can be disguised with tailored and fitted covers reaching down to the floor.

Although a fitted carpet is softer underfoot, and much the quietest option in a bedroom, hard flooring can be a successful option, especially if it is dressed up with a few rugs. If the house is properly sealed (well-fitting, draught-free windows, loft insulation and sealed floorboards and wainscots), then you needn't worry about hard flooring being cold underfoot. Strip and seal the boards or use other finishes such as liming for a soft white effect, or staining for something more colourful.

RIGHT: *To make the most of a dark, north-facing room, paint the walls white and use airy fabrics and pale flooring. The overall effect is that of light and space.*

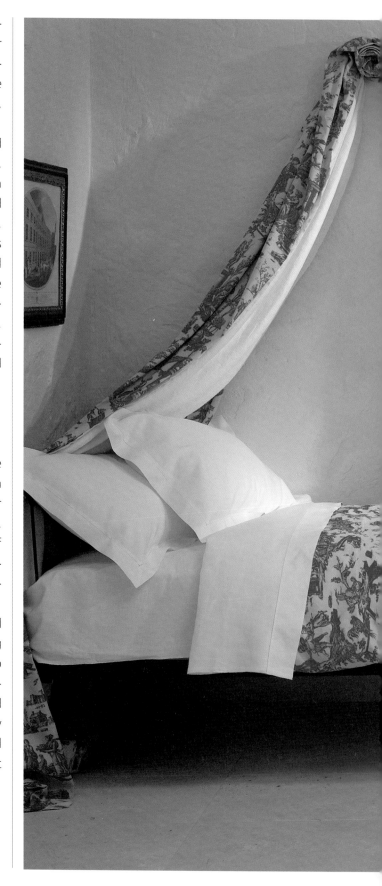

choosing flooring 172-177   ▶ treating floorboards 258-259

Added extras

BELOW: *Use brightly coloured pillow cases and blankets as the finishing touches and to unite other elements in the bedroom.*

RIGHT: *Socks are notoriously difficult to keep in pairs. Use a holder like this in a bedroom drawer to help conquer the problem.*

LEFT: *Make a feature of a fireplace by hanging a mirror over it. With a bed this large, such statements can be made elsewhere in the room.*

ABOVE: *Use storage chests with plenty of small drawers to help keep jewellery, hair ornaments and make-up in some sort of order.*

RIGHT & BELOW: *Bed linen has never been so varied. Choose a pale range of colours and mix them up or go for the monotone approach.*

LEFT: *A sofa by day, a bed by night, piles of cushions disguise the utilitarian nature of this piece of furniture. For small space living this is the ideal compromise.*

LEFT: *Oxford pillowcases look generous and luxuriant, especially when piled high on the bed. The borders can also be used to add variations of fabric and colour. Co-ordinated sets of bed linen and pillowcases are also available.*

Bedroom makeover

This bedroom has been designed specifically for a clutter-free existence. Paula and Laurence knew that once they had a baby on the way they would have to do something about all their excess paraphernalia, leaving their two-bedroom home as roomy as possible.

The first thing they did was to change the position of their bed and the resulting amount of floorspace amazed them. They decided to enhance the look by replacing the existing fitted carpet with plastic laminated close-fitted boarding. This work coincided with other current building work so they took the opportunity to replace the existing radiator with a smaller one that would take up less space and move it to a more convenient place for their new room plan. They also decided to replace the plastic-framed windows with wooden frames designed

Before: *A light bedroom that nevertheless lacks the adventurous sense of colour that is the trademark of the rest of the house.* BELOW

After: *Sunny and colourful, the bright orange wall behind the bed is a warm counterpart to the cooler aqua used on the rest of the room.* RIGHT

to match the rest of the houses in their street.

As ever in small bedrooms, storage was a major concern and to keep the walls as clear as possible they moved the wardrobe into the alcove to the left of the fireplace opposite the windows and Laurence then built small cupboards and shelves on the other side. Books

ABOVE: *To soften the wooden top to this simple dressing table, Paula lightly brushed a coat of watered-down white emulsion over the surface. To make it easy to clean, she then applied a few coats of matt acrylic varnish over the top.*

and family photographs are kept on the shelves and shoes and bags stored in the cupboard below, which houses a couple of shelves to keep everything in order.

The mini-dressing table beneath the mirror was also a replacement for Paula's bulky chest of drawers that she admits she found hard to let go because the drawers were the perfect size for all her potions and lotions. However, the new unit (readily available and simply customised with paint and specially chosen drawer handles) has proved a great success because of its many drawers, which enable her to still keep everything organised. The slim-line shelf on the top is another Laurence creation.

RIGHT: *The moulding details on the cupboard doors and running along the front of the shelves were bought from a nearby DIY store and simply cut to length and pinned in place. Buy a style of beading that matches the rest of your home.*

ORDER OF EVENTS

1 **Back to basics:** removal of the carpet and excess furniture for a more minimal lifestyle.

2 **Electricity:** As the room is mainly lit by bedside lamps and Paula and Laurence decided to keep the central pendulum for occasional extra lighting, an electrician wasn't required.

3 **Plumbing and heating:** a more compact radiator was installed in a new position to leave the walls as clear as possible for simple furniture.

4 **Flooring I:** the laminated close-fitting boarding was installed over the existing boards to keep the room as draught-free and simplistic as possible.

5 **Woodwork:** Laurence built the cupboard and shelves next to the fireplace and the dresser top beneath the mirror frame. The existing skirting boards were all intact and did not need repairing in any way.

6 **Surface preparation:** the paint on the fireplace was not too thick so there was no need to strip it back and there was no wallpaper on the walls so preparation was minimal.

7 **Decorating:** Paula and Laurence chose the colours with the aid of tester pots. The ceiling and woodwork have been painted white to retain the room's sunny character.

8 **Flooring II:** to retain the sense of minimal living the floor remains as bare floorboards – no rugs or carpet.

9 **Soft furnishings:** kept to a minimum and Paula chose the duvet cover and blanket on the bed for their complementary colours.

The bedroom faces onto the main street and has two sunny windows so Paula and Laurence felt they could paint the room with strong colours. Orange and aqua work well together and the single orange wall makes a great statement yet without being too overpowering. The fireplace and adjacent cupboard have been painted white to emphasise these features.

Although they wanted privacy in the room at night, they were loathe to block out the daylight. So Laurence and Paula have a pair of simple white roller blinds to soften the window plus check sheer curtains that still allow the sun to flood into the room.

Making changes

A guide to alternative decorative details

Window dressing: to block out the rising sun, use lined and possibly even interlined curtains. Blinds also help to preserve curtain fabric – especially useful if you have spent lots of money on your curtains.

choosing blinds 212-213

Flooring: for something softer and more luxurious underfoot choose a fitted carpet rather than bare floorboards. If you want to sleep in a more restrained interior than that featured on the previous pages, neutral and pale shades will complement any decorative scheme you plan.

choosing carpets 172-173

Wall covering: of all the rooms in a house, the bedroom is the one where wallpaper is most likely to be used. Shades of pale blue and pink are equally restful colours and whether you prefer a pictorial pattern or something more abstract you will always find something to suit.

choosing wallpapers 168-169

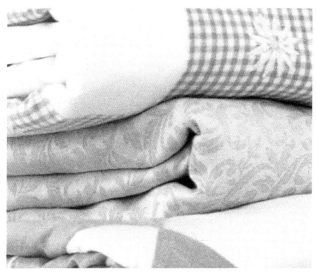

Bedcovers: use a complementary bedcover to successfully hide the old duvet cover you have yet to replace.

choosing bedroom furnishings 224-225

BATHROOMS

ABOVE: *A cupboard with glass-fronted doors is a great way to store a mixture of items in the bathroom. Practical and attractive, such storage is useful for towels and display items.*

Your bathroom is an important personal space. No matter how small, it is somewhere to relax, a door that can be closed and locked against the world outside. You can have great fun with decoration, too – in a room so small, it rarely costs much to re-paint or change the curtains – and you can indulge yourself in fantasy with accessories, whether you prefer classic Victorian style or bright, wacky colours. But first, you need to get the lay-out of the room right. If you are starting from scratch, consider the position and size of the WC, bath and basin, the amount of room you need to move around comfortably, and storage, along with good lighting and flooring. If you are moving into a house where these are established, it may be worth replacing or moving around major elements to make the room work better.

Start by looking at bathrooms you like, collecting magazine cuttings and visiting bathroom centres – although try to look past the decorative style to the basic ideas in layout and storage. Do you want clean modern lines or an elaborate period bathroom? Either spare, beautifully organised minimalism or expensive fabrics, elegant accessories and fabulous tiling can look

RIGHT: *A section of the outside wall in this bathroom has been built of glass bricks. They allow the sunlight to flood in and maintain privacy because the glass is textured.*

Right: *Floor to ceiling shelves have been simply hidden with white curtains. They effectively disguise clutter and are easy to use.*

Right: *Floor to ceiling shelves have been simply hidden with white curtains. They effectively disguise clutter and are easy to use.*

Right: *The exterior of enamelled steel and cast-iron baths can be successfully painted to match the rooms decor.*

luxurious. Whether you want to create a bathroom with the deep colours and dark wood of Victoriana or the sleek glass and chrome modernism, consider all the practicalities first. Your options may be limited by the current positioning of the plumbing or the fact that certain items, such as the bath, may fit into just one space or along one wall. But it is worth checking to see if there are other, possibly better, options.

The practicalities come first

The average bath is 1700mm long x 700mm wide, and you need space to get in and out. Where a basin is butted-up close to a bath, say in a small en-suite bathroom, don't forget that someone may be standing at the basin when another wants to use the bath, so run through this in outline to see if it works comfortably. A good designer tip is to use unravelled toilet paper to mark out where items would go and see if you can move easily in the floorspace left.

But before you even get to this stage it is well worth making a scale drawing of the bathroom on squared paper as described on pages 8-9. Then cut out tem-

plates of baths, basins, toilets and bidets (many bathroom fixture catalogues provide these outlines for you) to an appropriate size so that you can play around with different ideas. Sometimes, it is quite amazing what you can fit in and where, and the most unexpected arrangements come to light.

Odd shapes of room can work well – for example, a bath can fit into, or create, an alcove – but check that you have easy access to taps from the room. When siting the wash basin, don't forget elbow room, as shaving and cleaning teeth can use up to around 40cm (16in) of space on either side. This can make a corner an uncomfortable place to have a basin.

Choosing the fittings

Think about larger-than-average or small baths and basins, as well as showers. Usually, small baths are less satisfactory, but in a second or guest bathroom, they can be the answer. Sometimes you can do something unexpected with a small space – such as installing a large bath for extra luxury, and having very little else in the room. Small basins, however, can be very useful

choosing bathroom fittings 198-201

space savers. The big basins of the past were often used for washing small items of clothing, but now that few people do more than shave or clean their teeth in a basin, two small basins may prove more useful than one large one.

The most fixed item in your bathroom is the WC, because of its access to the soil stack. Some plumbers may say that it can't be moved. It can, but it will add significantly to the total cost, if, say you have to raise the floor (or, more cheaply, build a raised platform), so that a soil pipe can slope underneath it. But if it makes all the difference between the perfect bathroom and a compromise, then don't be put off. Ideally, you will need around 60cm (24in) of space in front of it. Likewise, if you want to install a bidet you will need to allow the same amount of space there too.

A shower cubicle is the most obvious space saver, and showers are increasingly popular. If you have a square 70cm (28in) square of space, you can install a shower – anywhere from in a wardrobe or broom cupboard to a loft, although you will have to have a fan to cope with condensation in places where there is no natural window. Higher up the house, you may need to invest in an extra pump to get the right water pressure (the tank should be 1m [1yd] above the shower head). Shower trays are between 700 and 900mm square, or 1200mm deep x 600mm wide, and come in ceramic (hardest-wearing), resin (slightly cheaper, less hard wearing) and acrylic (least expensive and warm underfoot, but not as long-lasting). Look for non-slip surfaces, but check how easy they are to clean.

Lighting

Bathroom lighting is a very personal thing but whatever you favour, think about it early on in your plans because very often wiring will need to be chased into the walls. Some people like brightly lit spaces and others prefer intimate, atmospheric pools of light in which to soak away the stresses of the day. The ideal scenario would be a mixture so you have good clear lighting by the mirror above the basin for all those daily cleansing and shaving chores, and more mellow light for bathing by.

LEFT: *Tongue-and-groove boarding is an excellent finish in a bathroom. Comparatively cheap to install, it will withstand condensation and can easily be painted to fit in with the rest of the decor. This kind of finish is also a very attractive way to disguise a not-so-beautiful bath exterior and all its plumbing.*

choosing lighting 180-181   choosing bathroom fittings 198-201

RIGHT: *There is no reason why a comfortable chair should be excluded from a bathroom. It is a place for relaxing in, which may well include conversation at the end of the day.*

For clear, white light, the best form of lighting in the bathroom is halogen. Such downlighters provide a form of light that is non-glaring and so comfortable to be with. If you don't want to install them in the ceiling, buy a track from which the bulbs are suspended. The value of the latter in particular is that you can organise the bulbs to point in any direction that you choose, making it a good form of task lighting as well as general lighting. For safety reasons, lights inside a bathroom must be switched on with a pull cord but there is no reason why you could not have a dimmer switch installed just outside the door if you want to have as flexible a lighting scheme as possible. Halogen lighting turned right down low is suitably atmospheric in the bathroom, or install an additional uplighter or two on a separate circuit for greater versatility.

The necessary extras

Now it's time to think about colour, accessories, window treatments and even the pleasure of co-ordinating towels and soaps. If you have inherited a bathroom you don't care for, and can't afford to change, distract the eye with these delights – curtains and towels are especially valuable assets in such a room. Bathroom windows are usually small so don't require large amounts of fabric, particularly if you are considering a simple treatment such as tab-heads or a roman blind. Window panes in many a bathroom are of the frosted variety so you may just want to think about using one of the brightly coloured muslins or sheers that are now so readily available. Fix them to a curtain rod with a gathered heading or – even more quickly – use café clips.

Because of the high levels of condensation in a bathroom you must take care with your wall coverings. Specially formulated paints to cope with just this problem are available and if it's a wallpaper that you are after, always buy a washable or spongeable product. (To protect any wallpaper by a basin, cover the immediate

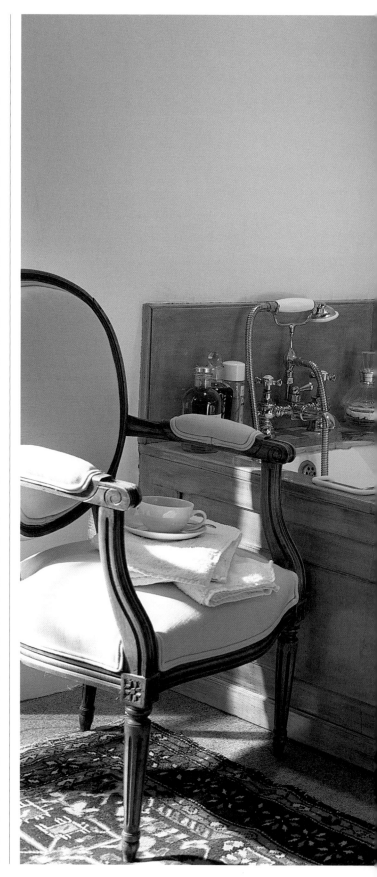

◄ planning colour 10-11   choosing paint 166-167   choosing light bulbs 182-183

surrounding area with a plate of glass.) For the same reason, your choice of bathroom flooring is important as it must be able to cope with higher than average amounts of water slopping about. There is no doubt that linoleum and vinyl are the most practical options and the range of colour and pattern is now very wide. As bathrooms are small, it is often possible to buy off-cuts or ends of more expensive flooring such as the recently developed rubber floorings manufactured for kitchens and bathrooms. Ceramic tiles look great but are slippery when wet, and carpeting must be purpose-designed – even so, you will probably have to take it up and air it after a flooded bath.

Cupboards and shelves are invaluable in bathrooms – to take towels, medicines and necessaries such as spare shampoo, bath oil and shaving kit. But in a relatively confined space you need to check their positioning. A common mistake is to put a bathroom shelf over the basin just where a child leaning forward to brush his teeth will hit his head. And most people like somewhere to position a cup of tea, a book or a shampoo bottle when they are in the bath, so don't forget that if you are installing a free-standing bath. Lastly, anyone getting in and out of the bath will want somewhere to hang a towel or dressing gown, and, in a shower, will need a shelf for shampoo and soap.

OPPOSITE: *What looks like a cupboard next to the bath is, in fact, an attractive disguise for radiator and plumbing. It has been given greater purpose by ensuring it is deep enough to be used as a shelf for displays.*

LEFT: *To give a large bathroom that extra special luxuriant quality, stand the bath in the middle of the floor. Remember to have a surface close at hand to make the soap and shampoo easy to retrieve.*

Added extras

LEFT: *The mosaic splashback behind the basin has been created to reflect the decor in this bathroom. Mosaic tiles can be bought from specialist suppliers and then adhered direct to a wall with tile adhesive or made as a panel to be positioned wherever you like.*

BELOW: *One of the best forms of lighting in the bathroom is good old-fashioned candlelight. There are so many styles of candlestick around that you will easily find one – or more – with which to light your bathroom.*

LEFT: *Choose a theme for decorating your bathroom and then spend time finding suitable fabrics and accessories. Here, shells are the order of the day, both real and in paintings and drawings.*

BELOW: *a display of blue glass bottles on a deep windowsill behind the basin is much more attractive than a mixture of old toothbrushes and half-used tubes of toothpaste.*

BELOW: *Search for canvas containers for your bathroom. Here, one is used for storing hand-towels, flannels and other items related to cleanliness; the other hides all those dirty clothes.*

RIGHT: *For something more colourful, look at the many contemporary plastic units that are available. Storage containers first and foremost designed for the kitchen can successfully double-up in a bathroom.*

RIGHT: *Smaller items are best kept in small containers so they don't become lost or jumbled up among larger bottles, jars and tubes. With several small containers or bags like these you can then divide your bathroom objects as you see fit.*

RIGHT: *Similarly, small nooks and crannies rather than one long shelf will help you keep order in the bathroom. By painting the interior of these shelves rather than continuing the tiling, they are more eye-catching.*

Bathroom makeover

Here is a fine combination of the old and the new. The Victorian roll-top bath and traditional pedestal basin have been installed in a bathroom with entirely white floor and wall tiles that are contemporary and timeless. To reach this stage, David and Martha had to overcome the avocado suite, a toilet perched right next to the basin, great swathes of greyed netting and an ancient and battered vinyl floor.

These last two items were easy to remove but the change to the fittings required a plumber. Before that, however, David and Martha had to decide on what sort of bathroom they would like. Did they favour white or would they like something more colourful? Having looked at lots of brochures from different manufacturers and at magazines they formulated their ideas and the picture opposite shows the end result.

The bath was a reconstituted antique that they found in a shop just around the corner, but the basin

Before: *Once the floral wallpaper had been removed from the walls it was easier for the owners of this house to decide in what direction they would go with their new decor.* RIGHT

After: *The simple approach was decided on and the clean white lines of ceramic tiles on both the walls and floor were chosen to maintain as simple a surface as possible.* RIGHT

and toilet are new. By moving the bath nearer to the window, they realised the toilet could be moved to a more private part of the room and as the plumber would be with them for a few days anyway installing the new fittings, they decided to put this plan into action at the same time.

When it comes to tiling a bathroom, the plumber and tiler have to work in close conjunction with each other because the final bath fittings can't be put in place until the tiles have been fixed to the wall and floor. To ease the work, David and Martha ensured their professionals were used to working together.

The moulded tiles used on the wall in this bathroom look terrific because their raised surface creates shadows, bringing added interest to the walls.

Once the surfaces were completed, David and Martha chose their eclectic set of accessories – a white plinth here for towels, a clear plastic pseudo-crocodile skin shower curtain, even a tall cactus plant and a pink proteus or two. In a contemporary setting such as this, anything goes. Finally, to round off the room and to retain their privacy, a piece of muslin has been hung from the bottom half of the window and a simple white roller blind suspended from the top.

ORDER OF EVENTS

1 Back to basics: a major stripping of wallpaper and flooring left the room sufficiently bare for David and Martha to be able to stand back and take stock for a while.

2 Electricity: David and Martha chose to install low halogen downlights across the ceiling on a dimmer switch to allow for different atmospheres to be created.

3 Plumbing and heating: the existing heating system and style of radiator suited David and Martha very well so they kept things as they were. However, the bathroom suite needed replacing and moving around.

4 Flooring I: this was laid at the same time as the wall tiles were put up. As it was such a large job and one that could so easily look dreadful if badly done, a professional tiler was employed.

5 Woodwork: the storage cupboard in this room was always going to be freestanding and turned out to be a chrome piece anyway, so there was no need for a joiner.

6 Surface preparation: with the exception of the window and door frames, there was none to be done as the bathroom was covered with tiles.

7 Decorating: just exactly as for surface preparation, Martha only needed to apply paint to the window and door frames.

8 Flooring II: to prevent slipping about on the floor when climbing out of the bath, a cork mat was found that lives on the floor next to the bath.

9 Soft furnishings: some minimal dressing to the window. The roller blind was fixed in the opposite direction to that which is normally associated with blinds so that the mechanism is hidden behind the end of the blind when rolled up.

Making changes

A guide to alternative decorative details

Taps: spend time looking through bathroom fitting catalogues: the finishes and tap mechanisms are numerous.
▷ choosing bathroom fittings 198-199

Mirrors: a mirror is more than a reflective surface to aid your make-up routine and teeth cleaning; the frame, shape and style will add to the rest of the room's decor.

Accessories: the small items you choose for something as small as a toothbrush or bar of soap or as large as a towel rail are almost as important as the larger bathroom fittings themselves. Take these opportunities to say something more about your style: introduce different colours or further the theme established on the floors and walls.

choosing bathroom fittings 198-201

Floor and wall tiles: with the myriad choice available for flooring and walls, you will need to have a very firm idea of the colour you wish to use in the bathroom. You can then decide on the size of each tile and whether you want to inject further pattern and texture.

choosing wall tiles 170-171
choosing hard flooring 176-177

CHILDREN'S ROOMS

ABOVE: *Make everything as cosy and comfortable as possible in the nursery to help while away those hours in the middle of the night.*

Children's rooms are fun, vibrant and filled with original ideas, and are an important part of growing up. Today's smaller families mean that most children can expect a room of their own – at least for a few years – so the child's room has become very much his or her special space, operating as a playroom and workroom as well as for sleeping. Gone are the days when you sent them to their room as a punishment!

Many people also believe that the right decor can be part of the learning process. For example, bright colours and bold shapes are designed to stimulate a baby (but take care not to over-stimulate; you do want your sleep after all), while older children can be allowed to express their personalities and develop their own sense of style. The most obvious way of doing this is through their choice of wallpapers and bedlinen – a pretty floral for a feminine little girl, or Disney designs for cartoon fans.

Studies have shown that children whose artwork is displayed on the walls gain confidence in their own abilities. Where children share a room, use changes in the decor, such as altering the colour or design around the room, to mark out separate areas. In this way, each child

RIGHT: *Over the years, traditional wooden toys and subtly designed fabrics have retained their place in the well-dressed nursery.*

has a space they can call their own. As they grow older, bedrooms become an important place for socialising and doing homework in – serious studies require peace and quiet, and most teenagers prefer to shut the door on the rest of the family when seeing their friends.

Building in growth

Children grow and change quickly, so before making any expensive decisions on wallpapers and fabrics, think about whether they will look too babyish in a few years time. For those who don't wish to re-decorate every few years, there are easy, fun ways of designing a room that is appropriate for any child from babyhood upwards and which can be adapted as they grow. One good method is to start with a fairly classic background, such as a striped wallpaper or a plain painted wall, and add elements that can be changed easily, like bedlinen, cushions, lampshades and borders. In a small room, the cost will not be too great, and many stores have excellent ranges of affordable children's designs.

The background can be as vibrant as you like – here's your chance to experiment with something you think is too outrageous for any other room. There is a huge range of stencils available, for example, especially for children's rooms. Big, small, flying kites, fluffy clouds,

teddy bears and dolls, whatever you are looking for, you are likely to find. Stencilling is a fantastically easy way to add colour to a room, and quick too. If you fancy something with a little more detail, look for transfers, which simply adhere with water.

Then introduce more colour and patterns with changeable accessories. After a few years, designs of teddies and bunnies can be replaced with favourite film characters, horses, ballet or trains. Out will go the mobiles, night lights and soft toys, in come rugged toy boxes, dolls' houses and bookcases. Instead of a changing table, room can be found for a desk. Even if your taste and that of your child don't coincide, try to give them the chance to develop their own sense of style and individuality. It may be galling to have to paint the walls sugar-sweet pink and fill the room with frills and roses if the rest of your house is a model of restraint, but it's a good way of giving children an investment in what their rooms look like.

Rooms for older children

Many people don't want to buy expensive furniture for children's rooms because they think children may wreck it, but that doesn't mean that children's furniture has to be dull and boring. Buy junk shop chairs, tables and cupboards and renovate them with paint, decoupage or stencils – which you can change when you tire of the designs. And children are much more forgiving of mistakes, so it gives you a good opportunity to practise. However, do check the serviceability of such furniture: deal effectively with wobbly legs and protruding nails.

You don't have to buy much purpose-built children's furniture, but small chairs and tables are far more comfortable for little legs, so it is well worth investing in a set that they will probably use until they are around six. Plain wooden coffee tables often make great toddler

tables, and can be re-painted or stained later on to have a second life in grown-up rooms. Little wooden chairs painted with the child's name have become increasingly popular as christening or birthday presents. And for something really special, you could even have pieces of furniture specially commissioned from a craftsman, creating an antique of the future which your children will be able to pass down to their children.

If you are buying new furniture, look at how it grows. Many cots turn into starter beds, and changing chests into standard chests of drawers. Make sure you see the conversion set up in the shop and check that you are happy with it in all its incarnations – and then don't forget where you've left the instructions and spare parts. You can equally easily adapt or use adult furniture – a single adult bed in a child's room, for example, will double as a sofa and spare bed, adding flexibility when people come to stay or if you need to spend the night with a sick baby.

If you don't have the space for a second bed look into the many space-saving ideas that are on the market. There are versatile bunk beds available with desks beneath and either a single seat that converts into a bed or – especially popular with teenagers – a sofabed adjacent to a pull-out wardrobe. Alternatively, buy a single bed that stores a second bed beneath it, complete with mattress. Once a child gets to school, 'sleepovers' become the greatest treat, so some kind of extra bed, even if it is only a spare mattress kept under the bed, is an essential requirement.

Solutions for storage

Storage is the biggest problem in children's rooms, because they are often the smallest rooms in the house and have to contain an ever-increasing amount of clutter. As well as a wardrobe or fitted cupboard and a chest of drawers, a toy chest, open shelves, wooden pegs, hanging bags and endless stackable boxes and cartons are vital for dressing-up clothes, building blocks, soft toys, games and jigsaws. If there isn't an easy place to put things, then tidying away will become even more of a chore – and children who really prefer things tidy will get very frustrated.

Of course, cupboards are the best form of storage because the doors can always be shut on whatever clutter is inside. Think carefully about your – or, rather, your child's – requirements and then search until you have found what you need. Cupboards are made with endless variations on hanging space, shelves, drawers and additional cupboards beneath or above the main compartment. You may decide that you need hanging rails that can start off low and be raised as the child grows (so useful for preventing the stepping-out-of-clothes-and-leaving-in-the-middle-of-the-bedroom-floor scenario), lots of shelves for sweaters and perhaps a few games, an additional drawer or two or a cupboard up high for storing a spare duvet and pillow.

If you can't find something to suit your needs, ask a local joiner to create something to meet your requirements. Such customised furniture is especially useful if the room is small or an unusual shape. MDF is an especially good material for such a construction. It is strong and easy to paint – you can really go to town on decorating it to match the rest of the room's decor.

choosing storage 184-187

LEFT: *A teenager will definitely want to stamp his or her own personality on their bedroom. Don't be surprised if the strongest and most unusual of colour combinations should suddenly come into play.*

Added extras

RIGHT: *For versatile and colourful storage, use hanging shelves such as these. They can be shuffled about at will and fit into the smallest of spare spaces if you want a little extra in the bedroom.*

ABOVE: *There are so many bright and lively desk accessories to choose from that it can be difficult to know where to begin. To prevent a room from becoming too much of a mixture, choose two or three favourite colours and buy accessories in that range.*

LEFT: *The space beneath a bed can all too readily be wasted and if your rooms are small then it is worth utilising it. Storage boxes and drawers on wheels keep items organised.*

ABOVE: *Keep drawings and paintings in order by buying a few art folders. They are great for storing homework too.*

Children's room makeover

Here is a room that has seen several reincarnations over the last five years. When the current owners of this house moved in, it was a spare bedroom complete with wash basin and gas fire. However, they had other ideas for this room and swiftly turned it into an office-cum-spare room so removed the basin. Now it has become their son's bedroom and the office has been moved downstairs. In a house where there is limited space, the arrival of a child or two can often mean that rooms are shuffled around and fulfil more than one use.

The end result is a room that any young child would love to be in. The flooring is perfect for easy cleaning and for creating complicated toy car traffic jams; the large cupboard houses both clothes and practically organised toy boxes; and the decor, although child orientated, is not going to be something that Leo will grow out of in a hurry.

Before: *A tribute to less design-conscious days, this bedroom showed a distinct disregard for its heritage.*

After: *Its fireplace, mouldings and window frame have now been restored to their former glory once again.* RIGHT

The inspiration for the large cupboard was a Victorian one that exists on the landing outside Leo's bedroom door. His parents hired a joiner to build a similar one so that the exterior would fit well into the style of the house. The interior, however, is a masterpiece of

ABOVE & RIGHT: Blue and yellow were chosen as the dominant colours, combined with a sailing theme. However, the matt yellow eggshell that was applied to all the woodwork turned out to be far too orange and overpowering. Leo's mother toned it down with a coat of white watered-down emulsion.

thoughtful contemporary planning. The top half of the cupboard holds all Leo's clothes on a range of hangers and shelves each of which can be moved around to accommodate increasingly large items as he grows taller and taller. The bottom houses clear plastic toy boxes resting on parallel lengths of doweling to make it easy for Leo to pick and choose his toys and lift them out of the cupboard.

Leo's parents also had fun decorating the room to make it a happy place to sleep and play in. The stencilled border running around the top of the walls was inspired by a collection of wooden boats owned by Leo's mother – here you can see them on the window frame – and the distressed wooden mirror surround was painted to continue the theme. They cut out the stencils themselves and each boat has been designed and painted to be different from all the others.

The ceiling, too, has been decorated with stamped stars. These were created by cutting different sizes of star from sponges with a stiff backing that were then stuck one by one onto the end of a long pole. By brushing paint onto the sponge, Leo's very own milky way has been created by simply raising the sponge to the ceiling.

ABOVE & RIGHT: A fine and flexible storage solution for clothes and toys. Leo can choose his clothes of a morning and then see very clearly which toys are where. By dividing them into farm animals, building bricks, cooking utensils and the like, he should always find what he is after.

ORDER OF EVENTS

1 **Back to basics:** having already taken out the wash basin, the next thing to do was to remove the gas fire from in front of the fireplace and take out the carpet.

2 **Damp proofing:** not really an issue as the house had been damp proofed several years earlier.

3 **Electricity:** the central pendant light was sufficient for a child's bedroom and any additional light for reading can be provided with a bedside table lamp or a clip-on fitting.

4 **Plumbing and heating:** the radiator was quite sufficient for this room and already in a good place so that was one less thing to think about.

5 **Flooring I:** Leo's parents knew they wanted a wooden floor but that the existing floorboards were very draughty. They bought new close fitting tongue and groove flooring that was positioned across the existing floor. After plenty of coats of clear matt varnish the end result is warm and durable.

6 **Woodwork:** the picture rail was reinstated and the toy cupboard built. The window frames were replaced with wood – more suitable for the period of the house.

7 **Surface preparation:** the old wallpaper needed to be removed, but the paintwork didn't need stripping just the surface roughened ready for a fresh coat of paint.

8 **Decorating:** working from the ceiling down towards the floor and painting the woodwork last, all the base coats of paint were applied. The white emulsion is washable so that all those grubby fingerprints can be easily wiped. The stencilling and sponging effects were then applied.

9 **Flooring II:** The striped rug was chosen to complement the colour scheme and to give the room a focal point.

10 **Soft furnishings:** so that Leo wouldn't grow out of his bedroom too quickly, the curtains have been made from fabric that will remain timeless. The pointy pelmet hanging down the front is a youthful extra that has been made a part of the room with the addition of small sea shells stitched to the end of each point. They were ready pierced with holes to make them easier to use.

Making changes

A guide to alternative decorative details

Flooring: fitted carpets are soft and warm underfoot in a child's room so if you don't want to install floorboards like these, go for the softer option.

choosing carpets172-173

Fabrics:you may prefer to choose a curtain fabric that co-ordinates with a border or a more obvious nursery design. You will probably have to change the curtains as your child grows up but if you have a simple curtain, the expense won't be too great.

choosing soft furnishings 204-205
creating soft furnishings 268-273

Friezes: choose one of the many paper borders that wallpaper manufacturers produce and in place of stencilling along the top of the wall, run a wallpaper frieze. Alternatively, stick the border around the wall as a dado.

choosing wallpapers 168-169

▷ wallpapering 252-255

Storage: in place of the toy box supports in these cupboards, use small plastic and cardboard containers. These can be stacked in a cupboard, beneath the bed or just in the corner of the room. Colour co-ordinate them with the rest of the room's decor.

▷ choosing storage 184-187

HOME OFFICES

ABOVE: *A home office with a difference. The occupier of this particular room is an artist who nevertheless requires a work area: stored neatly in a distant corner.*

The home office has become an integral part of the home – not just for work purposes, but because every home needs some kind of a centre for correspondence and bills. Working fully or partly from home has become a reality for many people, so the ownership of personal computers and fax machines has made some kind of a mini-office more of a necessity.

Home offices don't need to be large, but they do need careful planning. If you work at home, even for a few hours a week, then it will be irritating (if not impossible on busy days) to completely clear work away at the end of every day in order to use the room for something else in the evening. And, once installed, PCs cannot be moved lightly. So if you are creating a dual-use room – a home office-cum-dining room, for example – you will need to plan both uses equally carefully, and don't expect daily miracles of tidying from yourself.

The core of a good office

Ergonomics is an important part of office planning and these practicalities are just as important in the home.

RIGHT: *With the advent of lap-tops, a home office does not have to occupy a large space. With plenty of storage the area can be kept paper-free.*

Don't fall for a small desk because it fits into the space on the wall – start all your measurements from the size of your monitor, the position in which you will sit, and how much space you need so that both you and your computer can operate properly. Also make sure that whatever you buy to stand your PC on is sufficiently strong and stable. A personal computer is quite heavy and has a number of trailing wires, so however inexpensive or attractive a trestle-type set-up may be, you need to be quite sure you are not going to pull it over.

It is important, too, that the monitor is positioned straight ahead of you, with your eyebrows in line with the top of the screen. Their depth demands around 60cm (24in) of desk space just for the screen, and you will need a good extra 25cm (10in) in front of that for the keyboard and any paperwork you are using. Pull-out or pull-down flaps which can provide this extra work-surface and the L-shaped desk, with the personal computer on the corner where there is greater depth, are good solutions. But make sure that your chair can swivel around to face the monitor – don't allow yourself to spend much time with your keyboard in front of you and the screen to one side.

You should be able to sit in your chair with your elbows at right angles when you type, and your shoulders should not be hunched. If you have a chair with armrests, check that they are not getting in the way of this position. Your body, hips, knees and legs should also form a series of right angles, and you may need a footrest to achieve this. The chair should also be able to swivel and move, so that you don't have to twist and strain your body. However, this doesn't mean that you will need to spend a fortune on a smart office chair – you can often find perfectly well designed ones that fit all these criteria and are comfortable in second-hand office suppliers or inexpensive office furniture outlets.

As you plan your desk layout don't forget that you need space for paperwork – whether it is a bank account, notes or the letter you are replying to. You will also need a printer, which will probably need to be close by, and you may want a fax and a telephone. Printers and faxes are now fairly compact, but around 41cm (16in) square is average, with room needed behind for

LEFT: *If a desk faces a window, sunny days can cause problems with glare on paperwork. The ideal solution is a roller or roman blind, which can be pulled down just as far as is necessary.*

cabling. You may also want to consider installing an adi-tional telephone line, especially if you are planning on using a fax machine, modem and e-mail for sending and receiving work.

Disguising your assets

If you are installing a PC into an often-used room, such as a kitchen, and you want to be able to put it away, then consider converting a tall cupboard. It will have to be deep enough to take the computer with the door closed, but you can incorporate a pull-out or pull-down surface for the keyboard and work. You will also need to make sure that the shelf is strong enough to bear the weight, and that it is the right height to sit at, with room underneath for your knees once the desk is pulled out. Check, too, that you are not in everyone's way when you are actually using it!

There's a great deal of wiring and cabling to be hid-den away, too, so make sure that this can run easily to the power point, and that there's no chance of anyone tripping over it. If you are converting a cupboard or desk, you may be able to drill holes down the back to keep all the wiring stowed away. If you are installing the equipment in a cupboard, make sure that you can switch off anything electrical or that there are ventila-tion slats or similar. Electrical equipment always gener-ates considerable amounts of heat. Other ways of dis-guising the equipment if it is part of a family room is to pull a curtain around the computer at the end of the day or strategically position a screen or two around the work area. Vary the decor on each side as much or as little as you like.

Lighting and storage: two priorities

Lighting is the next important element. A traditionally lit room probably won't have a good enough light for working, but the addition of an Anglepoise-type lamp at the desk is all you need. As well as checking that you have enough light to see clearly, you also need to ensure that it doesn't shine onto the screen and cause reflec-tions. The same is true of strong sunlight – if you sit near

LEFT: *Boxes, baskets, ring binders and drawers are simple and effective ways to keep office clutter in order – and hidden away. Be as colourful or muted as you like: the range of designs is certainly all-encompassing.*

choosing lighting 180-181

a window, you may have to add a blind – vertical, roller or roman are the most versatile – to stop glare.

Storage is a more difficult part to plan. If your home office is simply a central place for running household affairs or a homework zone, this will be fairly straight-forward. If, however, you are creating a working home office from scratch, having only worked in an office before, it is almost impossible to tell what you will want to hand and how much storage and filing you will generate. Start with listing what you think you will need and then treble it.

Decorative detail

All this grey-looking equipment and piles of clutter hard-ly lifts the heart when it comes to decoration. All too fre-quently in the past, filing cabinets and shelves have been dismal-looking objects, but they are becoming less and less so. They can be both functional and attractive and shelves needn't be unforgiving planks covered in Melamine balancing on angled brackets. Look around for pieces of furniture that fit into your colour scheme and consider some of the extremely flexible shelving units that are available in every material from reclaimed pine to metal.

You may well feel that as you are spending so many hours in this room each day, it is worth having custom-built shelves made to meet your own specifications. If this is the case, take time to work out exactly what your needs are. Pay special attention to the depths of the shelves and their distances apart. It is probably worth having a variety of depths and heights to accommodate different sized books, pieces of equipment, and any-thing else that you may want to keep on them. Also keep an eye open for attractively covered boxes for stor-ing your CDs, disks and photographs or magazines and the fantastically wide range of stylish ring binders.

Aim to create a space that is as calm as possible to work in. Pale yellows, ochres and blues are all soothing for the walls and furnishings, and keep the flooring sim-ple – no wild patterns to make your eyes dance. Then plan your furnishings so that as much as possible is to hand and the desk positioned so that your view isn't of a blank wall (too dismal), although equally you don't want to be too distracted by the view through the win-dow if it is a busy spot. Keep window treatments unfussy and practical and ensure that fresh air is to hand, especially on hot days (if you don't have too much paperwork, you may want to install a fan somewhere), so that the room doesn't become too soporific. Finally, always make sure you have some flowers on your desk – they will be guaranteed to give you a lift, even on the darkest of days.

ways with windows 206-217   creating soft furnishings 268-273

Added extras

OPPOSITE: *The best bookshelves are divided into small compartments. Objects can be organised more clearly and so readily found when required.*

LEFT: *Wicker filing trays are much more natural affairs than all those plastic designs so beloved of corporate life. They look far more attractive in the home.*

LEFT: *This small seat has an impressive contents and has the advantage of doubling up its uses.*

ABOVE: *The ubiquitous hat box of course has a place in the home office. Large and small, they are perfect for storing rolls of sticky tape, staplers, and other such chunky parts of office life.*

LEFT: *Use photographs or other devices to remind you of the contents of your filing drawers. If you have seried rows of these it can be particularly frustrating to find the exact drawer you require.*

LEFT: *Use waste paper baskets for storing outsize items. Rubbish need not be their only contents.*

ABOVE & LEFT: *Desk accessories can combine style with function. Make sure that above all else your chair is at the right height and will be comfortable for several hours at a time.*

Home office makeover

An office can generate masses of paper. With careful planning and by making use of storage boxes and cupboards where you can hide things away, it is possible to keep an office at home as apparently paper free as possible. This is just what Debbie set out to achieve here when she created this working area in her home.

As you can see from the 'before' photograph shown below (the fireplace stands next to the newly installed cupboards in the 'after' photograph), this room was not in the greatest of shape when Debbie first moved into the house. There was a proliferation of damp nooks and crannies resulting in peeling wallpaper and the old battered floorboards had definitely seen better days. However, after much hard work – the rest of the house was no better and damp treatment was the first priority – a streamlined office for Debbie to work in is the result.

Before: *What a ruin. Peeling paper and aged paintwork took some stripping. But the alcoves on either side of the fireplace were destined to make the perfect place for shelves and cupboards.* RIGHT

After: *A few months later and this is the end result: a home office where anyone would want to work. Ordered, colourful and with a desk with a view: the perfect makeover.* RIGHT

ABOVE & RIGHT: Storage containers come in all shapes and sizes. Some are designed for specific items such as CDs, computer disks and magazines, whereas others have more miscellaneous uses in mind.

After removing all the wallpaper, Debbie sanded back the floorboards to discover some quite presentable woodwork, which she has now varnished to seal. She then concentrated on planning her storage units, which entailed hiring a joiner for a few days and hunting down an old school desk that she knew would be just the thing to place in front of the window. The view is of rolling countryside so it was important that nothing block this out and as the window sill is low anything larger would have done this. When she was out searching for the desk, Debbie came across the blue/green storage boxes and it is from these that she derived her plans for the colour of the room.

Cool and calm, the pale aqua used on all the walls and woodwork gives the room a restrained and peace-

RIGHT: A Victorian school desk with a difference: they certainly were never as colourful as this in the past. It is Debbie's intention to further the theme of her office by collecting other school paraphernalia such as ink wells, old school photos and slates.

ORDER OF EVENTS

1 Back to basics: preparation was the most time-consuming task as there was damp and aged wallpaper to contend with.

2 Damp proofing: along with the rest of the house, this room was treated very thoroughly so that damp would not recur.

3 Electricity: with technology requiring electric sockets and the necessity of good lighting at a desk, it was important to get the electrician in at the beginning.

4 Plumbing and heating: a complete new central heating system was installed when Debbie and Greg first moved into this house so by the time she reached this room, heating and plumbing were no longer a concern.

5 Flooring I: Debbie's chosen finish was stripped floorboards so the sanding needed to take place next, to avoid the resulting dust ruining any new paintwork.

6 Woodwork: to maximise storage potential, a joiner was hired to create shelves and cupboard space in the alcoves on either side of the fireplace.

7 Surface preparation: a certain amount of replastering had to be done following the damp treatment, but once this had dried out sufficiently there was little else to do before decorating.

8 Decorating: using just two colours of paint meant that this part of the room's transformation happened very quickly.

9 Flooring II: now that the room was all but finished, Debbie felt she would like to add a simple coir runner to the floorboards as an attractive finishing touch.

10 Soft furnishings: the length of muslin was hung at the window and Debbie is now looking for some bright fabric to make a cushion cover for a colourful highlight.

ful setting that is so necessary when concentrating on work. To help retain its aged qualities, the desk was painted with a coat of crackle glaze over the emulsion so that the paint would break up in a suitably old-fashioned style. The emulsion on the rest of the woodwork was finished with a few coats of acrylic varnish to render it wipeable. The walls looked disproportionately tall in the room, so the white on the ceiling also covers the top 20cm (8in) or so of the walls to improve the proportions. Debbie has also hung white muslin at the window to retain that fresh quality.

So that this home office can take up the least possible amount of space, Debbie chose a folding director's chair to accompany her desk. If she chooses, she can put it away in the nearby cupboard at the end of the day.

Making changes

A guide to alternative decorative details

Storage: pick and choose your containers to suit your purposes. Also use them as style statements in their own right, introducing colour and texture to your work space.
choosing storage 184-187

Waste: even wastebaskets will say something about your style. Look for brightly coloured, understated metal or something you have decorated yourself – don't forget the finishing touches.

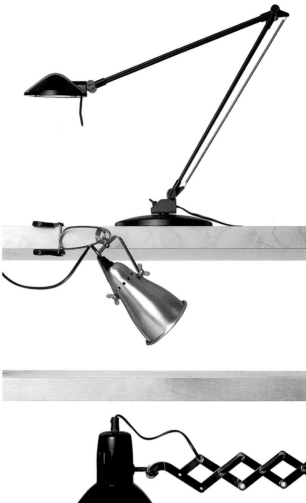

Lighting-up: a good desk lamp is an important part of any office and can be freestanding, designed with clips for the edges of desks or shelves, or fixed to the wall.

choosing lighting 180-183

CONSERVATORIES

ABOVE: *The checkerboard floor in this conservatory perfectly complements a restrained and sophisticated finish where white dominates the space.*

The change in the role of the kitchen from the servant's quarters to the heart of the home usually means that gloomy kitchens with very little access to the garden need to be replaced by light, bright rooms that children and guests can swarm in and out of. Removing most of a side or back wall, and replacing it with a conservatory adds floor space and allows light to flood into the darkest of kitchens, as well as allowing an excellent view of the garden.

However, there have been too many crude copies of Victorian conservatories, and it is important to recognise that if the conservatory is to become an extra all-weather room, then its building specifications are just as important as for any other room in the house. All too easily you can end up with something that is too hot in the summer and too cold in the winter and you will rarely want to use it.

There are three main types of conservatory based on a frame shape: square with a hipped roof, lean-to, or bay/hexagonal. When you are making your decision, keep in mind the style of your house as the finished conservatory really does need to blend in so that it looks as

RIGHT: *A conservatory is the perfect setting for a candlelit dinner. The reflections in the glass and lavish floral arrangement add to the romance.*

though it has always been there. If you have a choice of positions, avoid as many temperature fluctuations as possible by building on the west side of your home. A south-facing conservatory can easily suffer from too much heat in the summer – but if this is your only option you can help alleviate the problem with ventilation.

Indeed, proper ventilation is crucial to most conservatories. The traditional Victorian double roofed conservatory had a row of windows at the top acting as a chimney for hot air. If you don't have this, then you need around 40% of your roof area to be windows to maintain proper ventilation. Some designs are too delicate to hold the mechanisms of several roof windows, but the answer here is to persevere until you find a design that you like which can be ventilated properly. You will also need an air brick, vent, or other windows at a lower level, so that the air can circulate, or you can install a fan. Do check how noisy it is, first, however.

If you and your family tend to be out a lot during the day you may want to look into automatic roof vents that open and shut depending on the heat. There are electrically operated and other more low-budget sensors available which your conservatory supplier will be able to tell you about.

As well as becoming too hot, conservatories suffer from the other extremes of temperature – too cold in the winter and in the evenings. So be prepared to plan for heating as well as ventilation. If you are going to extend the central heating from the house, pipes may have to run under the floor so it is obviously important to plan them in advance of building the conservatory. And while you are at it, think about what other services you may require such as water supply, electricity and a TV aerial.

LEFT: Slatted roller blinds on the conservatory roof don't totally block out the sun. Instead, soft shadows are cast all around on the walls and floor.

RIGHT: Here a style reminiscent of a beach hut interior has been created with white rattan furniture and sheer curtains hanging at the door. It is refreshingly cool and inviting.

Double- or even treble-glazing is a must in conservatories, and you should also consider low-'E' (low-emissivity) glass, which helps prevent heat escaping in the winter. With the thinning of the ozone layer, many people now also install UV filters on their conservatory roofs. Experts suggest using laminated safety glass for the roof, which has a plastic film that holds the glass in place if it shatters. It is also preferable to use toughened glass for the sides, because if it does break, it bursts into lots of tiny pieces and is less likely to cut someone.

Finishing the conservatory

Internal roof blinds provide shade and help keep the temperature constant, but their mechanisms are complicated, and not a job for an amateur. It is best to have them made by a specialist blinds company, or by someone who has extensive past experience of conservatory blinds. Once you have decided what you want your blinds to do – do you want them to be simply decorative or should they provide shade, privacy, insulation and glare reduction? – you can then decide on an appropriate fabric and style. For the roof, look into more dense weaves than those used for the side windows and do make sure they are washable. For a total sun block,

◁ assessing the situtation 8-9   ◁ making plans 14-15

choose a thermal-coated blind, or consider acrylic, polyester or even PCV-coated fibreglass. There are many companies who specialise in blinds for conservatories so talk to a few to see what options you have. You also need to think about whether you want to operate the blinds by hand, cord, motor or even remote control. As for the style of the blinds, the most popular types include pleated, roller or roman, and for the side windows look at vertical louvre or Venetian blinds.

Your choice of flooring, too, can help keep the temperature constant, as flagstones and tiles act as 'heat bricks', retaining warmth on cold days, especially if you have underfloor heating. Ceramic tiles, vinyl and linoleum are cheaper options but bear in mind that they can become slippery when wet. Whatever you choose, ensure the surface is durable and easy to clean – as so many conservatories open out into the garden, dirt is more than likely to be trampled into the flooring. Carpet is probably the least appropriate material for a conservatory floor – and it will fade in the sun. Floorboards will fade too, but the effect will be less obvious and the patina of age on wood is often part of its attraction.

If you are planning on growing lots of plants in your conservatory – this was, after all, their original use – and intend to have plenty of pots and perhaps a raised bed or two in which to grow all your beauties, you may want to look into automatic watering systems. These come as fine gauge hoses that drip a slow but steady supply of water wherever you lay them. They can also be attached to timer devices. The real advantage of systems like these is that you can go away on holiday safe in the knowledge that you will come back to a green haven rather than a shrivelled desert.

Don't feel compelled to have purpose-designed conservatory furniture unless that is what you particularly want. If you are really going to enjoy the room, though, you will want chairs and sofas that are as comfortable as those in the living room, side tables for books, lamps and drinks, and possibly a dining table. Although the sunlight will fade fabrics, there is no other reason why any furniture should not be as appropriate for a conservatory as anywhere else, particularly if you have sorted out the problems of humidity and air flow.

choosing flooring 172-177   choosing sofas & chairs 222-223

LEFT: *When you are surrdounded with greenery, look to other shades of green – ranging from aqua to lime – with which to deocrate your space.*

Added extras

RIGHT: *As a kitchen extension a conservatory is an airy and comfortable dining area. Furnish it with plenty of natural materials and brightly coloured fabrics.*

ABOVE: *the conservatory is very often a place in which to sit and relax – and drinking a cup of tea and having something small to eat is the perfect way to do this. Look for colourful china to enhance the experience.*

LEFT: *Eat, drink and be merry. Colourful glasses abound, so choose some to match your dinnerware.*

RIGHT: *Wicker and wooden furniture made comfortable with piles of cushions is of primary importance in this, one of the most informal rooms in the house.*

2

The Home
Makeover
Directory

WALLS AND FLOORS

Paints

Decorating has never been such fun, all you need is a little imagination and product know-how to transform your home. Painting is all about colour and, with most major brands and DIY retailers promising to match virtually any colour, it couldn't be easier. However, choosing the most suitable paint can be confusing so to get the best possible finish for a surface, it's worth spending time studying the options.

Primer
This goes directly over bare wood or metal to form a protective layer. Don't skimp on this layer, quick drying versions are available. Use plaster primer or sealer on flaky or porous walls before applying emulsion.

Undercoat
This covers the primer or an existing colour. Choose a colour close to that of the top coat.

Gloss/top coat paints
Either water- or solvent-based and used on wood or metal finishes.
Solvent-based: these paints leave a high gloss finish but give off a strong odour while drying. Brushes need to be cleaned with a solvent or white spirit. Softer gloss finishes are available to imitate traditional eggshell paints known as satin finish or satinwood.
Water-based acrylic gloss: paints made in this way are becoming more popular because they are easier to use, are virtually odour-free and brushes can be cleaned in water. However, they are not as durable or shiny.

Emulsion paints
Water-based paints suitable for indoor walls and ceilings. Available in runny or non-drip, solid consistencies. Most emulsions now contain vinyl for greater durability and are available in matt (a soft, velvet appearance), silk (a delicate sheen) and soft sheen. Brushes and rollers can be cleaned in water. Emulsions suitable for external use may be called masonry paints.

Textured paints made from thickened emulsion are ideal for masking uneven walls and ceilings. Special effects can also be achieved using a texturing tool. Be warned, though, that once on, they are difficult to remove.

One-coat paints
Available as gloss or emulsion, these don't need an undercoat although you will still need to prime bare wood first. Although more expensive than traditional alternatives they do go further. If you use a brush, only one coat is necessary, but you will need to do two when using a roller.

Special paints
Anti-stain paint: used for covering heavy stains prior to painting. Usually solvent-based.
Bituminous paint: gives a long lasting protection to gutters and downpipes. It cannot be covered by another paint unless sealed with an aluminium primer.
Floor paint: covers concrete, stone, paving and quarry tiles. A heavy duty non-slip, grease resistant garage floor paint is also available.
Microporous paint or stains: can be applied to bare wood, outdoors. It is

flexible and expands and contracts at the same rate as the wood. Tiny pores in the paint allow any moisture in the wood to pass through the paint, preventing blistering and flaking. Primer and undercoat are not required.

Radiator paint: an enamel available in gloss and satin finishes, and in a range of basic colours. White does not yellow with the heat. Other enamel paints are available for covering metal areas such as kitchen appliances.

Spray paints: these are becoming increasingly popular and are ideal for covering different surfaces such as timber, metal, plastic and wicker. Stick to using over small areas or for decorative effects.

Traditional paints: these produce an old-fashioned, less uniform finish with antique tones and textures. Made from traditional ingredients (linseed oil, plant extracts and pigments), they mature well to give a soft, slightly chalky patina. Traditional oil-based paints, including eggshell, and water-based paints, including limewash and distemper, are available from specialist stockists. Currently there is a trend towards modern manufacturers simulating the traditional colours and textures in their paints.

WATCHPOINTS

◆ Buy all layers from the same brand to ensure compatibility.

◆ If you don't want wallpaper but like something more interesting than plain paint consider colourwashing or other paint effects.

◆ Allow 1 litre of standard emulsion or gloss to cover 12 sq m on walls and woodwork:
A door would be 1.5 sq m; a window 1 sq m; and 7m of skirting board, 1 sq m.

◆ For kitchens and bathrooms, it's worth considering an anti-condensation paint (known as kitchen and bathroom paint). These emulsion paints have a tough, water-resistant finish and reduce the risk of condensation and mould growth. Alternatively, use in children's rooms as they are easy to wipe clean.

◆ Don't wallpaper newly plastered areas, but use emulsion paint as this allows the plaster to dry out.

◆ If you want to transform old furniture or kitchen units, for example, try one of the fake wood kits which include a graining tool, base coat and grain coat.

◆ Instead of painting woodwork, use a coloured varnish or wood stain covered by several layers of clear varnish for protection. There is a huge range of colours and finishes available.

painting 240-243   creating paint effects 244-249

Wallpapers

Wallpaper is the fastest way to add a dramatic transformation to a room. You can add atmosphere, vitality and light by selecting the right colour and pattern. It is all about creative application, so experiment by hanging paper horizontally or using blocks of colour to create a specific mood or theme. Because of technological advances, textured effects such as plaids, natural fabrics, tiles on a roll and crackle glaze finishes are much improved. Instead of fixing picture or dado rails, add interest to a solid wall by using border papers. If you don't feel confident in matching colours, most manufacturers have co-ordinating wallpaper, borders, paint and accessories.

There is a huge range of patterns and textures available from traditional wallpaper (some pre-pasted), paper backed vinyl, embossed papers suitable for painting over, and textiles. First consider where you are going to hang it – in the kitchen and bathroom, for example, wallcoverings must withstand condensation. For children's rooms you may wish to choose one of the many novelty papers or spongeable types to remove scribble. Some even allow you to build-up scenes, by sticking animals onto a background. However, avoid being too adventurous if this is your first attempt: stick to medium weight or vinyl papers with random patterns, which don't need matching, such as a mottled paint-effect.

Embossed or relief papers
These have a self-coloured, raised pattern that can be painted over, so are great for hiding imperfections. They are tough and can be spongeable and they include:
Anaglypta and supaglypta: these have very pronounced designs and are made from paper, plus cotton or clay, or vinyl. Good dent resistance.
Blown vinyls: created by heating the vinyl in an oven causing it to blow or expand. Deep embossed patterns result. Use an adhesive containing fungicide.
Lincrusta: one of the first embossed papers, made from linseed oil and flax fillers fused onto a paper backing, with a pattern rolled into it. Hard-wearing, it is ideal for halls and other high traffic areas. Available either in rolls or as a panel and needs specialist adhesive.

Woodchip: this is the cheapest form and is good for disguising lumpy walls. However, because it is made from sawdust and woodchips bonded on to paper it can be difficult to cut and thin varieties can tear easily when soaked with paste. Paint when thoroughly dry with silk or matt emulsion.

Lining paper
Use as a base, for decorative paper or paint, on walls that have lots of filled cracks or other imperfections. Available in three weights: light (for painting over), medium (for most wallpapers) and heavy (under embossed papers).

Standard wallpapers
There is a huge range of colours and designs available, often with matching borders. Cheaper papers have designs machine printed onto the paper but

the more expensive designer papers are hand designed. Look out for the narrow width (26cm [10¼in]) papers for creating a stripe effect used vertically or horizontally – or both.

Textile wall coverings

Traditionally paper-backed hessian and flocked papers are incrasingly readily available as they are undergoing a revival in popularity. However, other textile papers, like grasscloth and silk, are much less common now because paper simulations have been so much improved recently.

Vinyl wall coverings

Paper-backed vinyl: the colour and pattern is heat fused onto the vinyl rendering it is more resistant to moisture than washable vinyl. This is the best choice for kitchens and bathrooms as the paper withstands grease and spills well.

Washable: the printed paper is coated with a thin, clear layer of PVC which forms a barrier against moisture. Paper like this can be sponged clean but avoid scrubbing.

Both types need a special adhesive for borders stuck over the top.

WATCHPOINTS

◆ Choose wallpaper before paint since it is easier to match a shade of paint to a pattern than the other way round.

◆ Try a pattern at home in the room concerned before making your final decision. Colours that seem subtle in a pattern book can suddenly become strong and overwhelming when used throughout a room.

◆ Get hold of as large a sample as possible. Some shops may allow you to take a roll home of a pattern that you like. If this is not possible, ask whether you can order a larger sample swatch.

◆ Always consider the size of the pattern and decide whether the scale is appropriate for the height and length of the walls in the room in which it will be used.

◆ You may also need to think about the colour of the main element in the design. On a small sample, a strong green may balance well with the reds and blues around it, but when used on a large area this might become much more dominant. Likewise, a small pattern that looks fresh and colourful might get lost on large expanses of wall, paling to insignificance.

◆ Bear in mind, too, the overall atmosphere you are trying to create and to look at how the pattern you like will influence this.

▷ wallpapering 250-253

Wall tiles

Don't restrict tiles just to the kitchen and bathroom! By combining different shapes, styles and colours, interesting effects can be created throughout the house. For example, use mosaic tiles to develop a Mediterranean theme. Tiles can be expensive, particularly unusual patterns or hand-painted designer tiles so to keep costs down just tile areas that get splashed regularly, such as above sinks and around cookers and worktops. Make these partly tiled areas into a design feature by finishing with a row of ceramic dado or strip tiles, wooden mouldings or plastic trim.

Make picture frame or panel effects with border tiles, edge around sanitary units in the bathroom or around fireplaces. Interlock plain colours with a randomly placed dramatic patterned one. The range of tiles is so wide you will have fun creating something different.

Ceramic

These are a practical alternative to paint and wallpaper in kitchens and bathrooms and are generally glazed making them hard-wearing, easy to clean and impervious to water and condensation. They are available in standard sizes (10-15cm [4-6in] square) although some specialist shops will custom make.

More interesting shapes include oblong, hexagonal, octagonal, diamond and interlocking curves. Smaller inset tiles and narrow border tiles can produce stunning effects. Picture tiles can also be built-up to create picture panels.

For something a bit more unusual, some kitchen and bathroom tiles have a raised motif such as a bunch of grapes or a shell, which can look effective when combined with plain tiles. Or go to a salvage yard where you may be able to find period reclaimed tiles. But remember that they may not necessarily be a standard size as period tiles can be smaller than modern designs.

Tile edging options are varied too.

Border tiles, slips or ropes are good for edging areas or for forming a mock dado or picture rail. Some have raised, embossed designs.

Cork

Cork provides a warm, soft surface and can be a cheap way of soundproofing walls and ceilings. Wall tiles are slightly thinner than cork floor tiles and are usually around 30cm (12in) square but are easy to cut to size. Depending on the finish you want, look for self-adhesive, sealed or unsealed tiles. They are ideal for making into a noticeboard for children's rooms.

Mirror

These are effective if you want the room to look bigger or add focus to one part of it. Sizes range from 10 to 30cm (4 to 12in) squares or come in mosaic form, and are also available in a range of finishes such as silver, bronze or a smoked glass effect.

Mirror tiles must be level when fixed to a wall because the gaps can't be sealed. So don't use them in an area that might get wet.

removing textures & tiles 234   tiling walls & floors 254-257

Alternatives

Replacing tiles can be expensive, so see if you can renovate your existing ones using paint or transfers. Paint existing wall tiles by first applying a tile primer sealer followed by an eggshell paint, using a roller. Stencilling patterns onto plain tiles is another option. Another way of keeping costs down is by using plain tiles with the occasional patterned one dotted around.

Mosaic

These are tough and hard-wearing like ceramic tiles but are much smaller, usually consisting of many tiny tiles glued onto a paper or mesh backing approximately 20cm (8in) square. Gaps are left between the tiles for grouting. These are easier to fit around awkward areas and look particularly good on curved surfaces such as arches and alcoves. For a really individual effect, create a mosaic from bits of broken glass or tiles. Fixing may require a great deal of patience however!

WATCHPOINTS

◆ Make sure the tile you have chosen is right for the application; check this with the supplier.

◆ Think about the effect you want to achieve, and does the tiling blend well with fixtures and fittings?

◆ Dark tiles in small bathrooms and kitchens will make these rooms appear smaller.

◆ Dark colours also mark easily and need constant cleaning.

◆ All-white tiles can look clinical so if you want more visual interest add the occasional patterned tile or edge with an interesting border tile.

◆ Brighten up white tiles by using a coloured grouting. Use either a proprietary coloured grout powder or add fabric dye to standard white grout. However, bear in mind that fabric dye will fade in steamy bathrooms and kitchens.

Floor flair

Flooring is an essential part of interior design and should be chosen before tackling colour schemes and furnishings. This is the case not only because of its expense but because, more than any other decoration, it has to endure the most wear. It is important to achieve the right balance between practical considerations and aesthetic appeal.

First look at the floor before the covering is laid. If it is solid, any floor covering can be fitted (although some may need 'priming'), but if it's a suspended wooden floor, it may not be strong enough for heavier flooring such as ceramic, quarry, terracotta and other stone tiles.

Choose your flooring by first considering who will be using the room and for what. Then think about what you can afford. Ask yourself – how much wear will it get? And how long does it need to last? For example, a study may have to become a nursery in a few years, or vice versa. How easily will it clean and should it be water-resistant? How important is noise, comfort and appearance?

Below is a list of the main considerations you should bear in mind for each part of the house. The best options are given in the box opposite. Flooring can be divided into three main types: semi-hard (cork, linoleum, rubber and vinyl), soft (carpets, natural matting and rugs), and hard (tiles, paving and wood). These areas are covered over the next few pages.

Bathrooms
Here, the flooring must be waterproof and non-slip when wet.

Bedrooms
It is always best for the flooring to be comfy underfoot.

Conservatories
Take care with wood in conservatories because of extremes in temperature. It can warp very easily if it has not been sufficiently dried in advance of laying.

Dining areas
Must be easy to clean and tough to withstand chairs being dragged across.

Hallways
Here the flooring must be tough, look good, be water resistant and easy to keep clean. It should link well with other rooms and stairs.

Kitchens
Flooring in the kitchen must be hard-wearing, water- and stain-resistant, and easy to clean.

Living rooms
Flooring must look good and be practical.

Playrooms
Flooring must be soft, durable, warm, easy to clean and fun.

Stairs
Safety is of the essence, as is durability as this is a very hard-wearing area.

choosing soft flooring 174-175   choosing hard flooring 176-177

Semi-hard flooring

For a versatile flooring consider any of the following. Generally warm underfoot they are each excellent for areas of hard wear and tear – and especially if there is likely to be some water spillage in the region. Each of these types is a good compromise in place of the harder wearing floorings described on pages 176-177.

Cork

A natural material that provides a warm, quiet and durable flooring with good sound insulation properties. Choose thick and dense tiles for greater resilience, bearing in mind they will need sanding down when beginning to wear. Unsealed and ready-sealed versions are available, some with a self-adhesive backing, other tiles have a clear vinyl surface that is impervious to stains and spills. Cork is easy to lay on a flat surface.

Linoleum

Made from natural ingredients, linoleum is undergoing a revival. It is tough, quiet, slip-resistant, hygienic, colourfast and has a good resistance to dents, scratches and minor burns. It is available in tile or sheet form and you can mix and match colours, incorporate small inset tiles, or add borders. Sheet linoleum should be professionally laid.

Rubber

Traditionally used in commercial building, this type of flooring is now becoming more common in the home because of its warmth and practical features. Available in sheet or tile form, it is quiet underfoot, water-resistant, durable and easy to clean. It is also easy to lay.

Vinyl

A flexible plastic material available in sheet (2-4m [2-4yd] widths) or tiles. It is the most practical and versatile choice and due to technological advances designs have improved beyond recognition. Ranges are available that mimic effectively the appearance of natural materials but without their coldness. Vinyl is easy to clean, comfortable and quiet underfoot and water-resistant.

Sheet vinyl can be plain backed or cushioned for greater comfort. The thicker the cushioning, the greater the acoustic insulation properties of the flooring. However, the extra layer of expanded PVC foam sandwiched under the vinyl layer can be dented and damaged by moving heavy appliances across the surface. To prevent this from happening, stand equipment on hardboard or castors. Choose the thickest cushioned vinyl that you can afford as lower quality can scuff, and also look for a textured, non-slip surfaced vinyl if you are intending to use it in wet areas.

Vinyl tiles are either flexible or more rigid than sheet vinyl. The more rigid types are very hard-wearing and offer exciting and original designs. These should be professionally laid, however, whereas softer forms can be laid by the DIYer.

tiling walls & floors 254-257

WATCHPOINTS

Best flooring options

✦ *Bathrooms:* vinyl, sealed cork, linoleum or carpet (with water-resistant backing).

✦ *Bedrooms:* carpet, wood with scatter rugs, sisal or jute, vinyl, cork.

✦ *Conservatories:* natural fibre matting, brick, quarry, ceramic or terracotta tiles, rubber, vinyl.

✦ *Dining areas:* stain-resistant carpet, cushioned vinyl, linoleum, sealed cork or wood, natural matting, polished boards.

✦ *Hallways:* wood (boards or parquet), unglazed ceramic, quarry or terracotta tiles, heavy-duty carpet, vinyl, linoleum, natural matting.

✦ *Kitchens:* semi-hard or hard flooring, stain-resistant carpet tiles.

✦ *Living rooms:* most types.

✦ *Playrooms:* carpet tiles, cork, rubber and cushioned vinyl.

✦ *Stairs:* heavy-duty carpet with short, dense pile, natural matting.

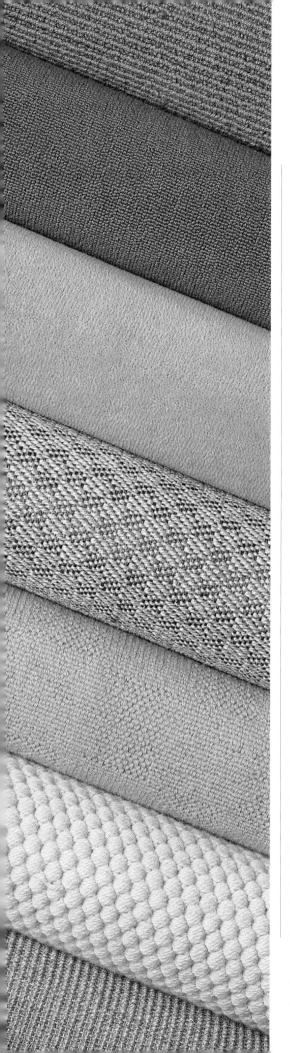

Soft flooring

With improved fibre and finishing technology, carpets are better value than ever. Whether you're a traditionalist or after one of the latest animal prints, like plain carpets or imaginative borders, there's one to suit. Even asthmatics, usually steered clear of carpets, will find one endorsed by the British Allergy Foundation (see suppliers).

Halls and stairs need the heaviest duty carpets, followed by living areas and then bedrooms, where you can get away with less robust types. There's currently no grading scheme, though a new European standard is expected soon and this is likely to pinpoint where carpet should be used. Use a professional fitter to lay carpets, who will also give an estimate of quantities.

Carpets are either woven, tufted (hessian- or foam-backed) or bonded, which means they don't have a pile. Woven carpets (Axminster or Wilton) are more expensive as the pile and backing are woven together giving extra durability. Tufted foam-backed carpets are less durable and suitable mainly for bedrooms. Alternatively, look at natural floor coverings: an inexpensive alternative. They retain their appearance well, are hard-wearing, anti-static and easy to maintain but need careful fitting. Rugs, too, are an excellent way of introducing variety to a large expanse of flooring.

Carpets: wool or synthetic?

Acrylic: acrylic looks and feels like wool and is often blended with other fibres. It has good stain resistance.

Nylon: very hard-wearing and will resist crushing if in a dense twisted pile otherwise once flattened the pile is difficult to restore. Top quality brands can almost feel like wool although cheaper ones attract dirt and feel harsh. Static is now much reduced.

Polyester: warm underfoot, it keeps its colour well and is abrasion-resistant, but the pile is difficult to restore.

Polypropylene: inexpensive and durable but it has a harsh feel so is often used in wool blends. It flattens easily so low loop piles are common. Carpets containing this fibre are non-absorbent, colourfast, they resist abrasion and are low in static.

Wool: the most expensive type of carpet with good insulation properties and resistance to soiling and flattening. Frequently blended with 20 per cent nylon for good looks, greater resilience and durability, it is ideal for heavy-duty areas. Like all woven carpets, it can rot if over-wetted.

Natural fibre floor coverings

Made from fibres extracted from grasses and leaves spun into a yarn and woven, most of these types of floor coverings are finished with a latex backing. They can be fully-fitted or used as mats.

Coir: matting woven using the thick rough fibre from the outer husks of coconuts. It is bulky and can be rough depending on the weave pattern. It can be natural, dyed or bleached.

Jute: softest of the fibres, it is made from the stems of sub-tropical plant. It is not very hard-wearing, but it is porous so dyes well although

choosing semi-hard flooring 172-173   choosing hard flooring 176-177

consequently stains easily too. Both coir and jute need adhesive to fit.

Rush: hard-wearing rush matting made from inland rushes. Medieval matting is made from plaited strips of rush, sewn together to give the required width and finished with a fine plaited border. It can be fitted or laid as loose mats.

Seagrass: a smooth, relatively impermeable fibre that repels dirt. The stems are twisted before weaving. It is warm underfoot but can be slippery. Dying is difficult but the natural colours of the grass – greens, beige and yellow – randomly appear in the weave.

Sisal: one of the hardest wearing, yet soft, natural floorings made from the leaves of a spiky sub-tropical bush. It dyes well and is available in a range of colours, as well as natural or bleached.

Rugs

There is a choice to suit all price ranges whether you want a cheaper machine-made rug or more traditional Oriental style. Use anti-slip backing to stop them moving. Choose between:

Afghan: bright reds and dark blues, geometric repeating patterns.

Chinese: standard designs of flowers, birds and dragons, in pastel colours with a sculpted pile.

Dhurries: Indian, hand-woven, cotton.

Kelims: Turkish or North African tapestry woven with no pile and featuring geometric patterns.

Persian: predominantly reds and blues with busy rounded, floral designs. Rugs are referred to by their region.

Turkish: soft earth colours and bold geometric designs.

WATCHPOINTS

◆ When you choose your carpet, take a photograph of the room or rooms with you to help find the right colour or pattern.

Underlay

Choose the best quality you can afford. A good underlay can prolong the life of your carpet so never use an old one with a new carpet. It will also prevent draughts through floorboards and act as sound proofing. Choose between:

Felt made from matted fibres: top of the range and will resist indentations.

Paper-felt: used under foam-backed carpets.

Solid rubber: hard-wearing but not as springy as waffle rubber.

Waffle rubber underlay: sold in different weights from light use to heavy-duty.

Carpet pile

◆ The closer the tufts the more hard-wearing the carpet. The pile of the carpet can be:

– looped in and out of the backing; low loops are very hard-wearing and often called corded if very tightly looped.

– cut, but short dense cut pile (velvet) is susceptible to shading and shows up tread and furniture marks. A less dense pile is known as Saxony carpet and shag pile is the longest cut pile and should be avoided on stairs. Twist pile is twisted cut pile, the more tightly twisted, the greater the durability and resistance to flattening.

– a combination of cut and looped for a textured effect.

– a Berber carpet that can be cut or loop with flecks of contrasting colour throughout.

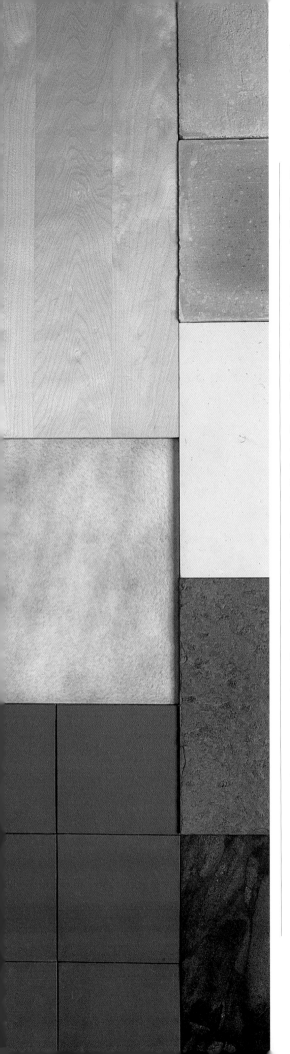

Hard flooring

Once laid, these floorings will give years and years of wear. Available in a huge range of materials, colours and textures, they are the ideal flooring solution for hallways, kitchens, bathrooms and conservatories. With recent developments in wooden floors, their versatility makes them suitable for almost anywhere in the home.

Brick paving

This is available in many shades and is renowned for its warm and rustic appeal. Not as cold and noisy as ceramic or quarry tiles, brick paving is non-slip and water-resistant when sealed. Must be laid on a solid floor.

Ceramic tiles

A huge variety of designs and colours are available ranging from mosaics and squares to larger hexagonal shapes. Check they are suitable for floors rather than walls: the thickness varies, and glazes are graded for abrasion resistance. Look for at least glaze grade 3 for kitchen use and 4 for bathrooms. Some have a non-slip textured surface, too. Ceramic tiles are comparatively easy to clean but cold, hard and noisy underfoot. Breakable items won't survive if dropped, and the floor itself is likely to crack or chip if a very heavy object is dropped. Have them laid by a professional.

Marble

In slab or mosaic form, marble is hard-wearing, cool and elegant but because it is very expensive, hard and noisy not especially suitable for domestic use.

Mosaic tiles

Made from small, irregularly shaped pieces of ceramic or glass, these are supplied in sheets about 30cm (12in) square. Basic designs can be laid by a competent DIYer.

Quarry and terracotta tiles

The different colours of quarry and terracotta tiles are achieved by the use of clays from different areas of the world, as well as the materials used to fire the kiln which bakes them. They can be machine or hand-made. Both types are very durable, and many Victorian and Edwardian houses still have their original floors intact.

Quarry tiles are more regular in appearance and harder and colder than terracotta tiles, which in turn are more porous. They are available unglazed or glazed for easier maintenance. Terracotta tiles must be treated or sealed using traditional linseed oil or an acrylic seal.

Tile shapes include squares (10-40cm [4-16in]), rectangles, octagonals and lozenge, with clipstones or insets and borders to complete the design. Victorian encaustic tiles, made up of different coloured clays, can be laid to produce geometric patterns just like an Oriental rug with border. Scour salvage yards for reclaimed tiles but do use a professional to lay either type.

Slate

Quarried naturally in Britain in Wales and Cornwall and also available from Africa, Thailand (a cheaper variety) and Samoa, many shades are available in a smooth matt, textured or with a slight sheen finish. Slate is hard, cold and noisy but inherently slip-resistant. It should be professionally laid.

choosing semi-hard flooring 173   choosing soft flooring 174-175

Wood

Properly cared for, wooden floors can look wonderful, be long-lasting, and softer underfoot than other hard flooring. The cheapest option is to sand, seal and varnish existing floorboards but ensure you make good any damaged areas or fill in small gaps using a proprietary wood filler. Alternatively, you can have new strip or blockwood flooring laid over existing boards or a concrete sub-floor. Tongue-and-grooved hardwood flooring should be laid at right angles to existing floorboards but don't forget that this will raise the level of the floor so you may have to trim doors. Parquet block flooring can be loosely laid over, or adhered to, a level damp proofed concrete sub-floor or hardboard.

Paler woods are currently popular, and strip flooring in ash, maple and oak, either with an oiled or lacquered finish, look impressive. However, there are many different colours and designs, including mosaics. Laminated wood flooring is increasingly popular, too, for its ease of maintenance. To help muffle noise, look for this kind of flooring with a natural cork backing and a tough vinyl layer on the surface.

Other easy-care alternatives are a pergo laminate floor, which consists of a wooden composite base with a laminate surface, and wood that has been treated with acrylic to make it extra hard so it is impervious to water and heels. These are all easy to lay and available in a range of designs and finishes, in block or planked styles.

WATCHPOINTS

✦ Dark colours and large patterns make a room look smaller; while pale colours reflect the light and make it appear larger. Bring home as large a sample of the flooring as possible to try out.

✦ To create a feeling of space, carry the same flooring colour throughout. For example, wood on the ground floor and neutral carpets in the bedrooms.

✦ Neutral flooring works well with all colour schemes. However, they may not be practical with a young family and pets.

✦ Patterned flooring should blend with the floors it butts up to.

✦ Use flooring to segregate areas, such as dining from food preparation, by using different materials or borders.

✦ If money is tight, paint and varnish a wood or concrete floor. Stencil checkerboard designs to look like quarry tiles.

✦ Although more expensive, if your room lacks a focal point, consider a flooring with a border.

tiling walls & floors 254-257   treating floorboards 258-259

FOCAL POINTS

Lighting

Used to define shape, colour and texture, lighting can affect how the room looks as well as how it functions. It can enhance the decor and be adaptable as the mood and activities change. So when choosing lighting there are three general considerations that need to be borne in mind:

1 The light source: the amount and type of light that the bulb emits.

2 The light fitting: its aesthetic appearance and how it controls and distributes the light.

3 The position of the light fitting.

You also need to keep in mind the main purposes of your lighting as this will affect the type of light that you buy. The four types are:

• General or background: to replace or boost natural light and give a general level of visibility.

• Task or localised: for specific areas and tasks.

• Accent: to highlight objects to emphasise their colour, texture and shape. This can be a narrow beam or broad spot.

• Information or utility: to improve safety; lighting like this is often found in areas of total blackness.

Ceiling lights

Not recessed, ceiling lights are shaped more like a globe. They are generally omni-directional.

Desk lights

Task lighting that concentrates directional light over a specific area. Look for ones with an adjustable arm so you can direct the light.

Downlighters

Directional light shines downwards. Normally recessed or semi-recessed in to the ceiling. Can be either a broad floodlight or narrow beam.

Pendant lights

Offer a good light source but can look obtrusive. Light distribution depends on the type of shade, of which there is a huge choice. Fit a dimmer switch to control the intensity.

Spotlights

These can be ceiling, wall or floor mounted or attached to a lighting track. Flexible and adjustable with light directed in a beam they made good accent lighting. Different bulbs are available for differing light effects.

Standard lamps

These offer omni-directional and semi-directional light depending on the lamp shade.

Strip lights

Offers omni-directional and semi-directional light for all types of lighting and generally fluorescent. Concealed strip lighting works well in alcove units and under kitchen wall cupboards.

Table lamps

Give out a soft omni-directional glow for general and accent lighting.

making plans 14-15   choosing light bulbs 182-183

Track lighting
Individual light fittings take their power supply from a continuous track suspended from the ceiling.

Uplighters
Semi-directional and directional light shining upwards. Beam can be bounced off a wall or ceiling for general lighting.

Wall-lights
Light can be distributed in any direction. Halogen lamp wall fittings cast a gentle wash of light across a wall. Again there is a good range from traditional to very modern styles. It is useful to have separate switches with dimmers on lights like this.

Wall washers
The wall is covered with an even stream of light. Usually ceiling-mounted, recessed or mounted on a lighting track, the light is directional. Add reflectors to angle the light.

Light bulbs

The strength of light given out depends on the wattage of the bulb and also how efficiently it converts energy into light, known as the lamp's efficacy. It is important to know how energy efficient a bulb is, how long it will last and the colour of light it gives out. There are two main types of bulb, filament and fluorescent.

Filament bulbs

Low-voltage tungsten halogen: these are very small and compact and so good for discreet display and accent lighting. They are the same colour and have a similar lifespan to mains halogen but to make them work you need a transformer to convert from mains to a lower voltage.

Mains voltage tungsten halogen: matter from the tungsten filament interacts with halogen gas and redeposits on the filament, which glows through a quartz surround. The bulb does not blacken so has a longer life than a tungsten or incandescent bulb at about 2,000 hours. It gives out a white cool light, so is good in spotlights.

Tungsten or incandescent: ranging from 8 to 200 watts, the filament glows white hot and radiates light through a pearlised or clear glass surround, eventually blackening the bulb and burning it out. The light is warm and flattering, like natural light. But it has a low life span of around 1,000 hours and is less efficient than other types because it produces a lot of heat.

Fluorescent tubes

The light can be warm or cool depending on the phosphorescent coating used on the glass. Unlike filaments, colour rendering is poor but because they give an even distribution of light and less glare they are suited to working areas. They are also more economical, burning for up to 7,000 hours. Compact fluorescent (energy-saving) light bulbs can be used in place of filament bulbs. These use about a fifth of the electricity that a filament lamp uses and last eight times longer.

Glass types

Coloured: great for parties, if not for everyday living!.

Decorative: plain or twisted, clear or opal, these look like candles.

Display-spotlight reflectors: these have a silver coating on the glass behind the filament to focus the beam. They are available as miniature low-voltage tungsten halogen lamps with two-colour reflectors.

Tubular: ideal for task and picture lighting. Choose warm colours to get the same light as tungsten filaments.

Tungsten filament: can be clear (harsh and tiring), pearlised (softer and diffuse), or softone, which are internally coated with pastel colours to enhance decor. Round and mushroom bulbs with a lustre coating can be used without a shade.

Fixings or caps

Bayonet cap: the most common fixing, it comes as standard or small for decorative candle bulbs.

Reflectors and compact fluorescents: have screw cap.

Tubular lamps: have two electrical contact pins at each end.

LIGHTING IDEAS AROUND THE HOME

Bathrooms

Here, lighting needs to be dual-purpose to help you feel energetic in the morning and relaxed at night. It should be task-orientated, centred around a mirror, and then work outwards.

• Mirror lighting should be soft and shadow free. Theatre-style mirror lights with low-watt pearl lamps fitted down the sides are a good choice. Cheaper and less dramatic is a fluorescent strip light with built-in shaver socket, but it can create shadows below the nose and mouth.

• The ceiling is best served by recessed downlighters. Avoid fluorescent strips and pendants because these aren't very flattering and can be dangerous.

Bedrooms

Here, you want to create an intimate setting for various activities requiring a high level of general lighting combined with task lighting, plus mood lighting. Ideally, you want overall light for activities such as cleaning and making the beds, soft background lighting for relaxing, and lighting for specific areas such as the bed and dressing table.

• Bedside lighting: look for a good source that won't disturb a partner. Try table lights, clip-on spotlights or overhead, recessed spotlights.

• Background: anything goes, so consider floor- or wall-mounted uplighters, concealed strip lights, ceiling spotlights.

• Functional lights: these could include tungsten strip lights and night lights for children.

Kitchens

Kitchens require a high level of shadow-free general lighting with task lighting focused at, for example, worktops, hobs and sinks.

• Fluorescent strip lights under wall cupboards prevent shadows on work surfaces.

• Ceiling-mounted spotlights, track lights and recessed downlighters work well in the same way overhead.

• If the kitchen is also used as a dining area, add table lamps and rise and fall fittings over a table.

Living and dining rooms

In these rooms, lighting must meet the needs of all the activities that occur, as well as creating atmosphere and enhancing furnishings. Keep it flexible, with lots of table top and freestanding lamps and uplighters. For reading, lighting should be above, behind or to one side of the reader to prevent shadows falling on the page. Experiment with table and floor lamps and swivel arm wall lights together with good background lighting.

• Dining lighting is best served by direct overhead fittings. Strong and harsh lighting is unflattering, so try an adjustable shaded pendant fitted with crown silver lamps to eliminate glare.

Stairs, halls and landings

Stairways are busy, so safety should be the main consideration. The quality of light should be as bright or brighter than the lights below without creating a dramatic contrast. So fix ceiling lights at the top of each flight of stairs, on each landing and at the bottom. Put on a dimmer for greater flexibility and ensure lights can be turned on and off at the top and bottom of flights.

• Mirrors and tungsten wall lights will give an impression of space, whereas central pendants will make a hall appear narrower.

• Wall uplighters are closer to eye level and give out a warm arc of light.

• Landings are often narrow so to create safe lighting, consider recessed lights, wall uplighters or angled spots.

WATCHPOINTS

✦ Choose the correct wattage for the light fitting or shade. If the lamp shade and base take a different wattage always use the lower one.

✦ Lighting can affect proportion successfully – uplights lead the eye upwards, making low-ceilinged room look higher, for example – so consider what effect your chosen lighting will have on the room before fitting.

✦ The wiring for wall lights does not always have to be traced into the surface but it does look better for it, so whenever possible plan your lighting in advance of the rest of the decor.

✦ Opt for two-way switching with dimmers in bedrooms so you can have one by the door and the bed.

✦ For good overall lighting look at ceiling-mounted fluorescent fittings, spotlights, downlights or track-mounted light fittings.

✦ Always remember in the bathroom that lighting must comply with wiring regulations: light switches should be outside the bathroom, or use pull cords inside.

✦ Use lights to pick out items such as pictures and special objects.

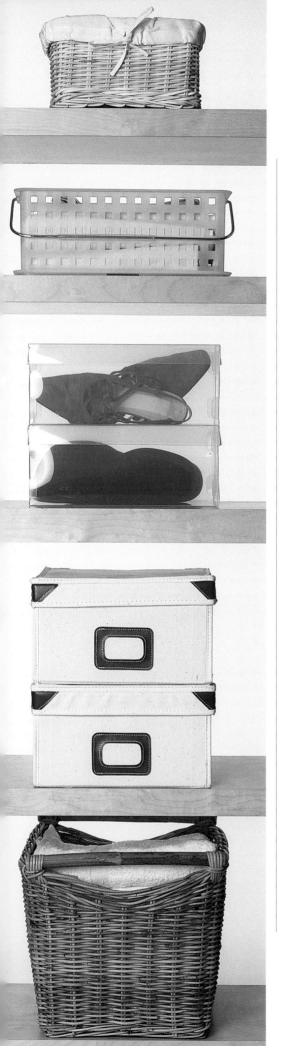

Storage

Whatever the size of your home, there never seems to be sufficient storage space. However, it is surprising, how, with a little thought and planning, you can make existing space work a lot harder. It's easy to miss out on potential space such as under the stairs and windows, under beds, in alcoves and the backs of doors. Avoid being a hoarder, those 'might come in useful' items hardly ever do! Look in any DIY store or mail-order catalogue and you will see there is no shortage or units, boxes or racks . As each room has specific needs here are ideas for creating storage around the home.

Bathrooms

In most houses, bathrooms have very limited storage space. Whatever options you choose they must be easy to clean. Wall-mounted shelving or cabinets should be away from the splash zone. Floor-standing units are useful for hiding pipework.

• Use narrow glass shelves (made from safety glass) for storing toiletries and wider wood or melamine for towels.

• There are many units, racks, cabinets and tidies available. Stacked wicker and bamboo storage boxes look stylish.

• Make use of any space under a window or at the end of the bath to build-in a locker or laundry bin.

• Make the bath panel into doors so you can store toilet rolls and cleaning materials around the bath frame.

• If you are short of wall space choose a cabinet with mirror doors and site at eye level above the sink.

• Spacious multi-rails for towels can be free-standing or fixed to the wall.

• Store children's bath toys in net bags and hang around the taps.

Bedrooms

Bedrooms soon become a dumping ground for odds and ends. Only store items here that you actually need. Pack away out-of-season clothes and store away in the attic or under the bed. But

first you must decide on the position of the bed. Is it better centrally or against a wall? Do you want individual pieces of furniture or fitted units? Large fitted wardrobes may seem the answer to your storage problems but often they make poor use of the space. If space is very tight you could fix a metal pole across an alcove for hanging clothes and then hide with a curtain.

• Wall beds are a good idea especially in bed sitting rooms. Alternatively, consider beds with built-in storage drawers or make good use of the space underneath for storing bedding and clothes in such things as plastic cases or cardboard storage boxes.

• If there isn't room for bedside cabinets, fix shelves above the bed with clip-on spotlight lamps for reading.

• Fit sliding doors to cupboards rather than ones that open outwards.

• For the interiors of wardrobes there are many different types of internal fitments available from sock tidies and shoe racks to full-length units. Fix rails at two heights to cater for full- and half-length items and use multiple hangers. Use the backs of doors for tie and belt rails. Build a shelf at the bottom for shoes.

• Look out for wire basket or bamboo racking systems and zinc or cardboard

boxes in free-standing units.
• Trunks and chests can usefully double up as seats.

Children's rooms

Virtually impossible to keep tidy because not only is it a sleeping area, it acts as a playroom or place to entertain friends. Furniture and storage systems need to be adaptable and expandable to cater for different life stages and fashions. Modular units can be fun and functional although they must be easy to clean, hard-wearing and safe. Wall-mounted shelving is good, but ensure it isn't used as a climbing frame.
• There are some wonderful children's bed units around from racing cars to the Sleeping Beauty! Raised beds with desk space or cupboards beneath are a good option. Bunk or fold-away stacking beds work well. Add bed-length bolsters and cushions to teenagers' beds to double as settees during the day.
• Babies and small children may only need shelves inside their wardrobes but for slightly older children have two rails at different heights to maximise space. Add wire baskets and shoe racks, too.
• Colourful crates and stacking boxes are cheap and invaluable. Store on low-level shelving which can be used for hi-fi equipment in later years.

WATCHPOINTS

✦ You may find that you need to have customised storage built for you by a joiner. This can be especially helpful for bookshelves and cupboards that need to fit into awkward corners. Use a joiner that you trust and get estimates before going ahead.

✦ The advantage of having such storage spaces created especially for you is that you can organise the height and depths or shelves to suit your needs.

✦ To help maintain order in cupboards use small storage containers within these larger spaces.

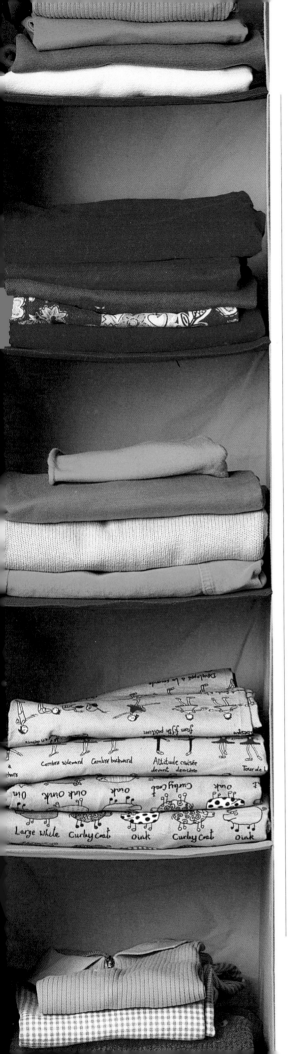

• Desks that fold-up or are hinged to a wall are useful. Alternatively, attach a wide shelf using strong brackets to the wall. Computer trolleys leave desk space for writing.

• Add lots of pin boards, hanging pockets and peg rails to the walls and backs of doors.

• Cheap pine chests, imaginatively decorated, make great toy stores, add castors for easy manoeuvrability.

Garages/sheds

Make good use of the walls and ceiling because floor space will probably be limited. Fit racking systems and hang tools from ceiling hooks. If there is space, old pieces of furniture or kitchen units are ideal for storing DIY and garden tools. If kitchen space is tight, a place like this may be a good place to have the freezer or washing machine.

• Store garden canes, timber and piping in the roof space.

• Brackets are available for attaching ladders and bikes.

• Keep nails and screws together in small plastic containers or jars or buy a small drawer filing system.

• Pegboards are useful for spanners and screw drivers.

Halls and stairs

These areas are under-used in most homes and it's relatively easy to construct shelving systems to fit. These can be either open or hidden away. Make the area into three separate cupboards each with its own louvre door and use the resulting spaces for storing:

• Wine – there are many different expandable wine racking systems available to build your mini-cellar.

• Coats, bags and shoes – include hooks at different heights for children's coats.

• Cleaning equipment, books and newspapers, phone and directories or DIY tools.

Alternatively, if you haven't a study, turn this space into a home office or sewing area.

Kitchens

Carefully plan where all your equipment should go, think how and where you store food, prepare meals and wash-up afterwards and, where possible, have task-related areas. Although units are generally fixed, there are a few things you could change. For example, you can make better use of cupboards by adding interior racks; to use wall space effectively fix shelves and bottle racks or plate racks at picture rail height for display; a traditional clothes airer suspended from the ceiling is ideal for hanging pans and utensils; and use the backs of doors for storing the ironing board and iron.

• In the activity areas around the oven and hob, aim to have storage for pots, pans, baking trays and utensils. Deep pull-out drawers are useful for pots and pans or insert wire baskets on runners. Alternatively, hang them from a rail or if there is lots of floor space purchase a free-standing pan stand. Lids can be strapped to the back of cupboard doors. Multi-pots and steamers are compact to store.

• Hang utensils above the work surface using magnetic knife racks, for example, or rails and butcher's hooks.

• In the sink area, you need space for cleaning products and waste disposal.

• Site small electricals near the food preparation area. Try to hang hand mixers and blenders on the wall to save on surface space. Even the microwave can be wall-mounted using brackets.

• If there isn't a utility room, at least have a separate laundry area. Stack the tumble dryer on top of the washing

machine – contact the manufacturers for details of stacking kits.
• For extra worktop and storage space, a butcher's trolley is a good option, although it does take up floor space.
• Make use of gaps between units for storing trays and tea towels.
• Add cutlery inserts to drawers. Convert plinth space into a drawer for baking trays, for example.
• Make the most of cupboard space: add clip-on baskets under shelves; fix spice-racks and wire baskets to backs of doors; screw-in hooks on the underside of shelves for mugs and cups; add extra shelves to base units; swing-out carousel units are useful in corner units; pull-out worktops, tables and shelves for mixers and food processors save space.

Living rooms
Depending on the activities that take place here, decide if you want individual, wall-mounted or free-standing storage systems. You may want some items displayed and others hidden. Make sure the shelving is strong enough for the purpose and be warned – open shelving is a dust trap.

• Wall-mount the television and speakers using swivel brackets.
• Fit low cupboards in alcoves with open shelving above.
• Make use of free-standing or wall-mounted corner cupboards, which are surprisingly spacious.
• Construct a window seat in a bay window with storage space beneath.
• Add glass fronts to open shelving.
• Make use of tables with drop down leaves or expanding flaps.
• Devote a whole wall to book shelving.

Lofts
These all-too-often underused space is are very useful for storing items that are seldom used. As well as requiring a sturdy ladder, though, you will also need to rig up a light and lay floorboards over the joists to make a walk-way. It is important when storing to spread the load evenly. This place is ideal for tea chests, suitcases and old books. If you decide to make something more of this space remember that if you want to add any windows, you will need planning permission.

Fireplaces

For centuries, an open fire was the standard form of heating. But because much of the heat escapes up the chimney, many people switched to more efficient central heating systems instead. Fireplaces were either removed or blocked off and the television rather than the fire became the focal point of the room. These days, most people opt for a gas fire of some description, with wood and solid fuel, electricity and oil next in popularity. If you want to make the fireplace the centre of attention in your room, look at the different types outlined here. Although some people prefer electricity, gas fires make a more attractive focal point, are far cheaper to run than electricity and, these days, are simple to install.

Electric fires

The one or two bar heaters of old are being replaced by more attractive models which combine radiant and convected heat. Many produce a flickering flame effect, but heat output is restricted as they plug into a normal 13-amp socket. Any higher and the circuit would be overloaded.

Gas fires

These are convenient because they provide instant heat and can be controlled. There is no fuel storage or cleaning and some of the flame effect fires look quite realistic. However, they should be serviced annually. Choice depends on chimney or flue and how much heat you want from the fire.

Cast-iron: combine the traditional look with the convenience of gas. They can also incorporate convected heat, so these stoves are more efficient than decorative gas and inset fires. They provide sufficient heat for one room.

Decorative fires: these are the cheapest option. They are sited within a fireplace and can provide some radiant heat to supplement central heating. However, because they are not covered, much of the heat is lost up the chimney.

Inset fires: these are sited inside the fireplace, flush with its edge. Convected inset live fuel-effect fires provide both radiant and convected heat – air is recycled within the fire – but as the heat output is low they cannot be the sole source of heat. Inset fires often resemble real log and coal fires.

Outset fires: these stick out from the fireplace and are often bulky and glass-fronted. However, outset fires are a good option if heating efficiency is your main priority.

If you have no chimney, a flue will have to be constructed and the type depends on where the fire is to be sited. If it's going on an external wall, you will need a fan to draw the air from the fire. If you only have an inside wall you are restricted to fires with skirting flues. These can be up to 4.5m (4¾yd) in length or 3m (3¼yd) with two bends and take the exhaust gases to the nearest outside wall.

Oil fires

This is a good option if you already have an oil-fired boiler. However, bear in mind that the heat output varies and they tend to be restricted to the glass-fronted style.

Stoves

Many people change to an enclosed, glass-fronted fire, room heater or stove which, because the fire is contained, reduces heat loss and extends fuel life, making them 80 per cent efficient. Log burning or multi-fuel, these fires produce a lot of heat so they are often combined with a ducted system, transporting heat to other rooms, either under the floor or over the ceiling. Glass-fronted fires need a self-cleaning air system to keep the glass clean and can also be used with the doors open.

You don't need to have a chimney to run a stove. Indeed, a stove can be put in the middle of the room with a twin-walled chimney system. This is a double-walled insulated pipe that runs from the outlet at the top of the stove straight up into the ceiling, through the loft and roof. For a large room this can form a neat divide.

Wood and solid fuel open fires

These provide a focal point in a room and can be a supplement to central heating. The fire radiates and reflects heat throughout the house while the flue removes fumes, hot air, smoke and gases. The flue also draws in air at the base of the fire to keep it alight. These fires are cheap to run because you can buy fuel off-season when it's cheaper but you do need to have room to store it. However, the fire needs regular stoking and is messy to clean and the chimney also needs cleaning about twice a year.

Types of fire vary from simple fire baskets which are very inefficient to enclosed Victorian style with integral sides and back, and sometimes an adjustable damper to control the chimney draught. Many reproduction ones are available, but take care with originals as these could be heat damaged.

WATCHPOINTS

✦ Consider if the fire is to supplement existing heating or be the sole heat source. When comparing heat outputs, bear in mind that 4kWh will give out enough heat for one average-size room. Below this will only supplement central heating.

✦ Before fitting a fire check that the fireplace and chimney aren't blocked. Have the flue tested – this must be in good condition as leaking smoke and fumes can be dangerous. It's worth installing a carbon monoxide detector.

✦ Always have gas appliances fitted by a registered CORGI installer.

✦ If your fireplace has been blocked off it should be relatively easy to open up. The Solid Fuel Association (see Suppliers) produce leaflets and videos to help.

✦ If you want an open fire but don't have a chimney you could have one built, although check with your local planning department to ensure it conforms to Building Regulations.

Radiant and convected heat

There are two sorts of heat: radiant heat, which feels stronger the closer you are to the heat source but over-heats your front and leaves your back cold; and convected heat (currents of hot air), which gives all-round warmth. All fires produce radiant heat and an increasing number are incorporating convected heat, recycling hot air via grills for more efficient heating.

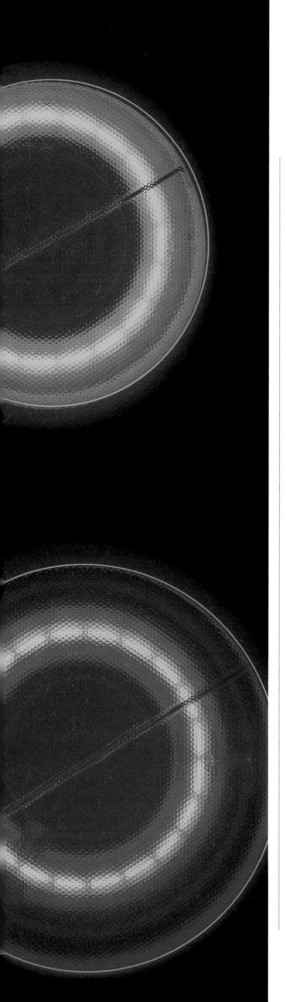

Cooking appliances

Kitchen appliances such as cookers, dishwashers and fridges are some of the most expensive items bought for the home. Making the wrong purchase can be costly and so with the huge number of products available the prospect of making the right choice is a daunting one. Not only do you have to select the right brand and model but choose the right design and colour. Gone are the days when kitchen appliances were just another white box, now they must be part of the room. Even dazzling yellows and blues or muted pastels are available to special order.

First you must decide if you want a free-standing cooker or a separate oven and hob which can be built into your units for a more streamlined appearance. The built-in option is more convenient because the oven can be sited at waist-level or built under the work surface if cupboard space is short. The hob can be positioned at the most convenient site: most only take up the depth of the work surface. You can also mix fuel types, combining a gas hob with an electric oven, for example. However, built-in is always dearer than free-standing. If you have the space, a range-style cooker is another option. These imitate the ranges of old, having side-by-side ovens, a separate grill and warming drawer.

Hobs

Electric: these have either heating elements under sealed plates or a ceramic glass top. Sealed plates are slower, less responsive and more awkward to clean. Look for ones with a red dot in the centre as these are speedier. Glass-topped hobs can cover conventional radiant rings or halogen bulbs. Halogen is slightly quicker and more responsive but not as fast as gas when it reverts to simmering.

Gas: these are the quickest form of heating but they are more awkward to clean. Models with lids have a safety device cutting off the supply to the burners if accidentally closed.

Specific modular units: such items as deep fat fryers, wok burners and griddles can be built into the surface.

Ovens

Built-in ovens: can be single (60cm [24in] high) or double-cavity (90cm [36in] high).

Built-under double ovens: usually 72cm (28in) high (smaller than built-in doubles because of height restrictions) and fit under the work surface.

Free-standing cookers: these can have one large single oven with a lower storage drawer or one main oven with a separate smaller compartment above which can be a second oven and/or grill. Be warned – the bottom oven is very low and you do have to bend to reach into it. If you often cook several dishes at once, bear in mind that a single oven has the grill in the main cavity and this can restrict your options (you won't be able to roast and grill at the same time). Eye-level grills are convenient to use. If you opt for a double oven, check the size of the smaller oven – not all will take a deep tin or roast.

Microwaves

There are three main types of microwave and the choice will depend on the type of cooking you want to do. Whichever type you choose, remember they cook more quickly than conventional ovens. Sizes vary from 0.4 to 0.8 cu ft (compact) or 0.9 to 1.4 cu ft (family). The wattage indicates the power output of the oven. The higher the wattage, the quicker the microwave will reheat. Look for power outputs of around 800-900 watts. Too high and food cooks too quickly and can burn at the edges. Food cannot be stacked in a microwave so it is the turntable size that is more important than the height. Useful programmes include auto-defrost and auto-cook;

auto minute; multi-sequence cooking; jet start and minute minder.

Microwave only: a good choice if you just want to defrost and reheat food quickly, but they don't brown the surface of food.

Microwave with grill: will also brown the surface of food. Grills are either radiant, similar to a conventional electric oven or quartz. Neither type are as powerful as a conventional oven grill, so cooking can be slow.

Combination microwaves: the most versatile, they combine a microwave, grill and convection oven, and allow you to cook by microwave, grill or convection; or microwave combined with convection or grill. They can be used in the place of a standard cooker.

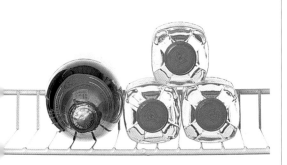

Refrigerating appliances

As well as heating and cooking food you will, of course, want to cool and freeze it. Fridges, in particular, are becoming increasingly colourful items to have in the kitchen and can be combined with freezing compartments in countless combinations.

Freezers

Chest freezers: these are less popular because they take up a large amount of floor space. However, they are ideal for freezing large quantities and bulky items such as joints and poultry. Because cold air sinks, they regulate the temperature more effectively than uprights. On the down side, items are harder to find and not all have a fast freeze compartment.

Fridge freezers: these combine a fridge and a freezer unit. The freezer is usually at the bottom unless less than 86 litres in size. There is a large combination of sizes available so consider which most reflects your lifestyle – do you want more fridge or freezer space? American-style units are wider than conventional models because the fridge and freezer are side by side with separate doors. However, they aren't as roomy inside as they appear. Extra features are incorporated such as drinks dispensers and ice-makers.

The two compartments may be controlled by a single compressor and thermostat or two separate ones. If you have separate controls it is easier to maintain the most efficient working temperature in each section. It is particularly important to have two thermostats if the unit is housed in a cold area.

Upright freezers: these either fit under the counter or are 120-170cm (4-5½ft) tall. Widths vary between 45 and 60cm (18 and 24in). They are easy to organise but are more suited to smaller, regular shaped items.

Look for:
• Drawers are easier to pack and clean than shelves.
• Solid drawers keep the temperature better than mesh ones.
• Fast freeze compartment. This is useful if the controls automatically revert to normal after a set period of time to save on electricity.
• Drainage tube for easy defrosting.
• Frost-free models have a heater that keeps the freezer sides from freezing and a fan circulates dry air so you never need to defrost. It can, however, be noisier and more expensive to buy and run than other types of freezer.

Fridges

There are a huge range of sizes available from table top (82 litres) and under counter to full kitchen height (385 litres). The widths vary from 44.5 to 60cm (17½ to 24in). There are two main types to consider.

Fridges with an ice-box: there is a small compartment at the top for storing commercially frozen food and making ice cubes. The fridge is coldest at the top, adjacent to the ice box.

Larder: These don't have an ice box and are the cheapest to run. The cabinet is coldest at the bottom, just above the salad box.

Look for:
• A good selection of adjustable, removable door shelves and range of shelf positions in the main cavity.

• A grill which encloses the condenser (the wires across the back) for quieter operation and easy cleaning.
• An enclosed evaporator plate installed behind the back wall. This creates extra storage space and easy cleaning.
• Auto-defrost for automatic defrosting. However, the ice-box must be manually defrosted.

WATCHPOINTS

✦ Don't site a fridge or freezer near your oven as it will have to work extra hard to keep cool.

✦ Think about how you use a fridge or freezer before you buy. Do you simply buy frozen food and store it or do you cook extra quantities to freeze for the future? Do you freeze fruit and vegetables that are in season?

✦ A freezer with drawers will suit you if you rely on frozen food, but one with moveable shelves will be more use if your freeze-ahead food is stored in varying shaped containers.

Washing appliances

Once you own a dishwasher it's hard to imagine ever being without one. Not only is it a more hygienic way to wash the dishes, because of the higher temperatures and powerful detergents used, but you can save yourself around three weeks a year on washing-up time! But knowing which appliance to choose can be difficult as there are so many different programmes available. The same goes for washing machines, tumble dryers and washer driers. This guide will help.

Dishwashers

Dishwashers are available in a range of sizes, so don't be deterred if you think your kitchen is too small. However, even if you are a small household it's worth buying the largest you can fit in, it's surprising how quickly you fill it.

Compact models: designed to sit on a work surface these small dishwashers will wash up to four place settings.

Free-standing models: these fit under the work surface and can be either full-sized (60cm [24in] wide) and suitable for washing up to 12 place settings (some up to 16), or slimline models (45cm [18in] wide) and suitable for washing up to eight place settings.

Slot-in models: 50cm (20in) wide, these models are designed to fit into a kitchen cupboard and have reduced height and depth so that all the pipework fits behind the machine and the cupboard plinth is kept in place.

Look for:
• The most commonly used programmes:
– Normal/Universal wash: cold prewash followed by a 65°C main wash, one or two cold rinses and a hot rinse. Used for average soiling that may have dried onto the china and cutlery.
– Economy/Super economy/Light/Bio/Daily wash: a lower-temperature normal wash (45-55°C) without a prewash. Uses fewer rinses with no drying cycle to make the programme shorter and saves energy. Used for lighter soiling, fresh food deposits and smaller loads.
– Intensive/Saucepans/Strong/Superwash/Universal Plus/Heavy Soil: operates at higher temperatures (65-70°C) and may include a hot prewash. It's longer and uses more energy than the normal wash. Used for pans and heavily soiled, greasy bakeware.
• Drying, which is carried out using residual heat, hot air or a condenser.
– Residual drying uses heat produced from the last hot rinse.
– Hot air drying uses a separate drying cycle. An element heats the air inside and evaporates it.
– Condenser drying uses a fan to draw warm, moist air on to a cooler surface, the water that's formed is drained.
• Adjustable top baskets with hinged cup racks to accommodate tall glasses.
• Sturdy baskets to take heavy pans and casserole dishes.
• Baskets that stay on their runners when pulled forward.
• Stage of wash indicators on the front panel that are useful to keep you informed of its progress. Other useful indicators will tell you when salt and rinse aid need topping up.

Washing machines

Most front-loading automatic machines are 60cm (24in) wide and will wash 5kg (11lb) cottons/2.5kg (5½lb) synthetics. Slimline models are available. They are becoming more and more sophisticated, energy saving and easier to use.

Look for:
• A range of programmes: all machines offer a range of wash cycles that correspond to wash care labels on clothes: 40°C cotton and 50°C synthetic are the most commonly used. Some useful extras include:
– a hand-wash cycle at a low temperature and reduced agitation cycle for items that would normally be hand-washed.
– deep rinse which adds an extra rinse or more water at the rinse stage to ensure all the detergent has been removed.
– rinse and hold/creaseguard to stop the machine during the final rinse, suspending the clothes in water and will not spin until reset.
– rinse and spin programmes for finishing-off hand-washing.
• Spin speeds of up to 1600rpm are appearing. But they are not always the best option as fast speeds cause more creasing. Look for variable spin speeds, suitable for different fabrics.
• Self-adjusting water level systems have replaced the half-load option. Sensors detect the weight of the dry wash and dispense the appropriate amount of water.
• Automatic foam sensors monitor if too much foam is produced and reduce drum agitation.
• If the machine has a PC update facility it can be upgraded from the engineer's PC to add new programmes, and faults can be corrected too.
• Fuzzy logic or intelligent technology is used in many machines. Information is gathered from the last few washes and combining this with messages received from its sensors, the machine decides on the correct wash temperature, most economical amount of water and can even tell if an extra rinse is needed. Each wash is tailored to the wash load.

Tumble dryers

Most are 60cm (24in) wide although there are slimline models available.
Condenser: this type of dryer doesn't need venting as the damp air is cooled in the machine and water collects in a reservoir at the top or bottom. Conveniently they can be sited anywhere. The container must be emptied regularly so check it is well-positioned. Drying times tend to be longer than in vented machines.
Vented dryers: must be sited near an outside wall or window so that damp air can be vented to the outside through a flexible hose. Vent holes can be right, left or rear.

Look for:
• Gas models must be connected to a gas supply. Although they cost more initially to buy, they are cheaper to run than electric dryers.
• Basic dryers operate on a timer system. You estimate and set the drying time for each load. More sophisticated models have sensors that monitor the dryness of the load and lower the heat as the clothes dry, or gauge the amount of moisture left and switch off when the washing is dry.

Washer driers

Prices for a combined machine compare favourably with buying a washing machine and tumble dryer separately but the performance is compromised. They will wash the same as a normal washing machine but will only dry half the amount. Also, because the drum is smaller than a tumble dryer, the drying results are less good. But they are space-saving and can wash and dry loads in sequence. During drying, water is condensed using cold water and pumped away.

Kitchen work surfaces

Kitchen worktops take as much wear and tear as the kitchen floor but the right type, treated with respect, should last for 25 years. Yet so often the worktop is an after-thought, chosen to complement the rest of the kitchen. We are becoming much more hygiene conscious, and as a consequence certain types of worktop are losing favour. Tiles, for example, where the grouting soon becomes dirty, are a safe harbour for germs. On the other hand, materials like stainless steel and granite are becoming more popular for their practical and aesthetic qualities, although both can be expensive. Whichever surface you opt for, it is essential to a use chopping boards for food preparation to keep your surface looking good for longer and easier to clean. You need several – one for meat, vegetables and bread. Don't mix them.

There are several different options from which to choose, each having their own strengths and weakness. Decide what your most important requirements are. You can mix different surfaces so you have task-specific areas with marble or stainless steel inserts in wood, for example. Most are between 3 and 4cm (1¼ and 1½in) deep (solid wood and granite may be less) and usually measure 60cm (24in) in width, although deeper surfaces are available for eating areas and island units.

Granite

A smooth, cool, natural solid surface sold in depths of 2-3cm (¾-1¼in). Because it is quite expensive it is often used for just one of the work areas. Joining thin sheets can be tricky, and the material is heavy so supports may need reinforcing. Granite has good heat and scratch resistance with medium resistance to impact and staining.

Laminate

This is by far the most popular choice and the cheapest. Layers of paper, resin-bonded with melamine, are bonded on to a core material, usually chipboard, MDF or plywood. Choose the deepest thickness you can afford – the weight is a good indication of the chipboard density. There is a wide range of colours and textures available. Most laminates can withstand temperatures up to 180°C, a few can take even greater, but take care with cheaper types which may damage quickly. Laminates have medium impact and scratch resistance, and resist stains well.

Lava rock

An interesting alternative to tiles, this surface is made from volcanic lava with a fired spray glaze that is easy to wipe down. If any chips occur these can be smoothed over professionally. Lava rock has good heat and stain resistance, medium impact and scratch resistance.

Solid surface

These consist of a solid composite material bonded on to chipboard, plywood or MDF. The worktop can be shaped, carved or inlaid and can incorporate drainer grooves and integral sinks. The joins are virtually invisible, so the finish is smooth and seamless. There is a good range of colours but the drawback is that this type of surface is expensive. Cheaper versions are available, known as solid surface veneers, which are not as deep. They have good heat resistance, medium impact and scratch resistance and although pale colours stain readily, marks are easily removed. Sand out scratches with an abrasive pad.

Stainless steel

Brushed or textured surfaces are available, the latter being more practical because it camouflages any marks. But it has some design limitations. The brushed surface scratches and stains easily, but the scratches will blend in over time. It has good heat and medium impact resistance.

Wood

Hardwood worktops look good but they are high maintenance and expensive. Seal them using two-part heatproof lacquer and avoid using softwood tops as these are not as hygienic. Wood should not be allowed to get over-wet, so it is best avoided near a butler's sink. If a dishwasher or washing machine is underneath, place a specialist moisture-resistant paper on the underside to protect the wood. Wood has good heat resistance and average impact, scratch and stain resistance, although scratches and marks can be sanded out.

WATCHPOINTS

✦ Consider whether the sink is going to be of the same material, otherwise will the colours and textures be compatible. Hobs can be cut into most materials, but think about the location carefully.

✦ Always have the work surface professionally installed. A good kitchen retailer will recommend a suitable installer.

✦ Be wary of having worktops delivered. Because of their size, they could easily be damaged on route.

✦ Check that the underside of laminate worktops have been sealed with a resin or foil lining.

✦ Once you've chosen your worktop material consider the edging you want to seal in the exposed chipboard. Laminated worktops can be bought with a pre-formed edge or square edge. Alternatively, hardwood mouldings are available to give a lipped finish.

✦ The height of the work surface is very important. If you are taller or shorter than the average person you might want to consider work surfaces that are higher or lower than average to prevent straining your back or arms unecessarily.

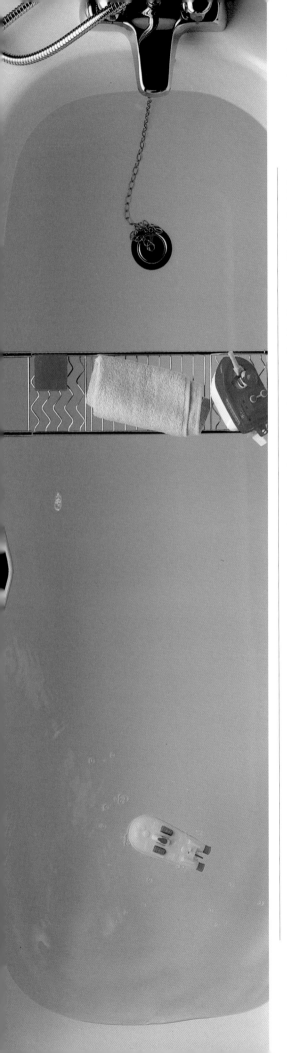

Bathroom fittings

Because it is usually one of the the smallest rooms in the house, the bath-room can be difficult to design. The permanent fittings, such as win-dows, doors and plumbing connections, can cause the greatest problems. But with planning and thought, it is amazing just how much can be squeezed into the room.

Baths

Choose between acrylic, enamelled steel or cast-iron. The standard bath size is rectangular and 1700mm long by 700mm wide, although smaller sit-in baths start at 1200mm long. Other shapes are available, such as corner units and contoured baths. The latter are shaped to trace the outline of the body and use less water. Traditional Victorian styles are free-standing with feet and a rolled edge. Taps can be either at the end or middle of the tub.

Acrylic baths: although lightweight, warm to the touch, less slippery than metal and stain resistant, acrylic will scratch easily. The moulded acrylic is reinforced with fibreglass and mounted on a galvanised steel frame.

Cast-iron baths: have a porcelain enamel coating.

Enamelled steel baths: coated with vitreous enamel and fired to give the hard finish.

Whirlpool baths: water is recirculated through jets around the sides; a spa is more gentle, injecting heated air into the water; a whirlpool spa combines both types. Performance is determined by the number of jets, their position and pressure. A self-draining system prevents the build-up of bacteria.

Bidets

A low-level wash basin made of vitreous china, which can be wall-hung or floor standing. Two types are available either of which may have an ascending water spray – the inlet nozzle is set in the base of the bowl giving an upward spray. However, you do need high water pressure for this. They must conform to your local water regulations.

Below-the-rim bidets: more like a toilet. Water is fed into the bowl around the rim.

Over-the-rim bidets: two taps or a mixer, plug hole and overflow slot. Work like normal basins.

Showers

The type you choose must depend on the water system in your house. If your hot and cold water are both supplied from a hot-water cylinder (in the airing cupboard) or a cold-water tank (in the loft) you can have a mixer shower or a power shower. If you don't have a hot water cylinder or constant hot water, choose an instantaneous electric shower. Different shower heads are available from fixed wall-mounted and slide rails to body-sprays.

Instantaneous electric showers: these work off the mains, heating water on demand. They are economical but have a lower flow rate. The higher the wattage, the better the flow of water, so look for at least 8kW. The mains pressure needs to be at one bar to deliver 8 litres of water.

Mixer showers: these rely on gravity to provide adequate water pressure, and draw water from the hot water cylinder and cold water tank. The greater the distance between the cold water tank and shower, the greater the pressure (should be at least 1m [1yd]). · Bungalows may need to add a booster pump. Look for 0.1 bar pressure and a flow rate of 9 litres per minute (based on a gravity-fed system at 1m [1yd]). There are three types:

• Manual – you mix the hot and cold water to suit, but if water is drawn off elsewhere (when the toilet is flushed, for example), the shower may run hot or cold.
• Thermostatic – more expensive but has a built-in stabiliser so water can't run too hot.

✦ Bathroom accessories are convenient, space saving necessities for any bathroom. Style is totally up to you as there is so much choice available. If the bathroom is small, avoid too many accessories or it will soon look cluttered. It is important, too, that they have firm fixings because all too often they are used as hand holds.

✦ Toilet roll holders and soap trays can be fixed onto or recessed into the wall. Ceramic tiles are available which have the holders moulded in one. Soap trays in shower cubicles should have drain holes for water to run through.

✦ Heated towel rails are one of the most useful accessory in the bathroom. They can be either heated by electricity or hot water. Hot water models are connected to the hot water system and are more efficient to run. Multi-rail styles are the most popular and provide heating as well as drying.

✦ Fold-down shower seats are useful for the elderly or infirm.

✦ Shower tidies or hanging racks, with water drainage holes, fix to the rail or wall.

✦ Gel/shampoo dispensers can be fitted to the slide rail of a shower.

• Pressure-balanced – maintains showering temperature against variations in supply pressure.

Power showers: either buy a mixer shower with an integral pump where the temperature is manually controlled or fit an additional electric booster pump to an existing mixer shower. This allows thermostatic control and can be fitted out of the way such as the airing cupboard. The pressure and flow can be adjusted to give spray patterns from needle jets to soft 'champagne foam' or strong body jets. These use more water than the others and can be noisy. When choosing, look for one that has a one-bar pressure and a flow-rate of 9-15 litres per minute.

Shower enclosures

The area around the shower needs to be protected from water spray. So if the shower is above the bath, fixing a shower rail and waterproof curtain is the cheapest option followed by a shower screen. These can be made from toughened plastic or glass, either as single panels or several hinged together.

Alternatively, shower cubicles can be built into a corner or alcove or be free-standing units. Square shower trays are between 70 and 90cm (27½ and 36in) square and rectangular trays are usually 120 by 60cm (48 by 24in). Curved or triangular shapes are also available. The strongest types are made from ceramic, followed by resin and acrylic.

Taps

Tap technology has come a long way. Many taps are now decorative features in their own right and there is a huge range of materials, styles and colours – but not all are easy to turn. Traditional cross-top taps are probably the easiest to use whereas the knob style can be awkward for soapy wet hands. Levers are easiest for the disabled or arthritic. Chrome or a gold-effect coating is the most common and very durable. Check it complies with BS5412/3 or EN200.

Water flow from the tap is controlled either by washers or ceramic discs. Washers are the most common but these wear out in time and need replacing. Ceramic discs are more durable and easy to operate if you have a weak wrist. They are usually found on quarter turn or single-lever taps.

Mixer taps: water is supplied via a central tap but taps like this need either a single hole (monobloc mixers) or two holes (twin-hole mixer). In either case, hot and cold water mixes in the spout or is kept separate until it leaves the tap. Bath/shower mixers have a diverter to send water to the attached shower head.

Pillar taps: water enters the tap vertically, so they must be mounted on a level surface. Small and neat with a twist or cross-shaped handle, they are available in pairs for hot and cold water, so two holes are required in the bath or basin.

Toilets

These consist of a cistern and pan, made from vitreous china and have a choice of flushing systems:

Macerating units: enables the toilet to be installed almost anywhere in the house. The waste is shredded so that it can be pumped through a narrower pipe. The discharge pipe can then be run behind the wall. An electrical connection is needed to operate the pump. Water efficient.

Syphonic: a quiet and efficient method where the water from the pan is drawn out by a syphoning action.

Wash-down: water washes down from the cistern through the pan.

There are also all sorts of sizes and shapes. Consider the following:

Back to the wall: the pan is flush with the wall and the cistern and pipework is hidden behind the wall. Easy to clean and streamlined.

Close-coupled: looks like a single unit, the cistern is connected to the pan which sits on a pedestal and it is flushed using a lever or knob.

High-level: the cistern is fixed high on the wall above the pan, and a long flush pipe connects the two. A pull chain is needed to flush the toilet.

Low-level with short flush pipe: the cistern is about 94cm (37in) above the pan and flushed with a lever or knob.

Toilet seats

There is a wide range available from hard and soft woods to coloured plastic. Some manufacturers offer different height seats, some of which are suitable for the disabled.

Wash basins

Made from vitreous china, kiln fired and glazed, the wash basin finish will crack or chip if mistreated. The main types include:

Counter top basins: the bowl is sunk to sit level with a wash stand or vanity unit. Cupboards underneath hide the pipework and provide storage. Semi-counter top basins are partly recessed into a custom-made unit.

Pedestal basins: as well as supporting the bowl, the pedestal hides the pipes. The bowl is fixed to the wall and stands about 80cm (32in) high. Different styles and shapes are available.

Wall-mounted basins: these can be put at any height and range in size from large to small hand basins. Because they are fixed to the wall the pipes may be exposed.

WATCHPOINTS

◆ Style and colour should be your last decision. Light, pale shades will give an impression of space whereas dark colours feel intimate and warm but show the dirt easily.

◆ If you are planning to re-sell your houses, install a white suite

◆ Mixer and power showers should conform to BS3456 and be installed by a registered plumber (Institute of Plumbing or National Association of Heating, Plumbing and Mechanical Services Contractors) (see Suppliers).

◆ Electric showers should have BEAB approval and be installed by a registered electrician (National Inspection Council for Electrical Installation Contracting) (see Suppliers).

◆ If you are converting a small bedroom into a larger bathroom, don't forget to remove all electricity sockets and replace light switches with pull cords.

◆ If you have always fancied having a roll-top bath but find the price of buying a new one prohibitive, look for an old one that has been re-surfaced.

SOFT FURNISHINGS

Soft furnishing fabrics

Soft furnishings are the decorative elements of the home that are made from fabric, such as cushions, curtains and upholstery. Experiment by combining different colours, textures, weaves and types of fabric. Don't be afraid to combine florals with checks or stripes for a dramatic effect and be bold with colours and trimmings.

Fabrics can create different moods depending on what style they are made up in. Think about the theme you want to create. For example, floral fabrics give a country feel to a room, and look better made up into comfortable cushions or curtains with a soft pelmet. Formal rooms with tailored furniture with lots of buttoning and piping need plainer woven fabrics.

Fabrics for soft furnishings

When choosing a fabric think about:
- Where is it going to go?
- How hardwearing does it have to be?
- Does it need good draping properties?
- Is it in sunlight?
- Is it resistant to fading and mildew?
- Ease of cleaning

There is also a wide range of different types of fabrics that can be used. Here are descriptions of the most popular types to help you decide which ones are the most suitable for what you have in mind.

Brocade: woven medium- to heavy-weight fabric with an embroidered, textured look. Made of silk, viscose or synthetic fibre. Sometimes a metallic thread is incorporated.

Calico: coarse plain weave, light- to medium-weight cotton.

Cambric: closely woven plain weave linen or cotton fabric. Uusually used as cushion covers.

Canvas: plain-weave durable cotton. Various weights available.

Chenille: heavy fabric of cotton, viscose, wool or silk with a soft velvety pile.

Chintz: tightly woven cotton with a shiny chemical glaze that drapes well.

The finish will wash off and fade, and once the glaze goes it cannot be restored. Some companies will clean and re-build an existing chintz finish and then re-hang.

Damask: elaborate jacquard weave of silk or cotton with a reversible pattern.

Dupion: looks like wild silk but made from synthetic fibres. Frays badly.

Gingham: plain weave cotton or cotton mix with equal width stripes of white and a colour. Reversible.

Hessian: coarse fabric of jute or hemp. Strong and hardwearing and available in various weights.

Linen: can be glazed or printed. Headwearing but creases badly so may be mixed with other fibres.

Moiré: watermarked effect silk or acetate. Do not wet.

Muslin: lightweight plain-weave cotton fabric available bleached (white) or unbleached natural).

Ottoman: heavy-weight fabric of ribbed cotton or cotton mix.

Silk shantung: light- to medium-weight silk with a slubbed appearance. Gathers and frills well.

Tapestry: heavy-weight, durable fabrics often depicting a historical scene. Heavy tapestries don't drape especially well.

Tartan: elaborate checked woven designs from wool, silk or cotton. Different weights available.

Velvet: synthetic (Dralon), cotton, silk or nylon with a soft pile. Hang so the pile runs down the length of a curtain or chair to show off the sheen. The denser the pile, the more durable the fabric. Dralon, unlike cotton velvet, is colourfast, but should not be ironed.

WATCHPOINTS

✦ When choosing fabrics and colour obtain as large a sample as possible from your retailer and drape in the room. See how it looks in natural and artificial light.

✦ Make sure that you have the right weight fabric for the application. Most retailers will be able to advise.

✦ If the fabric is washable, allow 10 per cent for shrinkage and wash the fabric at least twice before cutting out. Some fabrics have a shrink-resistant finish – check at point of purchase.

✦ Buy all the fabric you need at one time as colours may vary between batches.

✦ If you are choosing patterned fabric, check the pattern is correctly printed throughout the length before you buy.

✦ A woven rather than printed fabric is more likely to resist fading in sunlight.

✦ Small random patterning works out cheaper because you waste less matching pattern repeats.

✦ To help keep your soft furnishings looking good, have the fabrics treated for stain resistance or buy pre-treated upholstery and curtains.

creating finishing touches 274-275

Ways with windows

Window dressings offer great scope for the imagination and creativity. The huge variety of fabrics, headings, tracks, poles, pelmets and blinds available suit any style of decoration. And with so many ready-made ranges available you don't need to be a whizz with the needle. Don't worry if you don't feel confident at combining colours and patterns because many manufacturers have done this for you with ranges of co-ordinating soft furnishings, including curtains, tiebacks, valances, cushions, bedding and lampshades. If there is a problem, it's more than likely because there's too much choice. Before you make any purchase, decide on the effect you wish to achieve and evaluate your constraints. For example:

• What practical features are going to influence your choice, eg is there a radiator under the window? What style of window is it – french doors, dormer or pivot?
• What shape is the window – bay or square? How does it open?
• How many windows are in the room? Do you want to treat them all the same or as individuals? Do you need to maximise the light?
• How much clearance is there between the ceiling and top of the window? Obviously this will affect your choice of track or pole. Poles need space above and below to look effective. It may be worth considering a ceiling mounted track.
• Is the room over-looked, so is privacy important? You may want to screen the window during the day with blinds or sheers and have curtains that pull close at night.
• Are the curtains going to act as insulation? In this case they must be lined and maybe interlined.
• Would shutters or wood slat blinds look better than fabric?
• Is the window a feature, if so why cover it up? Many Edwardian houses have stained glass feature windows that look wonderful with the light filtering through. Translucent fabric draped round may look good.
• Is security important? You may prefer to install security grills or shutters on basement windows.

Curtains

Curtains are important not just for their functional properties – to provide warmth, keep out the light and to give privacy – but they pull all the other decorative elements together in a room. Before selecting your fabric consider what you want the curtain to do. For example, in children's rooms you want to keep out the light at night but in living rooms you want both privacy and light. Here you will need a combination of sheers and a top curtain, which can be closed at night.

Heading tapes

These are used to suspend the curtain from the track or pole and determine the drape effect (for example, a formal classical style using pencil pleats or a fuller, prettier effect from gathers) and the amount of fabric that is required. For example, using pencil pleated tape requires the width to be 2½ times the finished curtain width whereas for a gathered heading you only need to allow 1½-2 times the width. Most heading tapes have cords running through them which, when gathered, create the different pleats or gathers. Curtain hooks are threaded through pockets in the tape to attach the curtain to the pole or track. Allow five hooks for every 30cm (12in) of tape for good support. Heading tapes are

WATCHPOINTS

✦ Bay windows can be made from three separate units or curved. Consider covering with four curtains (two in the centre and one at each side); with three separate blinds; with blinds in the centre and curtains at the sides, or two curtains (but for this, the track and pole must bend around the angle).

✦ Bow windows are curved windows set in a straight wall. Curtains can be used to cut off the bow or used to emphasize the curved shape by hanging from a curved track.

✦ Dormer windows project from the roof. Often they don't let in much light, so opt for simple blinds or narrow curtains that pull back from the pane.

✦ French windows and garden doors need curtains that pull clear on either side so that the doors can open easily. Secure with tie- or holdbacks.

✦ Picture windows and patio doors may dominate the wall. Possibly you could cover the whole wall, rather than just the window.

available in different depths, in either cotton or polyester. Look for ones that have a coloured line running through them to indicate the sewing line. Flame retardant tape is also an option. The choices are wide:

Box pleat: generally used for valances.

Gathered or standard: shallow, evenly-spaced gathers that are often used behind a pelmet. Available in several different depths.

Goblet pleat: large individual pleats are stuffed with tissue paper to make them stand out and nipped at the base to form a goblet shape. Can be secured with buttons.

Pencil pleat: evenly-spaced tight gathers available in different depths.

Pinch pleat: fans of three or more pleats with flat sections between them. Fans can be secured with buttons. The heading tape is available in different depths.

Smocked pleat: for decorative headings.

Trellis and lattice: intricate pleating effects formed by drawing up four heading cords.

In place of using heading tapes consider one of the following simpler methods for hanging curtains.

• Tab top kits: available for use with your own fabric or fabric straps are supplied in a range of colours – no sewing necessary. Combine with buttons that you cover yourself.

• Make tie tops that are stitched to the top of the curtain and then fastened around the pole.

• Instead of using heading tape, create curtains by clipping café clips onto the fabric and hooking them onto any size curtain ring. Decorative clips are available which look good with voiles and sheers as café curtains.

• Heading tapes for fixed curtains: an adhesive tape that sticks to the wall or a wooden batten so you don't need to fix a pole or track. The heading, sewn on to the curtain, is then pressed on to the wall tape.

Curtain fabric

Most fabrics are suitable for curtains, but avoid very lightweight material unless it is for a decorative rather than functional effect. Also avoid heavy upholstery fabrics because of their poor draping qualities: they are best left for seating. If your budget is tight, the secret of economical window treatments is to use fabrics and materials not normally associated with soft furnishings. Never skimp on the amount of fabric you use to save a few pounds – luxury is associated with the amount of fabric you use not the price per metre.

Lightweights (cottons and polycottons) suit bathrooms and kitchens. In living rooms and bedrooms, use lining and interlining to improve the curtains' drape, insulation and light exclusion. Hem weights help the curtain to hang properly. Sew into mitred corners and hem, or lay tape into the hem fold and secure at intervals. Heavier-weight fabrics and tighter weaves offer better insulation, but they can be heavy to hang if lined.

Muslins, voiles and sheers

For decorative impact there is nothing better than muslin, calico or cotton voile, and because they're cheap you can use metres and metres. Don't feel that you have to use them by themselves, they are often used together with another set of curtains to filter the bright light. Make them in the same way as unlined curtains but use a flat fell seam or french seam because they are see through. Or simply sew a channel at the top to thread a wire or rod through or just drape over poles or through swag holders. Stencil designs using fabric paints, or dye or embroider motifs.

Muslin makes wonderful bed canopies. But don't skimp on the amount of fabric you buy because you will want it to look as voluminous as possible. Make a top channel in the muslin, thread a ring of garden wire through and hang from a hook in the ceiling using satin ribbon. Put weights in the hem to help it keep shape.

Curtain ideas

• To economise, use cotton sateen or silk lining as a top fabric. They are available in a good range of rich colours although they may need weighting.

• Indian bedspreads or saris work well at windows to add an ethnic touch.

• Don't forget dress fabrics – plaids, ginghams, stripes and spots all look good.

• Lightweight cottons and translucent fabrics can be twisted and knotted to create wonderful effects around curtain poles. Just stitch or staple in place. However, remember that these can't

choosing curtain tracks & poles 214-215   creating soft furnishings 268-273

WATCHPOINTS

What's in a heading?

✦ There are two categories of heading: fixed and drawn.

✦ Fixed headings tend to be more decorative and tightly gathered. It is this last factor that makes them fixed. The weight of the fabric and amount of material at the top of the heading means that they are much best hung, arranged and then left to look magnificent. The bulk of the curtains are then secured with tie- or holdbacks.

✦ A blind or sheers can be hung behind the main curtains for increased privacy.

✦ The headings for drawn curtains range from the very simple, such as tab heads, ties or clips, to the more ornate like goblet and box pleats.

✦ The headings can be left uncovered – especially if they are suspended from an attractive pole – or disguised with a pelmet, valance or swags and tails.

be opened and closed so they must be held back at the sides. They are easy to dismantle if you get tired of them.

• To keep sewing to a minimum – simply turn over the top edge of the curtain to make a pocket to thread the pole through. Alternatively, sew brass rings, loops of tape or make eyelets at intervals along the top of the curtain and thread ribbon or tape through to lace the curtains to the pole.

• Create an integral valence by attaching rings or tape to the back of the curtain some way down from the top edge and allow the fabric to flop over in soft folds. Allow for hems at the top and bottom; curtains that draw need fabric width of 1½ to 2 times the window width.

Linings

It is worth paying a little more to have the curtains lined. The extra weight not only helps block out the light at night but improves the drape and protects the top fabric from fading and condensation. It can also act as a buffer against noise. If made from contrasting or co-ordinating fabric the lining can be decorative as well as functional.

The lining can be permanently attached to the top fabric or detachable. Detachable linings are the more practical choice for areas where frequent washing is necessary, such as the kitchen. It can also be useful to be able to remove the lining during the warmer months.

Blackout linings: similar to thermal linings (see below) but they block out the light completely. They are useful for children's rooms or for shift workers as they also act as a noise buffer. However, they have poor draping properties.

Cotton sateen: the most common fabric, in cream or white for deflecting the heat of sunlight. Buy at the same time as the top fabric to ensure a good colour match.

Flame-retardant linings: these really are self-explanatory as they do exactly what they say they do.

Interlinings: used between the main curtain and lining to add body and insulation. Use with satin and silks but check that the curtain track can take the extra weight.

Thermal linings: these can be effective as a form of double glazing, saving up to 17 per cent more heat than unlined curtains. Similarly, they will keep the room cool in summer. They are made from cotton or blends of polyester and cotton, which have been flocked with a dense compound of acrylic or polyester. They are supple with a velvet pile. Hang the coated side away from the window.

Ready-made curtains

There are many ranges of ready-made curtains available from cotton chintzes to velvets and viscose. Many are supplied ready lined, and if not, linings can be purchased separately. However, if you want anything other than a pencil pleat heading you will be out of luck. Many manufacturers also offer a complete co-ordinated range from curtains and tiebacks to lampshades. Choose with care because the quality of the fabric varies greatly. Hold the fabric up to the light to see how translucent it is.

If you have unusually shaped windows you may also find that sizing is restrictive. Ready-made curtains do vary slightly between brands and ranges but most have a curtain drop or length of between 120 and 275cm (4 and 9ft) and a width of 110-330cm (43-130in) (each curtain). Most retailers offer a made-to-measure service in an excellent range of fabrics, which can also be bought by the metre (yard) for accessories.

measuring-up 262-265   creating finishing touches 274-275

Tiebacks

These are both useful and decorative and add the finishing touch to curtains whether they are formal or fun. They keep the curtains neatly in place and allow the maximum amount of light in to the room if attached away from the edge of the window. There is a ring at each end of the tieback so that it can be attached to a hook on the wall when in use. Check where you want to position the hook as this will alter the effect of the drape. But whatever position you go for, ensure the hook is hidden as much as possible.

There is a wide range of ready-made types available from specialist curtain stores and soft furnishing departments, but it is easy to create your own unique look using matching or contrasting fabrics and any manner of trimming. Braids, ropes and tassels are especially effective.

Shaped tiebacks are basically a shaped piece of stiff material covered with fabric. The stiff material is usually buckram (an open-weave cotton, starched and treated with a resin) that can be ironed-on or sewn-in. Kits are available if you don't feel confident cutting out your own. These include buckram with ready-drawn tieback shapes printed onto them. However, it is simple to make your own template out of paper. Cut out a style and hold it around the curtain to ensure that it is the right length and shape before cutting out any material.

WATCHPOINTS

Tieback variations

✦ To vary the effect have different shapes. Try squares, scallops and points.

✦ Add interest to plain edges by inserting a narrow frill or piping. Make in a contrasting colour or textured fabric for added interest. Alternatively, add braid, beading, fringing or tassels.

✦ Instant tiebacks are quick and easy to make. Natural hessian type materials look good tied back with rope. For lighter fabrics try muslin, silks or gauze.

✦ Plait different coloured lengths of ribbon, cord, raffia or fabric.

✦ Ropes and tasselled cords looped over hooks or cleats make good tiebacks.

✦ Tie a flouncy bow or sash of contrasting or matching fabric.

✦ Combine velvet and cord for a regal look.

✦ Make scrunchy velvet tiebacks by sewing a piece of velvet into a tube and threading a shorter length of elastic through. Secure the ends together.

▷ choosing pelmets & valances 216-217   ▷ choosing trimmings 220-221

Blinds

These can be plain and simple or highly decorative depending on where they are to be sited. If you want the blind for a specific purpose, such as to block out the light or help keep windows draught-free, check carefully as not all types will do this successfully.

Most soft blinds are easy to make and kits are available. Venetian blinds are generally bought ready-made, or made-to-measure. Roman and louvre blinds are not generally ready-made because they must fit exactly. Other blinds can be adjusted by altering the gathers or cutting the roller.

Austrian

These look like a curtain but are pulled up from the bottom by a series of vertical cords. They are made longer than the required drop of the window, and this extra fabric ruches up from the bottom to form a swag-like effect. The top is gathered using curtain heading tape.

Conservatory

Around 70 per cent of the sun's heat enters a conservatory through the roof. A blind won't eliminate wide temperature fluctuations but it will help to control it. On sloping panes blinds are held on tension wires to stop them sagging and these can be tightened if they slacken over time. The wires running through the blinds are secured to battens at the top and bottom. They can be cut to shape around pipes. There are several different fabric types from metallic coated to honeycomb structures. Discuss with your retailer what is the best type for your situation.

Festoon

Similar to Austrian blinds, but they use more fabric because they are ruched all along the complete drop. Suitable fabrics include lace, voile or other lightweight fabrics. As with Austrian blinds, dust and dirt can soon collect in the folds so vacuum regularly using the upholstery nozzle.

Roller

These are a good choice for kitchen windows, where curtains could be a hazard, or bathrooms as long as the fabric is PVC-coated to resist moisture. Roller binds can be made from fabric, paper or cane. Ready-made blackout roller blinds are also available.

They are cheap and easy to install, basically consisting of a spring-loaded roller which rolls up the blind. They can be decorated and trimmed to match the decor or a top curtain and personalized blinds are available where you add your own border to the bottom of a plain ready-made blind. If it is to go in a recess, choose a type that can be trimmed to size; alternatively, if it's over the recess, allow an overlap of 15cm (6in) on the sides and bottom.

Clean using an upholstery shampoo but avoid over-wetting. Proprietary blind cleaners are available from specialist curtains shops.

Roman

These look like roller blinds when hanging to their full drop but when raised, by a system of vertical cords at the back, they pleat into neat horizontal folds. The cords are wound around a cleat at the sides. They are usually made from fabric.

Venetian

A series of horizontal slats which can be made of plastic, wood or metal. The latest ones have wavy slats for a softer, more abstract look. They are operated by a cord system at the sides which raises or lowers the slats and they can be totally raised to the top of the window in the day time. Good for regulating the amount of light, however they are quite awkward to clean. Special brushes are available or, wearing cotton gloves, run your hands along both sides of the slats.

Vertical louvre

Similar to Venetian blinds, but the slats are vertical. They can be drawn to either side or some part in the middle like curtains. They are often used in conservatories.

Kits

Roller blind kits are available which include a tension sprung roller and end cap, lower batten, brackets and cord pulls. Fabric stiffener is not generally included but it is useful to have to prevent the side seams fraying. The kits are available from leading department stores and specialist curtain outlets and sizes vary from 60cm (24in) with a 2.4cm (1in) diameter pole to 240cm (94in) with a 3.8cm (1½in) pole.

Austrian, festoon and roman blind kits are also available for widths up to 224cm (88in). These include tape, curtain rings, cord, acorns, a cleat and screws, screw eyes and Velcro, but not the fabric, doweling rods, batten or track. Most specialist outlets will supply the individual components if you wish to make your own.

WATCHPOINTS

Simple blind ideas

✦ Tack a heavy striped cotton to the window frame at the top, and use long ties to keep the rolled lower edge in place. Add a pelmet to hide the top.

✦ Use plain, slightly translucent, fabric and sew in a series of evenly spaced horizontal pin tucks. This gives a textured, striped effect.

✦ Dress up your blinds with interesting ring pulls: use bows, tassels, buttons, brass rings or fabric covered rings. Many retailers offer custom-made ring pulls such as shells, stone animals, beads and rings.

✦ Add a contrasting border around the main fabric before making-up the blind.

✦ Buy a roller blind kit and customise it with fabric paints and pens to match your decor.

measuring-up 262-267   creating soft furnishings 268-273

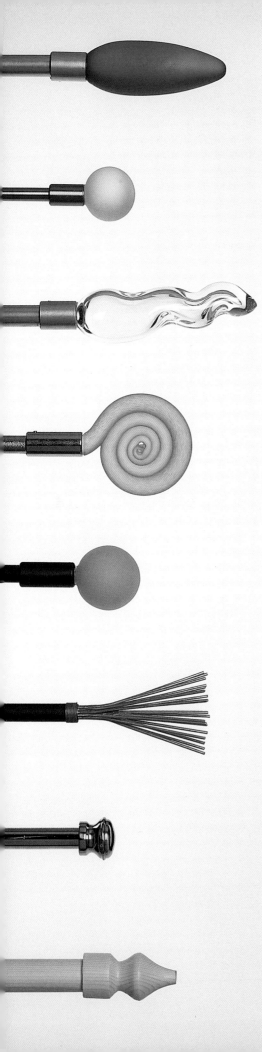

Tracks and poles

Make sure you buy the right type to suit the fabric and window shape, and the wall too. You must ensure that it can take the weight of the fabric and the pole. For example, if you are buying a track for a bay window check that it can be bent to the right angle. Curtain poles are designed to be displayed but tracks are often best hidden by a heading or pelmet.

Whichever type you choose, it will probably come in a kit form that includes the mounting brackets, endstops (fitting inserted into the end of a track to stop the hooks or gliders running off) and hooks or gliders. Some may have matching decorative finials (decorative endstop used on poles and some tracks). Fittings aren't interchangeable between different makes of tracks but curtain hooks to attach the curtains to the track or pole usually aren't included. Most heading tapes use plastic C-hooks, but pinch-pleated curtains need special metal multi-pronged or split hooks.

Curtain tracks

Tracks are made from plastic, aluminium, brass and steel. Check that you choose the right grade for the weight of the curtain fabric. Variable lengths are available or they can be made-to-measure and some tracks can be extended to take away the problem of having to cut to fit. Tracks can be ceiling or wall-mounted, and some can go round gentle internal and external curves. Plastic tracks are designed for straight runs and bay windows. To help bend plastic track for bay windows, immerse the section to be bent in hot water until it becomes more flexible. Then bend it into shape around something which has the same radius as you require, such as around a stool. Some tracks have an integral valance rail, for fitting fabric pelmets, or they can be attached separately. If the track is going to be visible, try covering it with one of the decorative track tapes available from DIY stores.

Curtain poles

Poles are made from a wide variety of different woods (teak, black ash, pine, beech, rosewood, walnut) or metal, in a range of diameters from 12 to 38cm (4¾ to 15in) depending on the fabric: long, lined curtains need substantial poles to bear the weight. Long poles (over 2.4m [2½yd]) need a central support to prevent them sagging, or two pieces can be joined together. Poles can be purely decorative, which means they conceal a track that holds the gliders. Half rings on the poles are attached to the gliders. Alternatively, they can be functional, which is best for short, straight runs, though it's possible to buy poles that bend around a bay using special elbow joints. They can be fixed to the wall or ceiling-mounted. More unusual styles of curtain pole include marble lacquered effects with a glossy finish, square poles and medieval.

Sprung rods are available to fit inside a window recess. These include café rods for café curtains and lightweight tension rods for lace curtains. For curtains over doors, used to prevent draughts, fit a portière rod to the door. This allows the door to be opened and closed freely.

choosing soft furnishing fabrics 204-205   choosing curtains 207-211

Cord sets

Useful for drawing hard to reach curtains and to reduce handling of delicate or expensive fabrics. Tracks and poles are available pre-corded or sets can be fitted to existing systems. The draw cord can be at either end of the track. Electric cord sets are available, useful for the disabled or, if combined with a timer, they act as a security device when you go out. Remote controls are available.

Control rods

These are rigid alternatives to a cord set. A pole is used to open and close the curtains to avoid handling them. They clip to the outermost hook or ring and hang out of sight when not in use.

Finials and holdbacks

Finials and holdbacks are used to make the pole into a feature. There are some quite spectacular wrought iron poles and finials currently in the stores. Other unusual combinations include: woven willow, macramé finials made from knotted jute and porcelain finials with iron pole; hand-blown glass or oak with a polished aluminium poles, and nickel and lead crystal poles and finials.

For children's rooms there are many novelty products such as wooden poles with colourful wooden car finials and matching holdbacks. Unlike tiebacks, these last are solid and attach to the wall. They are available in wood or brass, from plain, simple designs to the hugely elegant and ornate.

WATCHPOINTS

✦ Look out for an exciting new product which consists of coloured cotton or natural hemp wrapped around an inner steel core. It is easy to bend around corners.

✦ Fit circular shower rails above corner or free-standing baths or above a bed to make a canopy effect. They are available in gold, chrome or nickel finishes.

✦ Customise wooden poles using paint, wood stains, gilt or varnish. Use doweling to hang very lightweight materials. Finish with an unusual finial.

✦ For a rustic look, suspend a branch of weathered driftwood from the window frame to support a length of muslin.

Pelmets and valances

Adding a flourish at the top of a window dressing is an economical way of livening up dull curtains. They are ideal for hiding standard heading tape and so help you to make the most of a limited amount of fabric because basic tapes require less material than more elaborate headings. They will also alter the proportion of a room or window, making a high window look wider if fitted over it or taller if fitted above. Pelmets are the fixed variety, whereas valances are soft gatherings of fabric. Technically, swags and tails are more elaborate forms of valance.

Pelmets

A pelmet is simply a rigid box that is fixed over the top of the curtain, hiding the curtain track. Traditionally, these were made of wood, but now buckram tends to be used. This has the advantage of being easier to cut if you want to have a shaped front edge. The rigid material is then covered with similar or contrasting fabric to the curtains. Basic kits are available although it is relatively simple to construct from scratch. Other ways to use a pelmet are:

• For a very basic frame use three battens joined at the corners with angle brackets. Use two more angle brackets to secure this frame to the wall. Make the pelmet facia using as basic a material as you like; even corrugated card looks effective. Just attach it to the frame using glue and spray with gold paint.

• The simplest shape to make yourself is scalloped. Using a strip of lining paper the overall size of the facia, fold it into a concertina, cut a gentle curve, then open out. For more elaborate symmetrical shapes, fold the lining paper in half and cut through the two layers. This is your template. When cutting out, tape it to the facia panel for more accurate cutting.

• Card pelmets are a good base for covering with fabric, and add padding for a more opulent effect. Wrap the fabric around the card and glue down the edges on the wrong side. To cover intricate shapes, cut notches into the fabric edge so it turns over neatly. To finish, stick bias binding, braid or ribbon on the fabric following the contours of the pelmet.

• Alternatively, use wooden panels and stretch fabric over a layer of padding. Then staple in place around a simple wooden frame and trim with braid.

• Or try Pelmform, a stiffened material that is self-adhesive or velour lined. There is a choice of five different styles of front edges ranging from scallops to squares and sweeping curves. These are pre-printed on the backing paper.

• Attach fabric pelmets by using self-adhesive Velcro fastening. Stick the hooked part of the Velcro to the front of the frame or facia and the looped strip to the fabric heading tape. Press the two layers together.

Valances

These create a much softer, more feminine effect but can look fussy if inappropriate fabric is used. They are made in a similar way to curtains but hang on a second track in front of the main track. Use matching or contrasting fabric to the main curtain. Like pelmets, these should be about one-sixth the length of the curtain.

Swags and tails

These can be very formal and dramatic or very soft, pretty and feminine. The window area becomes the focal point of the room, especially if you mix colours, fabric lengths and textures. At their simplest, they are lengths of fabric draped across the top of the curtain to form folds of fabric or swags, and each end falls at the side to form the tails. When made like this they are easy to make as no sewing is required except for hemming the fabric which is then literally draped over the curtain tail and allowed to drop down at each end. Alternatively, instead of having a tail at both ends, create an asymmetrical look, swathing fabric along the curtain pole and down one side of the window.

More formal tailored styles take up a lot of fabric and can be difficult to assemble so are best left to the professionals. Whatever the style, the fabric should be cut on the cross and lie evenly and symmetrically across the window. An arched swag gives a formal finish and admits plenty of light. Alternatively, use corbels to hold the swags in place.

WATCHPOINTS

No-sew fabric pelmet

✦ Allow enough fabric to create soft gathers across the window. The length should be about one-sixth the total length of the curtains.

✦ Apply a strip of iron-on interfacing (about 20cm [8in] deep) to the reverse side along the top edge. Then use iron-on hemming tape to secure the hem on the bottom edge.

✦ Turn over the top edge and press in place. Cut vertical slits along the top edge about 4cm (1½in) apart. Thread a wide ribbon through these slits creating a soft gather as you go. Staple or tack directly onto the window frame.

choosing tracks & poles 214-215   measuring-up 262-267

Cushions and throws

Cushions can transform a dull, dark room by adding colour, individuality and style. They draw together all the different colours and textures used in the decor and improve the comfort and appearance of most sofas and chairs. Use them in any room of the house, from decorating a plain bed to softening a hard chair in the kitchen. Liven up an old sofa by adding vibrant cushions in rich opulent fabrics such as velvet, brocade, silk and satin.

Cushions are the most inexpensive of all soft furnishings to make and you don't need any great sewing skills or even a sewing machine – most can easily be made by hand. There is great scope for experimentation without the fear of making expensive mistakes.

Cushion styles

The most conventional cushion is square and simply made with two pieces of fabric joined together. This need not be the limit of innovation, however.

Alternative shapes: consider rectangles, circles and hearts; add gussets or leave them plain. Use the same fabric, but combine different shapes to pile them deeply on your sofa, chair or path.

Bolster cushions: these can look really exotic and give back and neck support. They are practical and simple to make. Leave each end of the bolster cover open and use drawstrings and tassels as closures. Alternatively, leave the ends ungathered and finish with a circular piece or fabric. Add contrasting piping for interest.

Oxford pillow: traditionally made as pillowcases, the wide border that isn't padded gives the cushion a generous quality.

Cushion pads

Cushions are either gusseted or ungusseted. Ungusseted pads consist of two pieces of fabric, the same size and shape, joined together – just like a pillow. Gusseted pads have another strip of fabric to join together the two shaped pieces.

Ready-made cushion pads are widely available in a variety of shapes, sizes and fillings. To be totally individual make your own using a heavy feather-proof cambric and filling with man-made fibre or feathers from an old cushion. The pad should be slightly larger than the cover size because they will flatten over time.

Curled poultry: the least expensive feather filling although you'll get a more comfortable cushion when combined with down. Feathers can be fluffed up and filled with air to restore their shape. You will need about 1kg (2lb) feathers or 0.5kg (1lb) down for a 50cm (20in) square cushion.

Foam: for a harder filling for box cushions use foam or a combination of foam and fibre. Cover with muslin before fitting a top cover.

Polyester fibre filling: a good choice for asthmatics because it is non-absorbent and washable. But it can lump together quickly. Use 0.75kg (1½lb) for a 50cm sq (20in sq) cushion.

Cushions fabrics

The beauty of a cushion cover is that you can use whatever fabric comes to

choosing soft furnishing fabrics 204-205   choosing trimmings 220-221

hand. Remnants are especially useful because in this way you can use fabrics that you might not otherwise consider because they are too expensive.

Fastenings

Cushion covers can be made into one piece but having an opening does give the option for cleaning. The fastenings can also be used as decorative additions: even a large and colourful chunky zip could be made into a feature.

Decorative buttons: the latest trend, you can make these into a feature by overlapping the cushion ends and securing with buttons or folding the fabric like an envelope around the pad and fastening with a button.

Fastening tapes: use either Velcro tape or popper tape, which has a series of small plastic or metal press studs.

Ties: made from ribbon, matching or contrasting fabric.

Zips: use nylon zips for lightweight fabrics and metal for heavier weights. Conceal these in the fold of the fabric or by the piping.

Throws

Whether the style is contemporary or traditional, a room can be transformed simply by adding a throw. Until recently much under-used, the throw is now undergoing a revival as a furnishing accessory. Don't just stick to one, several draped over a bed can look stunning. Any fabric can be used from old bedcovers and blankets to unusual lengths of fabric from all over the world. Indian and African cottons and Persian rugs always look spectacular. Textured fabrics such as tartans and chenilles work particularly well, adding a touch of luxuriance to old sofas and boring beds. Drape over old chests or storage boxes to add a focal point to a bedroom.

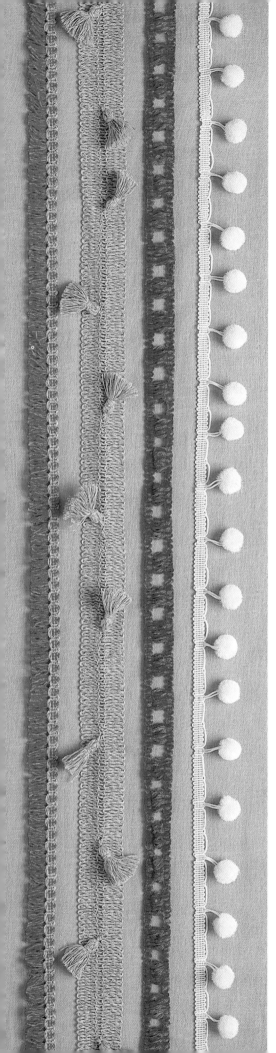

Trimmings

Haberdashery and home furnishing departments have a whole range of different tassels, cords, fringes and braids that can add stunning finishing touches to curtains, cushions and covers. They are available in all colours and sizes and some of the more straightforward ones like tassels and bows are easy to make at home. If you are interested in doing this, make use of unusual materials such as strips of lace or ribbons to create a unique look.

Use trimmings wherever you please – on curtains, cushions, throws, bed dressings. But while it is tempting to buy up an entire haberdashers in your enthusiasm, remember that a few frills and fancies go a long way. A tassel tieback here or a buttoned cushion cover there is usually sufficient to make a point.

Beads: glass, wood, plastic – use them individually or joined in strips and patterns.

Braids: from the simplest of rick-rack to the most ornate, 7.5cm (3in) wide decorative style with or without bobbles, these are perfect for adding as borders and strips on furnishings.

Buttons: self-covered or ready-made, the range is huge. Small or large, plain or colourful, novelty or traditional they are especially effective on simple soft furnishings because they make a statement in their own right.

Cords: stitch flat to the edge of cushions, curtains or pelmets, or make into more ornate loops at corners. Use fine cord to create three-dimensional shapes on covers and blinds.

Fringes: made from wool, cotton or synthetic yarns, these are available with straight edges or cut into shapes like fans and waves. They are available as single colours or mixtures, depending on what you require.

Tassels: large or small, attach to soft furnishings or use in their own right as tiebacks.

choosing curtains 207-211   choosing blinds 212-213

Using trimmings

• Appliqué shapes onto a solid background or sew or stick sequins or glass beads for a shimmering effect.

• Many manufacturers and retailers offer a fantastic range of curtain jewellery from which sheers or lightweight drapes are suspended. Shells, clear or frosted glass, brass teardrop and stone pebbles hang from fine steel hooks. The back of the hook is attached to the top of the drape allowing the decoration to dangle on the front. For best effect, allow one hook every 10cm (4in).

• Insert matching or contrasting piping or a frill around the edges of a cushion cover as you sew. Cover your own piping (stripes cut on the bias are especially effective) or buy one of the ready-made varieties. While not as exciting, they are quick to use.

WATCHPOINTS

✦ When shopping for trimmings, always take your fabric with you for an accurate colour match.

✦ Keep in mind the finished effect of your furnishing so that the trimming accurately reflects the mood and style.

✦ You can use the colour in your trimmings to emphasise one of the colours in the fabrics. They can also help to unite a disparate mixture of furnishings.

✦ Some trimmings require dry cleaning, and others need to be removed altogether. Bear this in mind when buying or making them as you might not want to take such trouble in the future.

Sofas and chairs

Sofas and chairs are a major investment and will probably have to last many years. When choosing, look beyond the fabric, they must be comfortable, practical and hardwearing. There are many styles ranging from traditional, formal tailored suites to more informal boxy styles with soft squashy cushions and loose covers.

Whichever your preference consider:
• Is the size right for the room? Too small and it will look lost, but too large and it will dominate the room.
• Do you want a two- or three-seater sofa or prefer several chairs? There should be about 1m (1yd) clearance at the front and sides of chairs and sofas.
• Does it offer enough support? It should support your back, base of spine and head and be easy to get in and out of. Firmness depends on the filling used. Foam cushions will be resilient and keep their shape, whereas feathers will be soft and need plumping up regularly.
• Seat height is important, too. You should be able to rest your feet flat on the floor while sitting back in the chair. If it's too high, legs will dangle, putting pressure on the underside of the thighs. Too low and it's difficult to get out of. If the depth of the seat is too great it will put pressure on your calves and restrict circulation to your legs.
• The style and design of furniture are extremely important considerations. Modern and traditional don't always mix. Too gimmicky and it will date quickly. Bold and fussy patterns can be tiring, make the room look smaller and restrict your choice of soft furnishings. Do you want a high back or more boxy style? If you have specific requirements, many retailers will tailor-make styles.
• Loose covers are very much in vogue, and are ideal if you have a family or pets. However, take care to follow wash instructions or they could shrink or fade. One upholstery manufacturer has developed two man-made materials with good stain-resistant properties. They both incorporate Teflon and look and feel like suede so are ideal for sofa covers, especially as they are washable at 40°C without losing stain resistance. Liquid spillages roll off and stubborn stains can be rubbed off with a soft cloth and special cleaning solution.
• The thicker and denser the foam, the more resilient it will be. Check by feeling the weight of the cushions.
• The cover should fit well without being over-stretched. Seams should be straight without puckering.

The fabric weave
Before buying your furniture look at the fabric weave. Textured fabric will snag more easily than a smooth, dense pile. A closely woven fabric should wear the best. These are the most used types of fabric for sofas and chairs:
Acrylic (Dralon): look for dense piles.
Cotton: as long as the fabric is tightly woven it is durable but shows stains and burn marks. Pile fabrics are more durable.
Linen union: a blend of cotton and linen, this is good for printed patterns, but has a poor resistance to abrasion.
Polyester: crease resistant and reasonably resilient.
Polypropylene: wears well and resists dirt but will melt if burnt.

creating soft furnishings 268-273

Viscose: durable but creases and shows dirt and stains.
Wool: wears well, is flame-, crease- and stain-resistant but choice is limited.

Sofabeds

These are an ideal solution to space problems and can be a life-saver over Christmas and family get-togethers. However, because you are buying both a sofa and a bed you tend to have to compromise on sitting or sleeping comfort. As a general rule, the more expensive the sofabed, the better the comfort in both modes. They are classified according to their method of opening into a bed.

A-frame: foam or sprung upholstery is supported by a metal frame and wooden slats. To convert into a bed, the cover is unzipped at the sides and the A-shape frame pulls out to lie flat. The seat is very upright and only suitable for occasional use.

Foam pull-out: consists of three foam pads, which concertina into the sofa. Hard and low as a sofa and as a bed, it is however suitable for occasional use for younger guests.

Futon: a thin mattress is used either on the floor or with a slatted base. Fillings can be cotton, wool and cotton or polyester. Suitable for frequent use but both the seating and bed is low.

Lengthways fold: here the box base of the sofa supports a metal frame and foam or sprung upholstery which doubles as a mattress. The frame pivots and opens out and it is comfortable enough for frequent use.

Pull-out drawer: the bed pulls out of a drawer in the sofa's bottom. Quite low, it is suitable for occasional use.

Three-fold: seat cushions are removed and the frame unfolds from the seat. The frame is usually metal, with a polypropylene or mesh base. Good for occasional use but the mattress is thin.

Two-fold: this mechanism unfolds from the body of the sofa. The frame is metal, with either a wire-mesh or wooden slatted base with webbing. The mattress can be either foam or sprung and is suitable for frequent use.

WATCHPOINTS

✦ Always use 'cups' under the feet of heavy sofas and armchairs or they will permanently dent your carpet or mark a hard floor.

✦ When choosing your furniture, think of the practicality of the colour and pattern and check the covers are removable for cleaning. If not, look for darker, patterned designs. Also look for fabric with a stain repellent finish.

✦ Comfort is crucial, so test the sofa in the store by sitting on it for as long as possible. If it doubles as a bed, open it out and lie on it. When you're lying down, the bed should be stable and you shouldn't feel the frame through it.

✦ Models on castors are easier to move but if it's a sofabed it won't keep still when opening out.

✦ For leather upholstery, the trend is towards softer styles rather than traditional Chesterfields. Softer, paler leathers are more prone to damage and staining so you need a long lasting finish. Unfortunately you have to rely on the dealer's knowledge because it is difficult to tell what finish has been used. It all depends on the origin of the hide and tanning process used.

✦ There are two main types of leathers: Natural-grain are soft and comfortable (semi-aniline and colour-coated full-grain are the best) whereas artificially grained leathers are less comfortable (but colour-coated corrected grain is hardwearing) because of the layer of protective coating. But they are easy to maintain.

Bedroom furnishings

There is no doubt that changing your linen is the quickest and cheapest way to revamp your bedroom! Over the last few years this area of soft furnishing has undergone a dramatic transformation. Bed-dressing has become an art in itself. All the elements – duvets, sheets, throws, pillows and cushions – interact to produce stunning effects that are simple to change as your mood takes you.

Bedheads

Bedheads either fix to the bed frame or the wall behind the bed. Whatever you opt for, ensure you can clean it easily and if the cover can be removed, make sure this is easy to do. If making one yourself, use pre-shrunk fabric or wash it a few times before making up into the cover. As an alternative to the more traditional bedhead, try one of these ideas:

• For a simple bedhead, fit box cushions, using tab headings, to a pole behind the bed or hang with ribbons attached to coat hooks in the wall.
• Use two large, well stuffed pillows to prop up against metal or wooden cane boards that aren't very comfortable.
• Hang an old quilt or rug from a pole above the bed.
• Cover old headboards with several layers of padding that are stuck in place. Then stretch a top fabric to match your decor across the front and staple at the back. Cover the back if it is likely to show. Trim with cord, tassels or braid.

Blankets

Blankets are becoming very popular once again as the traditional bedroom is becoming fashionable. Consequently, manufacturers are being more adventurous in their use of colour and texture, with colours mimicking those of clothing fashions. Blankets are being used as throws, so becoming a decorative feature as well as functional. Wool, cotton, polyester fleece, cotton waffle structures and non-woven acrylics are the most popular fabrics used for blankets today.

Tog values (see below) are not given for blankets but as a general rule three good-quality blankets are roughly equivalent to a tog rating of 13.5.

Duvets

Duvets are graded by 'tog' ratings – the higher the tog rating, the warmer the duvet. It is a measure of warmth, not weight or quality.

Tog rating	Suitability
4.5	Summer use
10.5	Spring and autumn or winter if you have central heating
13-15	Winter

All-season duvets consist of two duvets (one 4.5 and the other 9-10.5 tog) which can be used separately or attached together. There is also a three duvet system available, which allows you to combine doubles and singles: ideal if your sleeping partner likes different temperatures.

Duvet fillings

The important part of a duvet is the air inside and how the filling traps it. The air – and its moisture content – controls the temperature, as well as softness. In general, the better quality the duvet the less filling is required, which means it has a light weight-to-volume ratio. For example, a 13.5 tog goose-down duvet, is not as heavy as a 10.5 tog polyester one.

Duvets are usually filled with feathers and/or down, or polyester, but other natural fibres such as wool, silk and cotton are becoming popular. The main types of blend are polyester/cotton; polyester/silk; silk/wool.

Cotton: good for lightweight duvets. It is quick drying and a good choice for allergy sufferers. It is warm and moulds around the body well, but flat.

Down: pure down gives warmth without weight but you do have to pay for the luxury. However, this filling will last much longer than others. The best qualities are Hungarian followed by European goose down.

Down and feather: (at least 51 per cent down) followed by feather and down (15 per cent down) are cheaper versions but still soft, light and warm as other types.

Polyester: not as light or warm. They are generally cheaper and washable but may compress slightly. Like pillows, look for branded hollowfibres.

Silk: an ideal summer duvet because it is airy and cool. It breathes and absorbs moisture. Lightweight but flat.

Wool: can absorb up to 30 percent of its own weight in moisture before feeling damp. But it is flat and not particularly cosy.

WATCHPOINTS

✦ Buy washable blankets as they are softer and more hygienic.

✦ Bed linen patterns can be co-ordinating or contrasting, but try to keep a common colour running throughout.

✦ Always measure your bed before buying bedding. Check that bottom sheets can be tucked in adequately. Duvets should be wider by 35cm (14in) for a single, 65cm (26in) for a double and 75cm (30in) for a king-size bed.

✦ If you have an allergy sufferer in the family, many manufacturers have brought out bedding ranges that are non-allergenic and can be washed at high temperatures.

Duvet construction

It is not just the filling that is important but how the duvet is put together. Early duvets were just an envelope of fabric filled with a stuffing, which was able to move about, resulting in cold patches. Now a more sophisticated type of construction uses channels and pockets, which follow the way the body lies to keep the filling evenly distributed.

Top quality duvets will have walled pockets keep the filling in place. If you want to be able to shake the filling down in summer, for example, look for duvets with walled channels.

Electric blankets

Electric blankets are hotting up! There's now a choice of under, over or fitted blankets to fit different sized beds. Some can even be machine washed using a 40°C woollen programme, then tumble dried. Fitted under-blankets can be used to warm the bed and some brands can be left on all night. However, check how comfortable the blanket is to lie on because sometimes the wires can be intrusive. Also check that the controls are at the right side for your electricity supply – some can be on either side.

Pillows and pillowcases

The average pillow size is 50 x75cm (20 x 30in), although slightly longer 50 x 90cm (20 x 36in) pillows, designed so that two will reach across a double bed, are now available. The biggest change is the popularity of the square pillow (65cm sq [25 in sq]), originally only common in the rest of Europe. Pillowcases can be either housewife-style, where the case fits snugly around the pillow, Oxford style – which have a frill, edging or border – and square or button pillowcases.

Whether to go for a natural or synthetic pillow is very much a personal preference but as a general rule the more feathers, the firmer the pillow.

Curled poultry feathers: crunchy and less comfortable than down.

Down: the softest and most luxurious pillow filling, but the most expensive because birds produce only 12g (less than 1oz) of down each. Blends of feather and down are cheaper. Goose feather and down are smaller than duck and weigh less so the pillow will be lighter and softer.

Foam rubber or crumb: have a short life and soon go lumpy.

Polyester: non-allergenic but vary in quality and support. Look for the branded hollowfibre pillows which consist of hollow tubes of polyester fibres capable of trapping large volumes of air, making a lighter, softer pillow.

Wool: a relatively new filling for pillows and has the advantage of being very absorbent.

If you sleep on your side you need a firmer pillow for neck support. Opt for a high feather-to-down ratio; all-feather or synthetic pillow. If you sleep on your stomach, a very soft pillow is best so look for one with more down. And if you sleep on your back, opt for a medium-firm pillow with equal amounts of feather and down. There is a brand of pillow that is firmer on one side than the other.

Sheets and duvet covers

The choice of bed linen is now overwhelming, from romantic embroidered white and cream to colourful florals and bold checks. Patterned and coloured bed linen is available in two types. It can be woven, using dyed threads, so if you turn the sheet over the pattern is just as clear on the back. Alternatively, the pattern is printed on to one side only, which is often cheaper but less durable and more likely to fade. Duvet covers with a printed pattern often have one style on the top and another on the bottom, making them reversible. Quality and choice of material will depend on how much you wish to spend.

Combed cotton: this has been treated to remove a high percentage of short fibres, leaving a finer stronger yarn. Often combined with polyester.

Cotton flannellette or brushed cotton: these may sound old-fashioned but they are wonderfully warm and soft for winter.

Easy-care sheets: polyester/cotton sheets (usually a 50/50 blend) are popular because if hung straight from the machine you don't need to iron them. However, they absorb less moisture. Buy the best quality you can because cheaper brands will 'pill' over time due to abrasion and become uncomfortable. Cotton-rich blends (80/20) are worth considering but they

will need ironing. Some have a special easy-care finish.

Egyptian cotton: the best quality, though little now comes from Egypt. It is smooth and strong because it has longer fibres than other cottons. The higher the thread count, the closer the weave and better the quality. Top brands will be around 200 per square inch. It is harder to iron, however.

Percale: refers to any cloth (cotton or poly/cotton) which has a thread count of at least 180 threads per square inch.

Pure linen and cotton and linen blends: these fabrics feel luxurious and wear well but they are expensive and very hard work to iron. Pure cotton bed linen is more reasonably priced, however. Its beauty is that it stays warm in winter, and cool in summer because it can absorb up to 10 per cent of its own weight in moisture without feeling damp.

WATCHPOINTS

✦ If you are buying an electric blanket check it is BEAB approved and has an automatic cut-out, in case of over-heating.

✦ Make the bed into the focal point of the room by:

✦ Creating a swag against the wall instead of having a bedhead. Simply drape fabric over a pole fixed high above the bed.

✦ Create a canopy above the bed. Fix a pole to the ceiling at the foot and head of the bed. Drape fabric between the two. Allow it to cascade at either end.

✦ Make a coronet effect bed heading by tying the fabric to three hooks, set in the wall to form the points of a triangle. Use rosettes to hide the hooks.

3

Practical Know-how

PREPARATION

Stripping paint and paper

Surface preparation is the key to a professional finish but it creates large quantities of dust so empty the room to be decorated as much as possible and cover everything that is left behind with newspaper followed by dust sheets. It is not always necessary to strip paint before re-painting but you will probably need to remove paint from mouldings. If there are too many layers of paint, the mouldings lose their details and shape. If you are not stripping paint you will at least have to prepare it for the next coat. Wash thoroughly with sugar soap or detergent and rinse with fresh water. Dry the paintwork, sand and wash the surface one more time. If there is flaking paint on a wall, remove as much as possible with a scraper and then sand the surface smooth. Dust and wash, leave to dry and you are now ready to paint – assuming there aren't any holes and cracks to fill.

ABOVE: *With narrow rolls of wallpaper you can create unusual effects. But to reach this stage, the walls must be prepared thoroughly first.*

Stripping paint

You will need
- Blowlamp or hot air stripper or chemical stripper
- Scraper
- Shavehook
- Sandpaper

1 For large surfaces, use a blowlamp to soften the paint, removing it with a wide bladed scraper. Keep the flame moving to prevent scorching and never set down when it is alight.

2 To remove paint from the nooks and crannies of mouldings use a shavehook, which is shaped specifically to work into these gaps. To reduce the chances of scorching woodwork, use a hot air stripper in place of a blowlamp.

◀ making plans 14-15   making good 235

3 As a final precaution, rub down the mouldings with a flexible abrasive block, which takes the shape of the moulding.

Stripping paper

Alternate the soaking and stripping of wallpaper so that while you are removing the paper from one area, the next patch is softening up. Once you are under way, the stripping paper routine speeds up immensely. Seeing large areas of colour being removed in this way is very satisfying, only really surpassed by the subsequent hanging of new paper or covering with paint.

You will need
• Wallpaper stripper
• Steam stripper
• Serrated scraper (optional)

1 Soak normal wallpaper with warm water and some household detergent using a sponge and pressing it firmly onto the paper. Leave the water to soak in and apply some more water if necessary. Once the paper is sufficiently soft, scrape it off using a wallpaper scraper, working up from the bottom of the wall to ease the paper's removal.

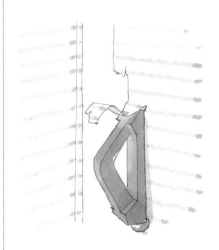

2 If you are removing washable paper, score the surface with a serrated scraper, wire brush or a coarse abrasive paper before wetting the surface. Take care not to press too hard or you will damage the surface beneath the paper. Scoring in this way allows water to penetrate through the top layer to the paper below.

3 For larger areas or stubborn paper you might find it easier to use a professional steam stripper. These can be hired from tool companies and are very efficient. They force the steam through a large plate to penetrate the top surface of the wallpaper, reaching the paste beneath. Work on a small area at a time and to prevent scalding, wear a rubber glove

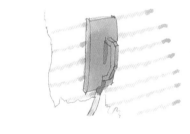

Stripping heavier papers

To strip vinyl paper, loosen the top surface – the vinyl coating – and peel it off first. Then strip the backing as for a normal wallpaper. It is best not to leave the backing if you are re-papering as it may no longer be sufficiently well stuck to support the new paper.

Removing textures and tiles

Removing ceramic tiles and textured finishes generally create a lot of mess and these surfaces can also be very hard work to remove. Never try to sand a textured finish as a huge amount of dust will be created. Also, in older versions of this product there may be asbestos fibres, which should on no account be inhaled. Before going to the trouble of removing ceramic tiles you might want to consider painting them instead, or sticking more tiles over the top. If you choose to painting them, there are some wonderful tile transfers on the market that you can use to add pattern to the paintwork.

ABOVE: *With care and attention, the most old-fashioned and tattiest of decor can be transformed into a calm and serene living space.*

Removing textured finishes

You will need
• Texture paint remover
• Paintbrush
• Paint scraper
• Rubber gloves
• Safety goggles
• Wire wool

1 Brush generous amounts of texture paint remover over the paint ensuring a good coating. Leave the remover to soak into the paint.

2 Scrape off the softened paint with the broad-bladed scraper. If you are working on a ceiling, wear rubber gloves and safety goggles as the remover contains abrasive chemicals.

3 To remove any remaining flecks of paint, use wire wool dipped in the paint remover.

Removing ceramic tiles

You will need
• Hammer
• Bolster chisel
• Club hammer
• Eye goggles

1 Crack a tile in a suitable place on the wall so that you can strip off the rest from here. If there is an edge to the tiling, start there.

2 Use the bolster chisel and club hammer to chip the tiles off the wall. Wear protective goggles. You may need to re-plaster the surface before continuing the decorating.

choosing wall tiles 170-171

Making good

Filling cracks and holes

Before applying paint or paper you now need to make the surface as smooth as possible as all minor lumps, bumps and cracks will show through the final covering. This may not be the most exciting of decorating tasks but it is an important one if you want the best finish possible. Whether you are filling defects in wood or plaster, the principle is the same – but ensure that you use wood filler for one and plaster for the other.

You will need
- Putty knife
- Paintbrush
- Filler
- Sandpaper
- Sanding block

1 Clear out any loose material from cracks and holes, using the putty knife and then the paintbrush, if necessary, to help you.

2 Fill splits and cracks with the appropriate filler using the putty knife and working the filler into the recesses. For smaller areas that are difficult to reach, use a finger and a small amount of filler at a time. Make the filler as smooth as possible before it dries to reduce the amount of sanding you will need to do later.

3 Leave the filler to harden and then use sandpaper wrapped around the sanding block to smooth the repair flush with the surrounding wall.

Filling large cracks and holes

If you are filling large holes, apply the filler in layers allowing it to dry thoroughly between applications. To fill chips in mouldings or at external corners, use a wooden strip held flush to one surface and fill the hole created. When the filler is dry, move the strip to the other surface and fill the hole as before. Leave to dry, sand back and paint.

WATCHPOINTS

✦ Removing old polystyrene tiles is a comparatively straightforward task that only requires a scraper to lever away the tiles. If blobs of adhesive are left over, use a hot air gun to soften the glue and remove it with the scraper.

✦ If knots are showing through the painted woodwork, sand the paint back to bare wood and apply knotting to the knot, and prime and undercoat as before until it is level with the previous paintwork.

✦ If the knot is resinous this can only be put right by stripping back, as above, and drying out the knot with a blowlamp.

✦ Before applying filler to a crack in plaster, dampen the edges to prevent the filler from drying out too quickly. This causes it to crack.

✦ If ceilings have been stained by plumbing leaks, seal the area with an aerosol stain sealer. This prevents the stain from showing through the next coat of paint.

stripping paint & paper 232-233

Stripping floorboards

A well-maintained and cared for wooden floor is very beautiful, but getting to that stage of mellow, varnished wood can be time-consuming. Before stripping the boards, assess whether it is even worth spending all this time on the job. Old floors can be very draughty and if many of the boards need repairing (see box, opposite) it might be just as well to cut your losses and cover them with another surface such as woodflooring laid in strips or squares. Central heating can dry out timber so much that the boards shrink, resulting in gaps and squeaks as the boards rub together.

The end result can be patchy, however, and a varnished floor might not look especially attractive. Clear varnish need not be the only finish, though, and if you want a more colourful floor, consider staining or painting the floorboards, or for a more restrained effect look into liming and waxing. Whichever finish you opt for, you will first need to hammer down protruding nails, fill in nail holes, remove sharp edges or splinters and then sand back the surface. Industrial sanders and the smaller, rotary sanders – useful for edges and corners – are available for hire.

BELOW: *Floorboards painted with watered-down white emulsion that is varnished to seal look totally fresh. But preparation is just as important as the creative finishing touches.*

Sanding floorboards

You will need
- Masking tape
- Face mask
- Ear plugs
- Industrial sander
- Coarse, medium and fine sandpapers
- Small rotary sander
- White spirit

1 As sanding a floor is such a dusty and dirty job make sure you wear a face mask at all times. It is also noisy, so ear plugs are advisable. To prevent dust spreading through the house, fix masking tape around the door frame and block the gap beneath the door with newspaper.

2 Follow the manufacturer's instructions for fixing sandpaper to the sander. Start with the coarsest paper and make sure that it is secure before you begin, otherwise it will rip off when you start sanding.

3 Sand diagonally across the floor working from one corner of the room to the other. Always work across the wood grain, never at right angles to it. Tilt the sander back before you switch it on and then lower it gently to the floor. For safety's sake, keep the lead behind you, trailing it over your shoulder. To turn the sander, lift the drum off the floor, and work back from where you have just come.

4 Sweep up the floor and then repeat the whole process but using the medium grade sandpaper and working across the floor on the opposite diagonal. For a smooth finish, sand for a final time with the fine grade sandpaper, but this time work along the length of the boards.

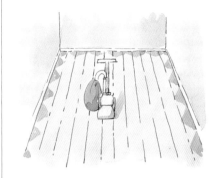

5 To finish the floor, work around the strip that is left at the edge and in the corners with the small rotary sander. Again, start with the coarse grade sandpaper and work down to the fine.

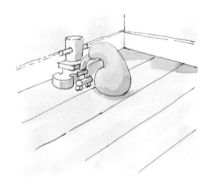

6 Once you have finished, sweep the floor very thoroughly for one last time and then wipe over it with white spirit. It is now ready to be varnished, stained or painted, depending on your requirements.

WATCHPOINTS

✦ Never allow the sander to stand still with the motor running. This is a very common mistake and it leaves very clear marks on the floor – and overheats the motor at the same time.

Pre-sanding preparation
✦ If only one or two of the boards squeak, try screwing the board to its neighbour or to the nearest joist – but take care to avoid wires and pipes, which may lurk beneath.

✦ Seal small gaps in the boards with wood filler and then sand level with the surround when dry.

✦ Cover larger gaps with wedges of wood coated with wood adhesive and coloured if necessary.

✦ Once everything is dry, plane and sand the wedges level with the floor.

CREATIVE FINISHES

Painting

For a great paint finish on any surface, follow two simple rules. One: prepare the surfaces as the slightest raise or crack tends to be highlighted by a smooth coating of paint. Sand the surfaces until they are as smooth as possible. This may require several weights of sandpaper, starting with the coarsest and working to the finest. If you have holes or cracks, fill them with an appropriate material – wood or plaster filler – in advance of the sanding. Two: keep everything scrupulously clean. This means that after sanding a surface you must always wipe it down before starting to paint, and ensure that your brushes and/or rollers are washed thoroughly as soon as you have finished with them or use them again.

ABOVE: *The conventional paint to use on woodwork is gloss, but with developments in water-based paints, acrylics and emulsions are viable. But seal the surface after.*

Tools and equipment

Paintbrushes: it is preferable to use a paintbrush for all woodwork for a truly neat finish; on walls and ceilings you may prefer to use a roller. Buy a range of widths of paintbrush (the most commonly used sizes are 25, 50 and 100mm [1, 2 and 4in]). A cutting-in brush is also useful for the edges of walls and ceilings and a long-handled brush for painting behind radiators. If you are planning some decorative paint effects, you might also want to add a stencil brush and some artist's brushes to your paintbrush collection.

Paint roller and tray: great for large areas such as walls and ceilings, but you need to have some smaller paintbrushes to hand, too, for the fiddly areas. Paintbrushes are also essential if you are painting on a heavily textured paper. Extension handles are available for rollers for high areas.

Paint pad and applicator: a small pad can be very effective for painting woodwork; they are available in different sizes ranging from 75 to 150mm wide (3 to 6in). An applicator – a sponge roller that rotates at the end of a paint tray – is useful because it ensures an even spread of paint on the pad.

Paint kettle or bucket: although not essential, these devices are especially helpful if you are spending a lot of time up a ladder – they have a handy hanging device – and they also allow you to use a wider brush.

White spirit: used in oil-based paints as a thinner and for washing brushes after use.

Masking tape: for window frames or other areas to be shielded from paint.

choosing paints 166-167   stripping paint & paper 232-233

ABOVE: *When painting a room, start at the ceiling furthest from the door and work down the surfaces to the floor. It is best to decorate the walls so that you are working away from the light source. Leave the woodwork and radiators until last.*

Order of painting

Whatever surface your are painting, whether it be walls, ceiling or floor, or windows and doors, you can make life as easy as possible by decorating each surface in the order suggested here. It is also best to paint the main surfaces first and then move onto the woodwork. Start at the top of the room with the ceiling and move down to the bottom – this prevents accidental paint splashes spoiling what you have already painted. If you are painting over a dark surface, you may find that you need to apply two coats of your new colour – or undercoat if you are intending to use one coat.

Ceilings

To help make this job as clean as possible use a roller and a solid emulsion paint. Cover yourself up well, too. If you have an extension handle for the roller, so much the better, but it can make roller control rather difficult. Instead, you may prefer to work from a plank that is laid on the steps of a pair of step ladders.

1 Paint a narrow strip. Using a narrow paintbrush – preferably a cutting-in brush – paint all around the edge of the ceiling, butting-up to the wall. It is difficult to paint neatly right to the edge of the ceiling with a roller and in this way you won't have to worry.

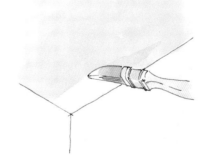

WATCHPOINTS

Applying paint

◆ With a paint brush: load the brush with paint, covering only about one third of the length of the bristles, and apply to the walls. Start at the top of a wall and work away from a natural light source making roughly square patches that you fill in with paint as you work across the wall.

◆ Before loading the brush with more paint, ensure that the paint is evenly applied across the surface and then lay-off, which means brushing from the leading edge back into the painted area. With matt emulsion, do this with criss-cross strokes. This prevents a hard edge forming.

◆ When painting on wood, follow the direction of the grain. Paint each item in one session and don't use too much paint at one time.

◆ With a roller: pour a small amount of paint into the paint tray and dip the edge of the roller into it. Run the roller up and down the tray until the roller is evenly covered, but not with so much paint that it drips everywhere. When applying the paint to the surface, make a criss-cross pattern to prevent creating hard lines.

◆ With a paint pad: use as for a roller but loading the paint from the special paint pad applicator. Apply the paint in rough squares, working in random directions.

making good 235   creating paint effects 244-249

2 Paint a wider strip with the roller. Start next to the window wall and ensure that the line is parallel to the previous strip but leaving a small gap between them.

3 When you come to the end of the run, work back in the other direction so that you can fill the gap. If necessary, gently paint over the area again to blend in the paint.

4 Repeat steps 2 and 3 until the whole ceiling has been covered.

Windows

Cover all glass with masking tape to prevent paint from getting onto the glass and to give you a neat finishing edge to the paintwork. Also aim to paint the frames as early in the day as possible so that you can shut the windows in the evening if it is too cool outside.

Casement windows
These are the most straightforward frames to paint and once you have prepared them and masked the glass you should tackle them in the following order:
1 Glazing bars
2 Opening window (if there is one)
3 Window frame and sill.

Sash windows
These need a little more time as the two halves of the frame need to be moved around so that you can reach every section with ease. Start by opening the window until the bottom and top sashes overlap by about 20cm (8in). Then paint the bottom of the top sash. Close the bottom sash and pull up the top so that the window is almost closed.
Finish the frame as follows:
1 Rest of top sash
2 Bottom sash
3 The frame, avoiding the sash cords.

choosing paints 166-167   stripping paint & paper 232-233

Doors

Before beginning to paint any door, it is important that you remove, or at least loosen, any door furniture as it can be extremely fiddly decorating around these parts of the door and you will invariably end up having to clean them up afterwards. For the best effect, paint the outside edge of the door to match the paintwork of the room that it opens into.

Flush doors

Start painting from the top and work down as shown in the illustration above right. So that each painted section blends in well with the next, make sure the paint edge is wet. Paint the frame last with a narrower paintbrush.

Panelled doors

The order of painting a panelled door (see below) is as follows:
1 Mouldings (if there are any)
2 Panels
3 Vertical strips in the centre
4 Horizontal strips
5 Sides, edges and frame.

creating paint effects 244-249

Paint effects

The wide variety of paint effects that can so readily be created bring added interest to walls, floors, ceilings and furniture. Indeed, paint effects can be applied to almost any surface and as water-based paints, acrylic varnishes and glazes are now widely available and easy to use, so the the tools you need should not be too inhibiting.

Before applying the paint effect to your chosen surface it is always best to experiment on a spare piece of board. First, colours always look quite different when they are applied over a larger surface than a paint swatch, and secondly they dry to a different shade. When combining two or more colours, this test run becomes even more important. Tester pots are excellent for just this kind of activity.

ABOVE: *Colourwashing can be strong or subtle depending on the contrast between the colours. The stronger the contrast, the less subtle the effect. Here, closely toning shades of blue and green have been used which give just a hint of surface texture, and a subtle play of light on the surface.*

Colourwashing

Colourwashing consists of a thin glaze applied over a base coat with a brush or roller, or even a cloth or sponge. The effect to aim at is gentle gradations of colour. Since the glaze that you buy comes in a fairly limited range of colours, you will be much better off tinting your own. If you are buying oil-based glaze, tint it with artist's oil colours or universal stainers, and if you are buying acrylic glaze, use acrylic paints. Good for large areas.

You will need
- Base coat
- Glaze
- Water
- Paintbrush
- Sponge

1 Apply the base coat (emulsion or eggshell, depending on whether a water- or oil-based top coat is being used) in criss-cross fashion.

2 When the base coat is completely dry, brush over a very wet glaze (tinted if necessary to the right colour) – 8 parts of water to 1 part emulsion, or 8 parts white spirit (mineral spirits) to 1 part oil paint – in random fashion. Allow the glaze to dry.

choosing paints 166-167   painting 240-243

3 Brush out a second coat of glaze in a closely related colour, going over any areas where the colour is uneven.

4 Seal with a few coats of clear matt varnish if the finish is to be waterproof. This is important in areas that receive high wear and tear.

Dragging

Dragging is often done as a pastel glaze over a plain white surface, or a deeper colour over a pastel base, so that the pale base coat shows through the dragged glaze. Good for smaller areas and on woodwork.

You will need
• Base coat
• Paintbrush
• Glaze
• Tint

1 Apply the base coat (emulsion or eggshell, depending on whether a water- or oil-based top coat is being used) in criss-cross fashion.

2 Tint the glaze if necessary to the required colour, and start to apply to the wall with up and down strokes, criss-crossing the brush in X-shapes. If you are working on your own, work in manageable sections.

3 Using a long, soft-bristed brush, ideally a purpose-made dragging brush, and working from the top downwards, smoothly and evenly bring the brush down through the glaze while the latter is still wet.

4 If you cannot drag the surface in one long movement, start at the top and drag most of the length. Then go to the bottom and drag upwards to meet the completed section. Feather the join by brushing gently into it.

5 If you wish to create a more hard-wearing finish, such as in a bathroom or kitchen, seal the surface with a clear matt varnish.

Rag-rolling

Like sponging, rag-rolling is a simple two-colour paint effect, but this time the second colour is applied and excess paint removed. Rag-rolling is a way of removing paint to create the effect rather than applying it. For best effect, the top coat should be a tinted acrylic glaze but because glazes dry quickly, work on small areas at a time. Good for large areas, and on furniture and woodwork.

You will need
- Base coat
- Glaze
- Tint
- Paintbrush
- Paint tray
- Lint free cotton or linen cloths

1 Apply the base coat and leave to dry. Tint the glaze if necessary (see Colourwashing) and mix with equal quantities of water. Stir thoroughly.

2 Randomly apply the glaze using a paintbrush, lightly brushing across the surface. If some of the base coat shows through this is not a problem.

3 Take one of the cotton or linen cloths, crumple it slightly and loosely roll it into a sausage shape. Then roll the rag across the surface in a continuous line. To further enhance the random effect of rag-rolling, change the direction of the rolling as you work and also dab over less well-covered areas.

Sponging

The variety of different effects that you can create with a sponge are wide and so it is worth experimenting with this paint technique on a spare piece of board covered with lining paper. It is important that you use a natural sponge rather than a man-made substitute as this last loses its shape when covered with paint. Good for large areas.

You will need
- Emulsion paints
- Paintbrush
- Paint tray
- Natural sponge

1 Apply the base coat and leave to dry. Soak the sponge in water until it swells to its full size and then squeeze out as much as possible. Pour your first emulsion colour into the paint tray.

2 Dip the edge of the sponge into the paint and dab the excess onto a spare piece of paper. Then apply light pressure to the surface you are decorating so that the areas of colour overlap each other. Constantly turn the sponge to create a soft and swirly finish. Leave the paint to dry.

3 Repeat step 1 with the same colour or a different colour – depending on the effect you are intending to achieve. A second sponged coat of the same colour will enhance the contrast; a different colour will add depth.

Stippling

The essential item when stippling is the stippling brush – a stiff bristled, stubby paintbrush. The glaze can be tinted as for colourwashing. When you have finished the stippling, apply a few coats of varnish for a tougher exterior. Good for smaller areas and on furniture and woodwork.

You will need
- Base coat
- Glaze
- Tint
- Paintbrush
- Paint tray
- Stippling brush

1 Apply the base coat and leave to dry. Mix the glaze with an equal quantity of water.

2 Generously – but not so that the base is completely obliterated – brush the glaze over the base coat. Work over a small area at a time so that the glaze doesn't dry out before you have a chance to stipple onto it.

choosing paints 166-167   painting 240-243

3 Hold the stippling brush parallel with the surface and pounce up and down to remove sufficient paint so that the base colour shows through.

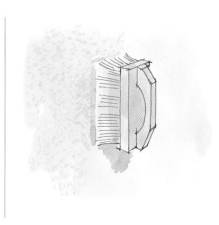

BELOW: *For a subtle rag-rolled effect choose two colours that are tonally very similar. By using a lightly crushed cloth the end result will grab the eye but not in an obvious kind of way.*

WATCHPOINTS

Rag-rolling

✦ Use the same type of cloth for the whole surface to prevent alterations appearing across the finished effect.

✦ Change the rags frequently so they don't become clogged up.

✦ Because the finished markings are so definite, it is best to work with colours that are subtly different such as pastel shades over a white or cream ground.

Sponging

✦ For the most subtle effect, sponge a lighter shade onto a darker one.

✦ To vary the finishing texture, use material other than a sponge such as pieces of muslin or hessian. Whatever you use, ensure it is undyed and lint-free.

Stippling

✦ For the best results, work on small strips at a time and with two people – one to apply the glaze, the other to stipple. Glaze dries quickly and it is especially important that the leading edge isn't allowed to become hard as the end result will be streaky.

✦ If you are working with two people, don't swap over jobs as the stippling will almost certainly look different.

Stencilling

Whether making your own stencils or using pre-cut ones, the end-result is always effective and no two stencils need ever look the same if you use a stencil brush and a soft pouncing technique, as outlined below. Slowly build up your stencils using small amounts of paint to create three-dimensional images. Good for small areas and on furniture.

You will need
- Stencil card
- Pencil
- Making tape
- Cutting mat
- Scalpel
- Spray adhesive (optional)
- Water-based paints
- Stencil brush

1 Draw or transfer the stencil outline onto the stencil card. Using pieces of the masking tape, stick the card on the cutting mat. Then cut out the design using the scalpel. Ensure you always move the scalpel away from your body in case it should slip.

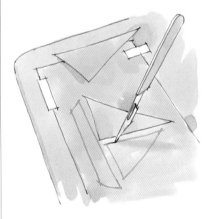

2 Position the stencil on the surface you are decorating and keep in place with more pieces of masking tape or the spray adhesive.

3 Dip the stencil brush into your first paint colour, dab excess paint onto a spare piece of paper and then lightly lift the brush up and down on the surface.

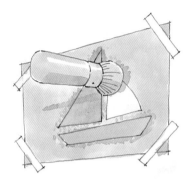

Stamping

As stamps are frequently applied so that they are equally spaced across a surface, take time and care to mark out their positions. As soon as this is done, the technique of stamping is remarkably quick and easy. In no time at all you have a decorated and decorative surface. Good for small areas and on woodwork.

You will need
- Pre-cut stamp
- Emulsion or acrylic paints
- Paint tray or saucer
- Small sponge roller

1 Pour some of the paint into the tray or saucer and then pull the roller through the paint. Move the roller backwards and forwards over a clean part of the tray or saucer until the roller is evenly covered with the paint – but not saturated.

2 Move the roller across the stamp a few times until the paint is evenly transferred across the surface. Press the stamp onto the surface you are decorating.

3 For an evenly stamped finish, repeat step 2 after each stamp. But for a more inconsistent or even faded finish, use the stamp two or three times before reapplying paint.

Using more specialised paints

Crackle varnish: to simulate crazing for a distressed look to any woodwork, apply a coat of crackle varnish over a dried base colour. Paint a second colour over the top and it will craze as it dries. Available as both water- and oil-based liquids.

Glitter varnish: make your own by mixing glitter with acrylic varnish or buy a ready-mixed spray varnish.

Metallic paints: there are an increasing number of these paints on the market suitable for walls, wood, metal or fabric. Silver, gold and bronze are the most popular and they can also be mixed with plain colours to give an added lustre. Try silver with pale blue or bronze with dark green. Use in small quantities, however.

Verdigris: available in kit form, this lovely metallic green finish looks good on pendant lamp fittings and pots and dishes.

choosing paints 166-167   painting 240-243

ABOVE: *If you are making your own stencil you can vary it not only through paint but also by cutting out shapes that differ slightly to each other.*

treating floorboards 258-259

WATCHPOINTS

Stamping

✦ If you have a simple image in mind for stamping consider making your own from a potato cut in half or cut out the shape from a piece of dense sponge.

✦ A gloss painted surface can be more slippery to stamp onto so make sure you hold the stamp firmly so that it can't slip about.

✦ Draw positional guides using a spirit level or plumb line if you are looking for a vertical line.

Stencilling

✦ If you are creating your own design remember to include some small 'bridges'. These are small pieces of stencil card that hold together the different elements.

✦ The secret of good stencilling is to use an almost 'dry' paintbrush – using the least possible amount of paint – and then to build up the colour as you work.

Wallpapering

There is such a huge range of wallpaper designs available that it can be a little bewildering knowing where to begin because colour, pattern and texture are the vital ingredients. Once you have formulated your ideas and found the perfect paper, use the table below to work out exactly how many rolls of paper you need to buy. If there is a pattern match on your paper, take this into consideration when placing your order, especially if the design is a large one. The store you are buying from will be able to advise you.

WALLPAPER QUANTITIES

Standard rolls of wallpaper measure about 10m (11yd) long by 530mm (21in) wide, but American and continental sizes may differ. This chart is based on standard wallpaper. Use it to work out the number of rolls you need.

Wall height from skirting	Distance around the room in metres (inc doors and windows)																	
	9	10	12	13	14	15	16	17	18	19	21	22	23	24	26	27	28	30
215–230cm	4	5	5	6	6	7	7	8	8	9	9	10	10	11	12	12	13	13
230–245cm	5	5	6	6	7	7	8	8	9	9	10	10	11	11	12	13	13	14
245–260cm	5	5	6	7	7	8	9	9	10	10	11	12	12	13	14	14	15	15
260–275cm	5	5	6	7	7	8	9	9	10	10	11	12	12	13	14	14	15	15
275–290cm	6	6	7	7	8	9	9	10	10	11	12	12	13	14	14	15	15	16
290–305cm	6	6	7	8	8	9	10	10	11	12	12	13	14	14	15	15	16	17
305–320cm	6	7	8	8	9	10	10	11	12	13	13	14	15	16	16	17	18	19

For ceilings: work out the area in square metres and divide by five to establish the number of rolls you require.

Planning papering

Start in a corner and then work away from the light. In this way, the joins between lengths are less noticeable. If there are no special features to be worked around in the room, it is best to start at the wall to the right of the main window and work around the room in a clockwise direction (if you are left-handed, of course you should reverse this).

Before starting, work out where the joins will fall and then if there are any awkward spots you can adjust your starting point. If you have a chimney breast, it is best to start in the centre, pasting the first length of paper down the middle of it and then work outwards from each side. This will minimise awkward joins.

Hanging wallpaper

Hanging wallpaper is a precision job and is something that really cannot be done in a hurry. You need to be methodical and meticulous in your approach – the curious thing about wallpaper is that it seems to know if you are rushing and it will refuse to do as it should. Air bubbles and wrinkles will appear as if from nowhere, and you can find yourself fighting with a soggy mess as it slowly slips its way down the wall.

Before you cut the first length of wallpaper make sure that you are organised with everything you need to hand. Position the pasting table in the centre of the room so that you won't have to keep moving it all the time and mix the paste to the appropriate consistency. This depends on the

◆ Buy all your rolls at the same time and make sure they have the same batch number, because colours may vary between printings.

◆ Buy an extra roll of wallpaper and keep it for future repairs.

◆ Small random patterns and textured designs may help disguise poor plaster.

◆ When hanging lining paper that will lie beneath wallpaper, hang it horizontally around the room starting at the top of the wall. This is known as cross-lining.

◆ Before wallpapering, ensure the lining paper is thoroughly dry; this could take up to a couple of days.

◆ When it comes to pattern matching, straight-match wallpapers line up horizontally whereas drop-match paper require adjoining lengths to be moved up or down to match. If you are using a random design, there is no need to worry about pattern matching.

◆ If you want to preserve the position of screws or picture hangers, insert match sticks into the holes and these will gently pierce the paper as you lay it in place.

Above: f you would like a paint effect on your walls but don't want to use paint, choose one of the paint effect wallpapers that are available .

weight of your paper and instructions are always given on the back of the packet. Follow them closely as you don't want to have lumps in your paste, nor have it too watery or too thick. Thin paste for a wood-chip paper, for example, would result in the paper coming down again rather too quickly; thick paste on lining paper means tears and gaping holes appearing when you touch the paper. If you are using a vinyl or plastic-coated wallpaper, use a fungicidal adhesive to prevent mould growing.

You will need
• Tape measure
• Pencil
• Pasting table
• Paper-hanger's shears
• Wallpaper paste and bucket
• Paste brush
• Step ladder (if necessary)
• Plumb bob and line
• Paper-hanger's brush
• Seam roller (to press down wallpaper edges)
• Rubber-based glue or similar adhesive (for repairs)

1 Using the paper-hanger's shears, cut a sufficient number of lengths of wallpaper to cover a wall at a time. Add 5-7.5cm (2-3in) to the length of each drop to allow for trimming at the ceiling and the skirting. Add more if you have a pattern repeat to contend with as well. If you are papering a staircase, don't forget to allow for the angle of the skirting at the bottom when you are measuring the drop.

choosing wallpapers 168-169

2 Roll the lengths of paper against the curl to encourage them to flatten, or lay the paper on the pasting table right side down, weighting down the corners before you paste on the glue.

3 Using the pasting brush, apply the paste, moving down the centre of the paper. Then brush the paste out from the centre moving the pasting brush away and towards you as you work until all the edges are covered. If you are using ready-pasted paper, simply lower the lengths into the trough provided and gently smooth onto the wall.

4 Leave the paper for 5-10 minutes (depending on how heavy it is) so that the paste will soak in. The paper stretches slightly and bubbles will then not occur. To make the paper easy to carry over to the wall, fold the ends in towards the centre of the strip so that the pasted surfaces meet. If you have a very long strip you will need to fold it up like a concertina. Remember which is the top end of the paper!

5 Using the blumb bob and line find the vertical line on the wall where you will be hanging the first strip and mark it lightly with a pencil. Then, using this line as a guide, hang your first piece of paper. Allow about 7.5cm (3in) to overlap on the ceiling and

2.5cm (1in) to turn around the corner (if this is where you are starting).

6 Gently slide the top half of the strip into place and smooth down with the paper-hanger's brush, pushing the paper well into the corner. Then release the bottom half and smooth into place without stretching the paper.

7 To trim the top and bottom, make a mark with the point of the shears, peel back the paper a small way and carefully cut along the line.

8 Continue along the wall in the same way, tightly butting up each length. The paper will shrink as it dries and this will prevent any gaps from appearing. Press the joins together firmly with the seam roller. If you are hanging relief wallpaper, do this with care so that you don't flatten the design. If you are hanging ready-pasted

paper the seams and edges may lift a little, in which case dab some rubber-based glue along the offending areas to encourage them to lie flat.

9 When you are papering around a corner, trim the width so that you don't overlap the next wall by more than about 2.5cm (1in). This prevents there being too much bulky paper in these awkward places. You might also like to consider gently tearing the edges of relief papers to soften them still more. Convex corners may need a larger overlap so that seams don't coincide at the corners, where they are all too likely to tear. Before trimming the width, measure the gap to be papered in several places (in older properties in particular this is important as the walls can be far from true) and use the widest point as your guide.

10 Light switches can be awkward to work around but by turning off the electricity and removing the switch cover you will be able to make a far neater finish. Hang the paper over the switch and smooth it into place. Then cut a square out of the wallpaper that is 6mm (¼in) smaller than the size of the switch. Cut from the centre diagonally towards each corner and then you will be able to tuck the excess paper neatly beneath the switch cover when you put it back in place after the wallpaper paste has dried.

◁ planning colour 10-11   ◁ planning pattern & texture 12-13

11 If you are unable to remove the cover, cut an X shape in the paper, trim the excess and stick the remaining 6mm (¼in) to the edge of the cover. If you are using a foil wall covering, you must always do this as foil conducts electricity and so must not be tucked under the switch cover.

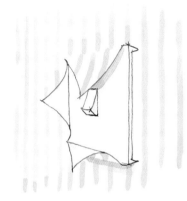

Papering ceilings

Unless you are very tall or have low ceilings, you will most likely need to balance a plank across a pair of step ladders in order to comfortably paper a ceiling. However, if you do need to do this, make sure the plank is very secure before you attempt to walk along it. Cut and prepare your paper in exactly the same way as for papering walls and draw a straight line on the ceiling that runs parallel with the wall you are starting against.

If there is a ceiling light, remove the bulb and shade and turn off the electricity at the mains. Smooth the paper over the fitting and make a cut in the centre. Clip regularly around the hole, unscrew the fitting slightly and tuck the edge of the paper beneath.

Borders

It is essential that a border is vertical, unless you are creating a false dado up a staircase, for example. You may also decide to follow the line of the ceiling if you are applying a border at the top of a wall. If you are unsure as to what would look best, experiment with masking tape, which will remove without spoiling the surface beneath. If you are working on a vertical line, use a spirit level to draw guidelines.

For a mitred corner, say around a door or window frame, paste one border strip in place leaving an overlap of about 15cm (6in) beyond the corner. Cut and paste the second strip also with a 15cm (6in) overlap. While the paper is still wet, gently lift the ends at the corner and place a piece of card beneath. Using a metal ruler and pencil, draw a diagonal line from the top corner where the strips overlap to the bottom corner. Cut through both layers of paper using a sharp knife, drawing the blade along the metal ruler. Remove the backing and smooth the border into place.

choosing wallpapers 168-169

WATCHPOINTS

✦ Bubbles form if the wallpaper hasn't been pasted properly or if it hasn't been left to soak for long enough. They can also form if the strip isn't smoothed out sufficiently well on the wall. It is possible to remove them by make a tiny slit in the paper with a scalpel blade. If they are tiny they may also disappear as the paper dries.

✦ Try removing small dirty marks with a white eraser or a piece of stale white bread.

✦ Peeling can be caused by damp and as long as it is only the edges that are peeling you can usually stick the paper back with some additional wallpaper paste.

✦ With some careful sticking (use rubber-based glue if it is only a small area and you have already thrown away the excess paste), tears can be repaired almost invisibly.

Tiling walls and floors

It can be very satisfying tiling expanses of walls and floors because once you have prepared the surface and planned which tiles are going where (see steps 1 to 3, right) the transformation is wrought relatively quickly. However, if you have very large areas to cover, especially if it's a floor, you might prefer to hire a professional tiler. Tiles can be expensive to purchase and to then lay a floor that is less than perfect would be money wasted. This would also apply if you have a particularly awkward shaped area to cover.

ABOVE: *Combine different sizes, shapes and colours of tile to make patterns and borders on the floor of your kitchen, hallway, conservatory.*

Tiling walls

Ceramic tiles are so durable that it makes them the perfect finish for walls in kitchens and bathrooms. They are waterproof and easy to clean so ideal as splashbacks behind the sink and cooker areas and around baths and showers.

You will need
- Metal ruler
- Pencil
- Wooden battens
- Spirit level
- Hammer
- Nails
- Tile adhesive
- Notched spreader
- Plastic tile spacers or matchsticks
- Tile cutter
- Tile file
- Pincers for cutting random shapes (optional)
- Sponge
- Grout

1 Wash and sand emulsion paint to provide a key. If there is wallpaper on the surface you will be covering, remove it.

2 Before sticking anything in place, work out where the tiles will fall and if you are aiming for a random effect, time spent now in ensuring that the end result looks sufficiently random will be well spent. If you find that you have very narrow pieces of tile left at the end of a run, adjust your starting point. Aim for tiles of equal sizes at each end.

3 Measure the distance of one tile up from the bottom of the area you

are tiling and use the spirit level to find the true horizontal. Mark this with a pencil and nail a wooden batten to the wall along this line. Do the same at the end of the last full row of tiles, fixing a vertical batten in place.

4 Start spreading tile adhesive with the spreader, working along and up from the marked corner. Only cover about a square metre (yard) at a time, combing the adhesive with the spreader until it is even.

5 Press the tiles firmly into place without sliding them. To ensure the gaps between the tiles remain constant, insert the plastic spacers (or the matchsticks) at each corner. If you should accidentally get adhesive onto the surface of a tile, wipe it off immediately with a damp sponge. Continue until all the whole tiles have been fixed, leave the adhesive to dry and remove the battens.

6 To cut tiles, mark the cutting line on the tile and place on a cutting board, right side up. Score along the line with the cutter against the metal ruler. Raise the tile slightly beneath the scored line using some matchsticks or a

pencil and press firmly on each side. The tile will usually snap neatly along this line. However, it won't always be the case and you can neaten breaks with a tile file or use some pincers to nibble away at the edge until you have achieved your desired size or shape.

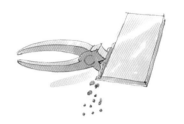

7 Once you have finished the tiling, let the adhesive dry as instructed on the packet. Waterproof adhesive takes longer. Then mix the grout, if necessary, and spread it over the gaps using a damp sponge so that you can push it well into the spaces. Work over about 1 square metre (yard) at a time and wipe away excess with a clean damp sponge before moving onto the next area.

8 If you want to mould the grout, draw a rod that is marginally wider than the gap, such as a piece of doweling or lolly stick, through the grout when it is almost dry. This will remove the excess and make the finish slightly recessed.

9 Leave to dry and then wipe once more with a damp sponge to remove the last traces of grout. Polish with a soft cloth for a gleaming finish.

removing textures & tiles 234

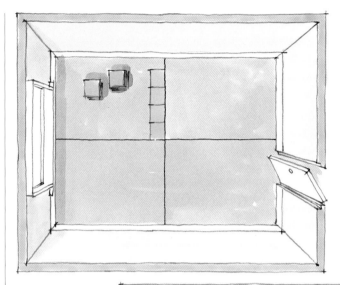

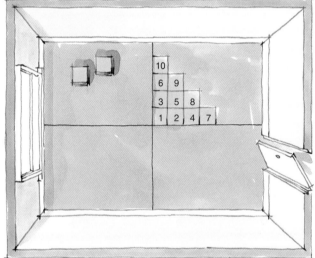

1 Divide the floor into four equal areas. Mark the centre point of one wall and that opposite it. Join the two points with a piece of string that has been rubbed with chalk, stretch the string and snap it against the floor leaving a mark from wall to wall. Repeat on the other pair of walls.

2 Before beginning to stick the tiles down, lay out a line of tiles from the centre outwards to see how they fall (see above left). The space left between the wall and the final tile should not be less than half a tile. If it is, adjust from the centre to avoid.

3 Starting from the centre and covering no more than c.1 sq m (yd) of the floor at a time, apply the tile adhesive with the notched spreader. Then start positioning the tiles. Lay the first tile at the point where the chalk lines cross, butt the next tile up against it, and work outwards towards the wall in the order shown left.

4 To fit edge and corner tiles, take the tile to be laid and place it over the last complete tile. Then take a spare tile and place it over the tile where the last cut tile ends, butting it against the skirting board. Mark the line of the overlap on the tile to be cut, remove the spare tile and cut with the DIY knife. Fix the tile in place in the same way as the rest.

Tiling floors

It is perfectly possible to lay soft and semi-hard or hard tiles yourself, although the first two are easier, especially if you have tricky shapes to negotiate. Whatever type of tile you are using, ensure that the sub-floor is absolutely flat. If you are laying over worn floorboards, for example, you may need to cover them with hardboard or chipboard screwed down to the underlying floorboards. If laying tiles onto concrete, make sure it has a damp-proof membrane (DMP) as any hint of moisture, and you will find that the tiles will lift from the floor.

Laying soft tiles

Whether you are using carpet, cork, linoleum or vinyl tiles, the principles are the same. If you are tiling a floor that is in constant use don't tile it all at one time. It is more practical to work on one end of the room first, let it dry, and then tile the other end.

You will need
• Tiles
• Tape measure
• String and chalk
• Tile adhesive
• Notched spreader
• DIY knife

choosing semi-hard flooring 173-174   choosing hard flooring 176-177

5 For doorways and architraves, make a template from thin card. Once you have an exact outline cut out of the cardboard, transfer it to the tile and cut with the DIY knife.

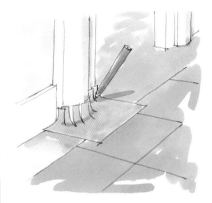

Laying hard tiles

The adhesive needed for laying hard tiles depends on which type of tile you are using. For ceramic tiles, you need ceramic tile adhesive; quarry and terracotta tiles are laid onto a bed of mortar. Calculate the number of tiles as described in the Watchpoints on page 255 and mark out the room as described in step 1, opposite.

You will need
• Tape measure
• String
• Chalk
• Tile adhesive/mortar
• Notched spreader
• Plastic spacers
• Tile cutter
• Tiling grout

1 As for soft flooring, start from the centre of the floor and work out to the walls. If you are laying ceramic tiles, use the notched spreader to apply the adhesive, and don't apply more than a square metre (yard) at a time. Mortar needs to be spread with a trowel.

2 Press down the tiles into the adhesive/mortar and put spacers between the tiles and at the corners to ensure they are evenly positioned. Use a spirit level at regular intervals to check the tiles are level.

3 To cut tiles, mark the cutting line on the tile and place on a cutting board, right side up. Score along the line with the cutter against the metal ruler. Raise the tile slightly beneath the scored line using some matchsticks or a pencil and press firmly on each side. The tile will usually snap neatly along this line. However, it won't always be the case and you can neaten breaks with a tile file or use some pincers to nibble away at the edge until you have achieved your desired size or shape.

4 Cut edge and corner tiles as described for soft flooring but instead of spreading the adhesive on the floor, put it directly onto the cut tiles, one by one. It can be difficult spreading adhesive right up to the walls so this is the best way to ensure the tiles will stick well.

5 Once you have finished the tiling, let the adhesive or mortar dry. Then mix the grout, if necessary, and spread it over the gaps using a damp sponge so that you can push it well into the spaces. Work over about 1 sq m (yd) at a time and wipe away excess with a clean damp sponge before moving onto the next area. Leave the grout to dry and then polish the floor.

WATCHPOINTS

✦ To remove a very narrow strip along the edge of a tile use pincers rather than a tile cutter.

✦ Special template formers are available from DIY stores to help cut around tricky shapes.

✦ If you are using cork or vinyl tiles on the floor, unwrap them and leave in the room in which they are going to be laid for 24 hours before sticking in place.

✦ If you are laying self-adhesive tiles covered by a protective backing paper, do not remove this until you are ready to lay the tiles. Then remove the backing one by one. Also, cut these tiles with the backing paper still in place.

stripping paper & paint 232-233   removing textures & tiles 234

Treating floorboards

If you are lucky enough to have new untreated floorboards you can consider any of the ideas on these pages. However, aged floorboards will need a little care and attention first for the best possible effect.

There are basically two finishes you can achieve: a neutral seal that brings out the colours and texture of the wood, or something that adds more colour to the room. For the former, choose a clear varnish or a waxed finish; for the latter, look into wood stains and paints and this is especially valuable if your floorboards are not particularly beautiful and need disguising. The coverage from paint is the denser of the two finishes. Before applying any finish to the floorboards, sweep up the surface and wipe the floor clean with white spirit.

ABOVE: *With planning and careful measuring it is possible to create the most intricate of painted designs on a wooden floor.*

Liming

Limed floorboards have a soft, chalky finish that look especially good in a light, sunny room. A rug or two laid over the top and textured soft furnishings in neutral shades accompany the effect extremely well.

First coarsen the texture of the wood by brushing along the grain with a wire brush. Then apply a liming paste or wax with some fine steel wool working in small circles to fill the grain of the wood. Work across a small area at a time leaving it to dry so that you can remove any excess with fine, clear-paste wax before moving onto the next part of the floor. To give some sheen to the surface, buff up the floor with a soft, lint-free cloth.

Alternatively, paint a diluted coat of white emulsion over the floorboards. Although not as durable as liming wax, the effect looks as good and is far easier to apply. If you want to add a stencilled pattern over the top this is the ideal background.

Painting

Paint floors in much the same way as if you were applying a stain (the sealing coats of varnish are especially important), but the end result is a lot denser and the paint tends to obliterate the wood grain. The advantage of paint is that it is much more flexible than stain to apply and you can paint more detailed patterns should you so wish. In addition to the stripes and checked patterns described below; stencils are a simple way to add pattern and can be especially effective as a border around the edge of the

stripping floorboards 236-237

room. Or why not paint your own unique and colourful rug in the centre of the floor?

Staining

Wood stains are available in an increasingly wide variety of shades and they add a protective coating and colour at the same time. If you choose to apply a wood stain that doesn't have a varnish combined with the stain, it is advisable to then paint three or four coats of varnish over the top to seal the surface. Apply the stain with a clean, lint-free cloth following the direction of the wood grain. Then use a small paintbrush to carefully fill in the edges and fiddly corners that you may have not been able to reach.

Wood stain need not be applied right across the surface. Consider staining every other floorboard for a striped finish, or score a checkerboard pattern into the wood and then stain alternate squares. Draw out your plan first and transfer it to the floor in pencil. Then score quite deeply into the floorboards using a very sharp craft knife against a steel rule. This prevents the stain seeping into adjacent areas.

Varnishing

Several coats of a varnish will leave a wooden floor looking rich and protected at the same time. Purchase oil-based polyurethane varnish as a clear gloss, matt or semi-matt finish, or matt acrylic varnish, both of which are applied with the good old-fashioned paintbrush. Both forms are equally tough after several coats have been applied, but water-based acrylic varnish has the advantage of being much easier to clear up afterwards.

WATCHPOINTS

◆ Apply wood stain along the grain of the wood using a small amount at a time.

◆ Although emulsion paints are easier to use than oil-based ones, gloss or matt paints plus primers and undercoats will give a more durable finish.

◆ Always start decorating a floor by starting at the end furthest from the door. Work backwards and you can then escape without having to walk over your precious handywork!

◆ When planning a pattern for the floor work on a scale drawing first, aligning the design along the wall that will be most obvious.

◆ If you ever want to paint over a stained floor, you will need to sand back once again, and then prime and undercoat.

LEFT: *Here, the floor and wall have been cleverly tied in to each other through using the same colours and design motif.*

SOFT FURNISHINGS

Measuring-up

The price of fabric is wide-ranging but even if you buy material from the cheaper end of the spectrum the sheer number of metres (yards) that are needed for making many forms of soft furnishings means that the money you are spending can all too quickly add up to large sums. By taking detailed measurements in advance of choosing your fabric you can work out the minimum amount of material you require and so tailor your budget accordingly.

On these pages and overleaf instructions are given for measuring-up windows for curtains, blinds and pelmets; furniture for loose covers and table covers, and beds for bedspreads and valances.

ABOVE: *Whether you are measuring-up for new curtains or a loose-cover for your chair it is important that you are as accurate and meticulous as possible.*

WINDOWS

Whether measuring for curtains or a blind, it is important that the pole, track or batten is in place first and that you have a preferred length for the curtains (see the box opposite). For floor-length curtains you may want to consider adding a couple of centimetres (an inch) to the bottom as curtains that just drape on the floor look luxuriant – and are also even better at keeping out draughts.

The position of the batten for blinds varies depending on whether or not there is a recess. For windows with a recess, screw the batten to the ceiling at the top of the recess. For windows without one, the batten is usually placed at the top of the architrave. However, if there is a wide wooden frame and you would like to see some of it, consider positioning the batten some way down so that moulding shows above the blind.

Always measure with an extendible steel tape or wooden rule rather than a soft fabric tape which often stretches over the years and so the measurements won't necessarily be as precise as you would like.

Curtains

Calculating the length for curtains
• Measure from the top of the track or just underneath the pole to your required finished length.
• Add 20cm (7½in) allowance for the heading and hem.
• Detract 2.5cm (1in) if you want the curtain to hang above the floor or sill.
• Windows are not necessarily square, so take a few measurements across the

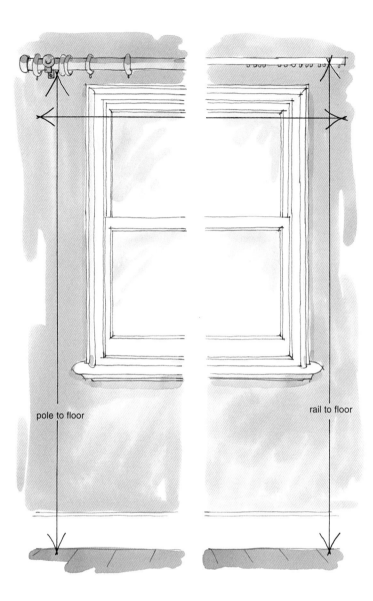

pole to floor

rail to floor

choosing tracks & poles 214-215

window to ensure the bottom edge will hang parallel with the floor.
• If the shape is too awkward, make the curtains as far as the hem and pin once the curtains are hung.

Calculating the width for curtains
• Measure the width of the pole or track.
• Multiply this figure by the amount of fullness you require in your heading. The most conventional fullnesses are:
Pencil pleat tape: 2¼ times
Triple pleat tape: 3 times
Box pleat tape: 2¼ times
Sheers: 3 times.

Calculating fabric requirements
• Divide the width measurement by a single fabric width.
• Round this up to the nearest whole number.
• Multiply this number by the length measurement.
• Allow extra fabric for pattern repeats so that you can then match the patterns across joined widths and adjacent curtains.
• Any lining or interlining you are using will require the same amount of fabric as the main fabric less the allowances for pattern repeats.

WATCHPOINTS

✦ As far as curtain lengths go there are no real rules, but traditional curtain lengths are:

Full-length: 2.5cm (1in) above the floor
Half-length (window): 2.5cm (1in) above the sill
Half-length (on surface): 2.5cm (1in) below the sill
Half-length (over radiator): 5cm (2in) to prevent discolouring. Or hang them 10cm (4in) below the radiator and tuck behind when the heating is on.
For an opulent and elegant look, let full-length curtains trail in folds on the floor.

✦ Never let curtains cover a storage heater as this can cause a fire to break out.

✦ If you are using patterned fabric, centre the pattern for each width of curtain and match up across the width. Parallel or horizontal lines need to be aligned with the walls and ceiling rather than furniture.

Blinds

Calculating the width and length

• For a roller blind, deduct 3cm (1¼ in) from the width across the glazed area to allow for the roller mechanism.

• Position the brackets 3cm (1¼in) from the top of the recess and measure the length from the top of the roller.

• For a roman blind, measure from the top of the batten to a fraction above the sill for the length.

• For the width, measure along the batten.

• Shapes of windows are not necessarily square so take several measurements along the depth and width and shaping accordingly.

Calculating fabric requirements

• Add 5cm (2in) to the length at the top and bottom for the hems.

• Add 5cm (2in) to the width at each side for the turnings.

• For the number of widths of fabric required, divide the width of the fabric by the width of the blind and join fabric lengths accordingly.

• Bear in mind, however, that blinds that are more than 1.5m (1½yd) wide can be hard to handle so plan to make blinds that don't require too many widths to be joined together.

Pelmets and valances

Calculating the pelmet size

•The first step is to fix the support board above the window (see right).

• This is a 10cm (4in) wide shelf cut from plywood and it needs to be positioned 5-7.5cm (2-3in) above the window and at least 5cm (2in) on either side of the curtain track.

• For the pelmet width, measure the length of the board and add 10cm (4in) at each end for the returns.

• For the pelmet length, this is entirely

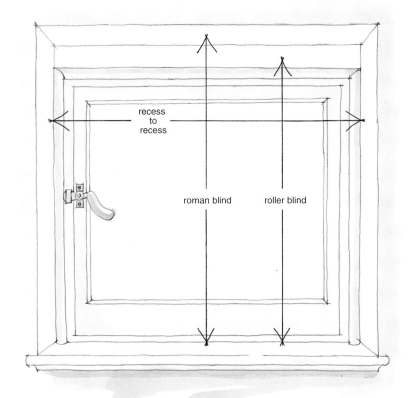

recess
to
recess

roman blind   roller blind

choosing blinds 212-213   choosing pelmets & valances 216-217

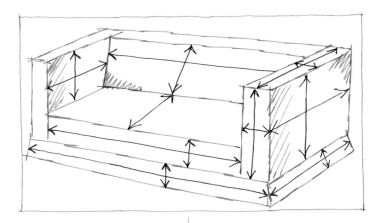

personal and to help you decide the best length in proportion to the window and curtain length, experiment with some cardboard.

• If you are using a patterned fabric, ensure the fabric design is centred to the pelmet length; and make up any additional length by joining fabric to each side, matching the pattern.

Calculating the valance size

• Measure the length of the track and allow at least 2 times the width for gathering.
• For the length (usually a sixth of the full drop), experiment with spare fabric.

FURNITURE

By far the easiest way of revitalising an old piece of furniture is by adding a throw, but if you want something more permanent, consider making a loose cover for your sofa or chair or draping a cloth over an old table. Here instructions are given for a sofa and a table for a full-length cover.

Sofas

Measuring-up for a cover

• Make a drawing of your sofa (as shown above) and measure the width and length of each section.

• Write these down, adding 3cm (1¼in) to each measurement for 1.5cm (⅝in) seam allowances.
• Some of the fabric pieces require an extra 10cm (4in) for tuck-ins to allow for a good fit when the cover is put on the sofa. These are:
inside back: bottom and sides
inside arms: bottom and back
seat: back and sides.
•For a tailored skirt, measure:
the length of the sides
the back
the front.
To each of these measurements add 18cm (7in) for pleats and seams. The depth of the skirt should be 15cm (6in) plus 3cm (1¼in) for seam allowances. You will also need four 18cm (7in) square inserts for the corner pleats.
• If you prefer a gathered frill, measure right around the foot of the sofa and double the length for the final measurement.

Measuring-up for cushion covers

• Measure the length and width of the top and bottom pieces and the gusset. To each piece add 3cm (1¼in) for seam allowances.
• If you are including a zip, cut one gusset panel of each cushion into two sections, with an extra 1.5cm (⅝in) seam allowance added to each. On seat cushions, a zip will be at the back, and on the back, it will face down.

choosing sofas & chairs 222-223

WATCHPOINTS

◆ As loose covers are easy to take off a sofa you will want to have the option of washing them so choose washable fabric. However, make sure this is pre-shrunk or wash it a few times before cutting out the pieces.

◆ For piping, wash the cord too or buy polyester piping, which doesn't shrink.

◆ When calculating the quantity of fabric remember that inside arms, outside arms and arm strips should be symmetrical. If you are making cushions, centre the motifs.

Calculating fabric requirements
• Scale down your measurements and draw each piece of fabric on graph paper, writing which piece is which in the centre of the outlines.
• Mark the direction of the grain – running top to bottom – and cut out the pieces.
• Cut out another piece of graph paper to the correct width of your fabric and lay out the fabric pieces taking into account the pattern repeat and ensuring that all the grain directions run the same way as the fabric.
• If you are going to include piping, add sufficient space for 5cm (2in)-wide bias strips to cover piping cord. To help in your calculations, you should be able to cut 30m (33yd) of strips from 1.5m (1⅔yd) of 140cm (55in)-wide fabric.
• To calculate the total length of fabric needed, convert the length covered on the paper to full-size.

Tables

If you are planning to cover a square or rectangular table with either a fitted or loose cover, the measurements that you need to take are obvious. For a circular table, however, the measurements are slightly more tricky.
• Measure the diameter of the table top.

• To this add twice the length of the overhang plus however much you want the fabric to cascade on the floor.
• Then add 6cm (2½in) to allow for a double hem all the way around the bottom edge of the cloth.

BEDS

Whether you are considering making a bedspread that reaches to the ground or adding a valance to hide the bed base and what lurks beneath, you will need to take several measurements.

Bedspreads

• Always measure the bed with your favoured bedding and number of pillows in place. A large and squelchy duvet can easily add a few centimetres (inches) to the height of the bed.
• Measure across the length and width of the mattress.
• Then measure from the top of the bedding to the ground (or however far you would like the bedspread to overhang).
• Add this to the length measurement and twice the measurement to the width.
• Add a further 1.5cm (⅝in) seam allowance on each side.
• If you would like additional fabric to

tuck behind the pillows, add as much as you see fit.

Bed valances

• Remove all the bedding and the mattress. A valance sits on the base of the bed and hangs down to the floor. It is made from two pieces: a flat sheet to cover the bed base and a gathered frill hanging down the side.
• For the base cover, measure across the length and width of the base.
• Add a 1.5cm (⅝in) seam allowance to the side and bottom edges.
• Add a 2cm (¾in) hem allowance to the top edge.
• For the frill, measure from the top of the base to the ground.
• Add a 1.5cm (⅝in) seam allowance for the top and 2cm (¾in) for the hem.
• The length of the frill depends on whether it is to be gathered or pleated and how many sides you want to attach it to. As a broad rule, frills require 1½ to 3 times the required finished length, and pleats 3 times the finished length.

RIGHT: *A bedspread (right) made from fabric that tones with the rest of your bedroom's colours makes a lovely finishing touch. The bed is the focal point, so make the most of it.*

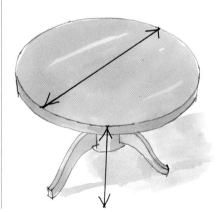
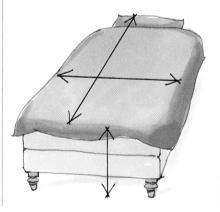

WATCHPOINTS

◆ To make a tablecloth larger attach panels to either side of a centre width to avoid a centre seam.

◆ If you are joining pieces together, a further 1.5cm (⅝in) on each edge that has to be joined.

◆ For a very wide bedspread join strips of fabric to each side of the main strip so that seams don't appear in the centre of the cover. Add a 1.5cm (⅝in) seam allowance along each seam.

◆ For a bedspread that reaches to the ground around three sides of the bed, cut the corners in a circle so that the fabric will drape more gracefully.

◆ The flat sheeting of a valance will never be seen so use a cheap piece of sheeting.

Creating soft furnishings

Despite the large amount of fabric that is required to make curtains, the actual method for making them is very straightforward. All you need is a table on which to spread out the material and a sewing machine for all those long seams. Although it is very tempting to work on the floor, it is more difficult to cut accurately – and you can end up with backache too. So even if it means you have to clear the kitchen table to work on it this is something that is well worth doing. Arm yourself with some heavy weights to stop the fabric sliding about and you can then cut the fabric with far greater ease and comfort.

Curtains with tab-heads

When you are making these it is best that they are as light as possible otherwise the weight of the fabric on the tabs distorts the top of the curtains. If the curtains are fairly small, they can be lined, but if you are making a curtain for a doorway or a pair that will stretch right down to the ground, it is best to leave them unlined. The instructions given here are for just such a curtain: light and airy, it would look great softly blowing in the breeze of an open doorway.

You will need
• Curtain fabric
• Contrasting fabric for tabs (optional)
• Sewing thread

1 Measure-up the curtain as described on pages 262-263, adding 5cm (2in) at each side

2 Cut out the fabric. You will also need to cut out the following:
• A facing strip measuring the width of the finished curtain plus 6cm (2¼in), by 8cm (3in).
• Tab strips measuring the circumference of the curtain pole plus 8cm (3¼in), by twice their finished width plus 2.5cm (1in). Use the contrasting fabric here if you wish.

3 Neaten the edges of the curtain by making a double hem of 2.5cm (1in) on each side. Fold and press and then lightly catch the hem to the main fabric with fine handstitching.

LEFT: *Tabs made from contrasting patterned fabric work well if the colours are the same.*

choosing soft furnishing fabrics 204-205   choosing curtains 207-212   choosing tracks & poles 214-215

4 Repeat with the hem and leave the top of the curtain raw.

5 Prepare the tabs by folding each strip in half lengthways and with right sides facing. Machine down the long edge taking a 12mm (½in) seam allowance. Trim close to the stitching line, turn through to the right side and press.

6 Prepare the facing by turning up 15mm (½in) of one long edge to the wrong side. Tack along the turn-up to keep it in place and press.

7 To assemble the curtain heading, lay the main fabric on your worksurface right side up. Take each tab and fold in half so that the raw edges are aligned with the top of the heading – again with all raw edges aligned. You will need to spend some time positioning them so they are regularly spaced – pin in place. Finally, place the facing on top, right side down and with raw edges aligned. The excess fabric should be equally distributed at each end.

8 Pin and tack all four layers together and then stitch securely taking a 15mm (⅝in) seam allowance.

9 To finish, fold back the facing to the wrong side, fold in the excess material at each end and neatly hand stitch in place down the side seams and along the top of the curtain. It is now ready to be threaded on to the curtain pole.

Roman blind

When making a roman blind, measure everything very precisely and double-check the width of hems before stitching anything in place. To ensure an accurate fit, you cannot do enough of this Make all the necessary measurements as described on page 264 and jot them down on a rough plan of your blind. To work out the positions of the rod pockets, see the box overleaf. It is important that you do this before cutting out the lining material so that you can then cut out the right length.

You will need
- Main fabric
- Lining material
- Ruler
- Pencil
- Sew and stick Velcro
- 1cm (½in) diameter doweling rods cut to width of blind less 2.5cm (1in)
- 5mm x 5cm (¼ x 2in) batten cut to width of blind less 2.5cm (1in)
- Plastic rings
- Nylon cord
- Metal screw-in eyelets
- 5 x 2.5cm (2 x 1in) batten cut to width of blind
- Blind pull

1 Lay the main fabric face down on your worksurface and turn in 5cm

WATCHPOINTS

Variations on the theme of tab-heads are wide and varied and as this particular heading is so simple to make and hang, you can vary the style with ease.

✦ Rather than inserting loops of fabric into the heading make ties, which can be as wide or narrow as you like, from the same or contrasting fabric. Stitch them between the main fabric and the facing strip.

✦ For something a bit more unusual, make the ties from ribbons or hessian taping.

✦ Instead of tab-heads that are stitched to the heading, finish off the ends of the tabs (either as flat ends or pointed) and make buttonholes in each end. You can then attach the tabs to the top of the curtain with buttons.

✦ If you go for this last option either cover the buttons yourself or choose from the many fancy buttons that are available. Glass, plastic and metallic finishes will all look very striking at the top of these curtains.

choosing blinds 212-213   measuring-up 262-267

(2in) all the way around the fabric. Pin and press the seams, mitring and stitching the corners. Set to one side.

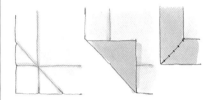

2 To the width of the lining fabric add 6cm (2¼in) to the finished blind width; to the length add 6cm (2¼in) plus 2cm (1in) for each rod pocket to the finished blind length. Turn in 4cm (1¾in) all around the fabric. Pin and press the seams and mitre the corners. Stitch hems as near as possible to the raw turned-in edge.

3 To make the rod pockets first measure and mark their positions working from the top of the lining to the bottom. Work on the wrong side and use the pencil and ruler to draw the lines across the width of the material. Draw the first line at the appropriate drop from the top and then the second 2cm (1in) below that. This will ultimately form the casing for the doweling.

4 Continue drawing pairs of lines in this way until you have reached the bottom. Check your measurements at several points across the width of the fabric. It is essential that they all run parallel to each other and at right angles to the sides.

5 To finish the rod pockets, fold the lining fabric with the wrong sides together and with the top-most pair of stitch guidelines on top of each other (see right). Machine together forming a channel that is 1cm (½in) wide. Repeat with the remaining pockets.

Working out the positions of rod pockets

Estimate how many pockets you will ultimately need bearing in mind that the ideal space between each pocket is approximately 20cm (8in). To work out the exact space between each pocket, use the following method:

- Subtract 10cm (4in) from the finished length of the blind.
- Divide this figure by twice the number of pockets plus one.
- This is the distance from the bottom of the blind to the first pocket.
- Regularly space the rest of the pockets at twice this distance above the first one.
- The amount of fabric left above the top pocket will be the doubled distance plus 10cm (4in). This extra piece of fabric prevents the plastic rings at the back of the blind from getting caught up in the screw-eyes in the mounting batten once the blind is raised.

6 Stitch the soft side of Velcro to the right side of the lining and as near to the top edge as possible.

7 Lay the main fabric face down on your worksurface and centre the lining on top with the rod pockets facing up. Put the 5mm (¼in) deep batten into the hem of the main fabric and slip stitch both fabrics together around all four sides.

8 Slide the doweling rods into the pockets and slipstitch the fabric ends so the rods can't slip out. Then sew a plastic ring to each end of every pocket. If your blind is more than 1m (1yd) wide you may wish to have an additional cord for pulling up the blind running up the centre. If this is the case, stitch plastic rings to the rod pockets here too.

9 To hang the blind, screw the small metal eyelets into the bottom edge of the mounting batten directly above the point where each set of plastic rings will descend. Screw in one more eyelet just to the left or right (depending on which side you want to pull up your blind) of the outside eyelet through which you will ultimately thread all the cords. Also stick the hard side of the Velcro to the front of the mounting batten. The top of the blind will be fixed to this.

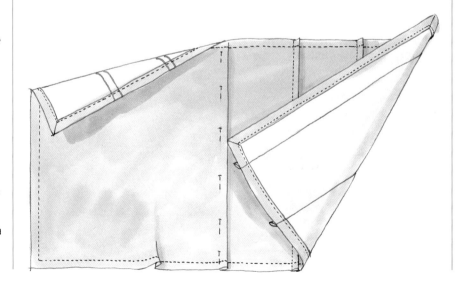

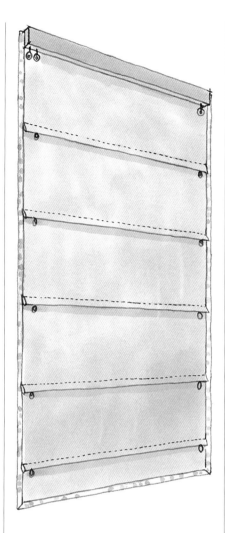

10 Cut appropriate lengths of nylon cord so that each cord can run up the length of the blind, across the width and have some left over for fastening off. Tie each cord to the bottom plastic ring and thread through to the top. You will now have to Velcro the blind to the mounting batten and thread the rest of the cords through their appropriate eyelets. Finish by uniting the cords in the blind pull to prevent them falling back down through the rings.

Sofa loose-cover with fitted skirt

Once you have measured-up your sofa and worked out your fabric requirements (see pages 265-266), it is time to cut out the fabric. However, if your individual pattern pieces are varied shapes that aren't square or rectangular, you will need to enlarge them to full-size and make templates from pieces of newspaper. If your pattern pieces are regularly shaped, you should be able to measure the size and transfer the dimensions to the reverse side of the fabric.

You will need
• Fabric
• Newspaper
• Tailor's chalk
• Sewing pins
• Hooks and eyes

1 Transfer the outlines of the pattern pieces to the back of the fabric using tailor's chalk. Ensure that all grain lines are correctly positioned, label each section and mark the top, bottom and centre lines. Cut out the pattern pieces.

2 If you are including piping in your cover – and this does make a very smart, more professional-looking finish – cut out sufficient bias strips for the entire cover.

3 Starting at the back of the sofa, pin the separate pieces to the sofa with right sides out. Ensure that you leave 15mm (⅝in) seam allowances wherever they are required and the centre lines are suitably positioned. Make sure, too, that all the pieces are the right way up. Pin them on carefully and in the following order:

WATCHPOINTS

When a roman blind is unfolded it is a simple, flat surface, so if you feel like adding to the effect, here are some ideas to consider:

✦ Use fabric paints to stencil or stamp a design all over the blind or just around the edges.

✦ Spray paints can be used as well but they can make the fabric stiff and may crack on the folds. If you would like to use this sort of paint, apply it only to the bottom and top of the blind where the fabric remains flat at all times.

✦ If you are feeling more ambitious and enjoy painting, apply a freehand picture or design using fabric paints in the centre of the blind.

✦ Appliqué pieces of fabric onto the surface. Do this before stitching on the lining so that all the stitching is hidden at the back when the blind if finally made up.

creating paint effects 244-249   finishing touches 274-275

- outside back
- inside back
- inside and outside arms.

4 Position the arm and back strips and pin all the pieces together but leave three-quarters of one back/outside arm seam open for fastenings. Using tailor's chalk, mark all the stitching lines.

5 Lift up the side and back tuck-ins and pin the base fabric onto the sofa so that all the tuck-ins are on the top. Trim them at the front of the sofa edge so that they taper from 15mm (⅝in) seam allowances at the top to 10cm (4in) at the bottom.

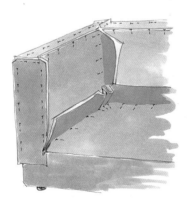

6 Unpin the cover and then pin and tack (following the tailor's chalk lines) together once more, but this time with right sides facing. Start by making one long piece of the arm and

back strips and also of the outside arm (that isn't a part of the opening) and back. The rest of the pieces can then be tacked together in whatever way seems easiest, reserving the seat and front panel for last. It is worth tacking all the seams so that you can check the fit. If you are piping the cover, position this at the same time.

7 Once you are happy that the cover fits well, stitch the pieces together sewing as near as possible to the piping cord.

8 Trim the seams, finish the edges and press. Re-fit the cover, right side out. Check the bottom edge is level and about 13.5cm (5⅓in) from the floor. Trim if necessary.

9 To make the back opening facing, cut a strip of fabric twice the length of the opening (excluding the skirt) and 7.5cm (3in) wide. Hem one long edge and then with right sides together, stitch the raw edge of the strip around the opening.

10 Turn the facing to the inside and hand stitch the hemmed edge to the seam line on the wrong side.

11 To make the skirt, pin and stitch the pieces together with an insert between each main strip. Each time take a 15mm (⅝in) seam

allowance. Do not join the insert and back seam at the back opening end. Hem along the bottom edge.

12 Fold each insert to make an inverted pleat and tack along the top edges. Press the pleats flat.

13 Pin and stitch the skirt to the cover with right sides facing and pleats matched to the corners.

14 Slip the cover back over the sofa once more and sew hooks and eyes down the back opening. You are now ready to make the box cushions (see box right)

Cushion covers

The most important style that you will need is a plain cover with a zip for easy removal for cleaning. The cover itself is straightforward and can be made from the plainest or most decorative of fabrics. Extras such as piping, cording and other braids, tassels and appliqué, covered buttons and beads can then be added in as restrained or liberal a manner as you choose.

You will need
- Cushion pad
- Fabric
- Zip

---

measuring-up 262-267   finishing touches 274-275

1 Measure the size of your pad and then cut out your fabric to exactly fit these dimensions. There is no need to add seam allowances as a well-fitting cover is best to ensure that the pad stays nicely plump at all times.

2 Cut out two pieces of fabric paying attention to the positioning of motifs if they are a dominant part of the fabric design.

3 Lay one piece of the fabric face down and lay the zip next to one edge for positioning. Centre it to the length of the fabric and cut snips in the fabric where each zip end lies. If the cushion will obviously have a right way up when it is finished, make sure this is the bottom edge.

4 With the two pieces of fabric aligned, right sides together, stitch from the corners to the snips taking a 15mm (⅝in) seam allowance. With the longest possible stitch also sew across what will ultimately be the gap for the zip. This will help ensure that the zip fits neatly and centrally to the opening.

5 Fold the fabric at the seam line with right sides together and extend the seam allowance of one side of the cover. Open the zip and with right side down tack it to the extended seam allowance centrally to the seam and with the teeth over the opening. With the zipper foot, stitch in place. Repeat with the other side.

6 On the right side, carefully remove the long machine stitches using a stitch ripper to reveal the zip below.

7 With the zip open, lay the two fabric pieces together with right sides facing and stitch around the three open sides and up to the ends of the zip on the fourth side. Take a 15mm (⅝in) seam allowance. Trim the seam allowance at the corners, turn the fabric through and press.

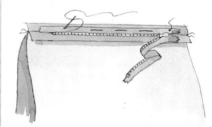

Making box cushions

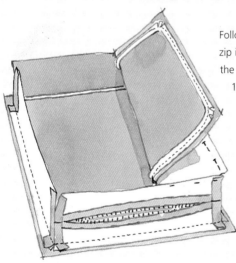

Following the instructions above, fit a zip in the back gusset. Pin and stitch the gusset pieces together leaving 15mm (⅝in) open at the ends of each seam. Add piping to the top and bottom panels.

Attach the gusset to the panels matching seams to corners and ensuring the zip is open. Finish the edges and turn the cushion cover right side out. Insert cushion pad.

WATCHPOINTS

◆ Put the zip in the centre back so that you can add more intricate borders, such as frills and flanges.

◆ Make an Oxford pillow with a generous flange around each side. Cut out fabric that is 5cm (2in) wider all around than the cushion pad. Make the cover as left (but put the zip in the centre back) and after it is turned through stitch around the cover once again to the dimensions of the pad. Make this stitching as decorative as you like, which is especially easy if you have a zigzag and other pattern making facility on your machine.

◆ Make an envelope back – or front – where two pieces of fabric overlap each other. Make up the back first and then attach to the other cushion piece.

◆ To make a feature of the closure, use large self-covered buttons or consider making ties from the same fabric or other scraps that you might have lying around. Ribbons too are attractive if used in this way.

◆ Instead of ties, try different openings such as Chinese-style fastenings or frog fastenings. Use two buttons with a loop between them.

◆ Use quilted fabric or add appliqué to the cover.

choosing trimmings 220-221

Finishing touches

When you are planning your soft furnishings think of what details you can add to make them even more interesting. If you are making your own curtains, blinds or cushion covers you can easily incorporate a button or tassel or two into your designs. Alternatively, if you are buying ready-made curtains or blinds, or have inherited them with a new home use some of the ideas given on these pages so that you can turn them into your own, unique creations.

To create your finishing touches does not have to mean hours slaving away at the sewing machine, they can be very simple, as demonstrated here. They can also be ready-made beads, buttons and bows or other trimmings that have taken your fancy at your local haberdashers.

Piping
The most time-consuming part of piping is cutting out the strips of fabric on the bias. It is important that the material is cut in this way, though, because it is then at its most stretchy enabling the finished piping to be shaped around curves and corners.

You will need
• Fabric
• Pencil and ruler
• Piping cord

1 To find the bias, fold the selvedge at right angles across the grain of the fabric. Press along the fold to make a crease, open out the fabric flat and draw along the crease with a pencil and ruler. Then draw parallel lines until you have sufficient quantities for whatever you are making.

2 Join sufficient strips to the required length by pinning two ends with right sides facing and so that the strips are at right angles to each other. Stitch together, taking a 6mm (¼in) seam allowance and working along the straight grain. Press the seams open.

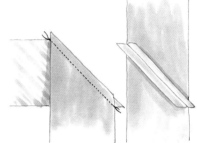

3 Wrap the bias strip around the piping cord with wrong sides together and raw edges aligned. Then use a piping or zipper foot to stitch close to the cord.

Self-covered buttons

Whatever size of button you are using, the covering principles are the same. If you are using a patterned fabric, position the motifs centrally.

You will need
• Self-covering buttons
• Fabric

1 Using the guide on the back of the button packet, cut out a circle of fabric that is a few millimetres (¼in) longer in diameter than the button.

2 Run a row of neat running stitches around the edge of the circle. Knot one end of the thread at the start and let the thread hang loose at the end.

choosing soft furnishing fabrics 204-205   choosing trimmings 220-221

3 Gently pull the thread to gather the circle sufficiently so that it slips over the button but without falling off.

4 Put on the backing and secure as in the manufacturer's instructions.

Tassels

There are a great variety of tassels available in shops to be attach to the corners of cushions, the end of a bolster and on a curtain heading or two. For something a bit more tailor-made, follow these instructions.

You will need
- Cardboard
- Yarn (wool, cotton or silk)
- Needle

1 Cut out two pieces of cardboard to the length of your finished tassel and 10cm (4in) wide. Place them together.

2 Put 30cm (12in) of your yarn to one side and then wind as much of the rest around the card from top to bottom until there is sufficient for the type of tassel you are making. Remember that the more you wind on, the fuller will be the end result.

3 Thread the set-aside yarn through the needle and then pass the needle through the top of the wound

yarn and tie at the top. Repeat several times so that you are left with a strong loop at the top of the tassel – it will be used later for attaching to the item you are dressing up.

4 Holding the bundle firmly in one hand, cut through the yarn at the bottom between the two pieces of card. Release the card and then bind the tassel as illustrated below as near as possible to the top of the tassel to ensure that the head remains firm.

5 To neaten, comb out the yarn using your fingertips and give the whole tassel a good trim.

Attaching cords

Just like tassels, cords are multi-coloured, multi-sized affairs. They add interest and a professional finish in next to no time and, of course, do not only need to be attached around the edge of a cushion. Here is some helpful advice on starting and finishing cording around a cushion cover.

1 Using a stitch ripper, make a small hole in one seam near to a corner.

2 Bind one end of the cord with sticky tape to prevent it unravelling and insert into the hole. Bind the other end with sticky tape in the same way.

3 Attach the cord to the cushion using buttonhole thread for added strength perhaps making loops at each corner as you reach them.

4 When you reach the starting point, trim the cord so there is 2cm (¾in) left to push through the hole adjacent to the start of the cord. Bind with tape, push through and stitch close the hole and cord where they meet.

creating soft furnishings 268-273

STOCKISTS

BATHROOM FIXTURES AND FITTINGS

Bathroom suites

Armitage Shanks Ltd
Rugeley
Staffordshire
WS15 4BT
Tel: 01543 490253

B&Q Plc
Portswood House
1 Hampshire Corporate Park
Chandler's Ford
Hampshire
SO53 3YX
Tel: 0181 466 4166

Dolphin Bathrooms
Bromwich Road
Worcester
WR2 4BD
0800 626717

Doulton Bathroom
Products/Twyfords
Lawton Road
Alsager
Stoke-on-Trent
ST7 2DF
Tel: 01270 410023

CP Hart
Newnham Terrace
Hercules Road
London
SE1 7DR
Tel: 0171 902 1000

Heritage Bathrooms
Heritage House
1a Princess Street
Bedminster
Bristol
BS3 4AG
Tel: 0117 963 9762

Ideal Standard
The Bathroom Works
National Avenue
Kingston-upon-Hull
HU5 4HS
Tel: 01482 346461

Spring Ram
PO Box 155
The Woodlands
Roysdale Way
Euroway Industrial Estate
Bradford
BD4 6ST
Tel: 01274 654700

Showers

Aqualisa Products Ltd
The Flyers Way
Westerham
Kent
TN16 1DE
Tel: 01959 563240

Caradon Plumbing Solutions
Cromwell Rd
Cheltenham
Gloucs
GL52 5EP
Tel: 01242 221221

Redring Expelair Creda Heat
Morley Way
Peterborough
Cambridgeshire
PE2 9JJ
Tel: 01733 313213

Triton Plc
Shepperton Park
Caldwell Rd
Nuneaton
Warwickshire
CV11 4NR
Tel: 01203 344441

CONSERVATORIES

Amdega Limited
Faverdale
Darlington
Co. Durham
DL3 0PW
Tel: 0800 591523

Appeal Blinds Ltd
6 Vale Lane
Bedminster
Bristol
GS3 5SD
Tel: 0117 963 7723

Bartholomew
Unit 5
Haslemere Industrial Estate
Haslemere
Surrey
GU27 1DW
Tel: 01428 658771

CURTAIN TRACKS AND POLES

Artisan Curtain Rails
4a Union Court
20 Union Road
London SW4 6JP
Tel: 0171 498 6974

Copes and Timmins Ltd
Angel Road Works
Advent Way
Edmonton
London N18 3AH
Tel: 0181 803 6481

Peter Brown Designs (Hasta)
Hussis Lane
Main Street
Long Eaton
Notts NG10 1GT
Tel: 0115 9460274

Speedy Products Ltd
Speedy House
Cheltenham Street
Pendleton
Salford
Manchester
M6 6WY
Tel: 0161 737 1001

Sunflex
Hunter Douglas Ltd
15-16 Bellsize Close
Walsall Road
Norton Canes
Cannock
Staffs
WS11 3TQ
Tel: 01543 271421

FIREPLACES

Real-effect, gas and electric fires

Berry
Unidare Environmental
221 Europa Boulevard
Westbrook
Warrington
Cheshire
WA5 5TN
Tel: 0800 072 1503

Cannon Industries Ltd
PO Box 446
Grindley Lane
Blythe Bridge
Stoke-On-Trent
ST11 9LU
Tel: 01782 385500

Dimplex
Millbrook
Southampton
SO15 0AW
Tel: 01703 785133

Flavel
Clarence Street
Leamington Spa
Warwicks
CV31 2AD
Tel: 01926 427027

Gazco
Osprey Road
Sowton Industrial Estate
Exeter
Devon
EX2 7JG
Tel: 01392 444030

The Platonic Fireplace Co
99 Amyand Road
Twickenham
TW1 3HN
Tel: 0181 891 5904

Valor Heating
Wood Lane
Erdington
Birmingham
B24 9QP
Tel: 0121 373 8111

Stoves

Aga-Rayburn
PO Box 30
Ketley
Telford
Shropshire
TF1 4DD
Tel: 01952 642000

Charnwood
AJ Wells & Sons
Bishops Way
Newport
Isle of Wight
PA30 5WS
Tel: 01983 527552

Dovre-Franco Belge
Unit 1
Weston Works
Weston Lane
Tyseley
Birmingham
B11 3RP
Tel: 0121 706 7600

Stovax
Falcon Road
Sawton Industrial Estate
Exeter
Devon
EX2 7LF
Tel: 01392 474000

Traditional fireplaces

Acquisition fireplaces Ltd
Acquisitions House
24-26 Holmes Road
London NW5 3AB
Tel: 0171 485 4955

Elgin and Hall
Adelphi House
Hunton
Bedale
North Yorkshire
DL8 1LY
Tel: 01677 450712

Farmington Natural Stone Ltd
Northleach
Cheltenham
Glos
GL54 3NZ
Tel: 0800 7310071

Weatherley & Foot
Unit 2
Little Dale
Colloers Green
Cranbrook
Kent
TN17 2LS
Tel: 01580 212124

FLOORING

Carpets

Allied Carpets
Tel: 0800 192192 for nearest
retail outlet

Axminster Carpets
Axminster
Devon
EX13 5PQ
Tel: 01297 33533

Brintons
PO Box 16
Exchange Street
Kidderminster
Worcestershire
DY10 1AG
Tel: 0800 505055

Carpet Depot
Tel: 0321 300306 for
nearest retail outlet

The Carpet Library
148 Wandsworth Bridge
Road
London SW6
Tel: 0171 736 3364

Kingsmead Carpets
Caponacre Industrial Estate
Cumnock
Ayreshire
KA18 1SH
Tel: 01290 421511
(Pristine Twist suitable for
asthmatics)

Lecaflor Carpets
Unit 1, Beza Road
Leeds
LS10 2BR
Tel: 0113 2775776

Stoddard Templeton
Glenpatrick Road
Elderslie
Johnstone
PA5 9UJ
Tel: 01505 577000

Tomkinson Carpets
PO Box 11, Duke Place
Kidderminster
Worcs
DY10 2JR
Tel: 0800 374429

Woodward Grosvenor
Stourvale Mills
Green Street
Kidderminster
Worcs
DY10 1AT
Tel: 01562 820020

Hard flooring

Attica
543 Battersea Park Road
London SW11 3BL
Tel: 0171 228 5785
(ceramic, quarry and
terracotta tiles)

Castelnau
175 Church Road
Barnes
London SW13 9HR
Tel: 0181 741 2452
(quarry and terracotta tiles)

Corres Mexican Tiles
29 Great Suffolk Street
London SE1 ONS
Tel: 0171 261 0941
(quarry and terracotta tiles)

Fired Earth
Twyford Mill
Oxford Road
Adderbury
Oxon
OX17 3HP
Tel: 01295 812088
(marble, quarry, terracotta
and slate tiles

Junckers
Wheaton Court
Wheaton Road
Witham
Essex
CM8 3UJ
Tel: 01376 517512
(wood flooring)

Kahrs (UK) Ltd
Unit 1
Timberlaine Estate
Gravel lane
Quarry Lane
Chichester
West Sussex
PO19 2FJ
Tel: 01243 784417
(wood flooring)

Marlborough Tiles
Elcot Lane
Marlborough
Wilts
SN8 2AY
Tel: 01672 512422
(ceramic tiles)

Paris Ceramics
583 Kingís Road
London SW6 2EH
Tel: 0171 371 7778
(stone, limestone and
terracotta tiles)

Perstorp Flooring (UK) Ltd
39 The Green
Banbury
Oxfordshire
OX16 9AE
Tel: 012995 252580
(wood flooring)

Pilkington Tiles
PO Box 4
Clifton Junction
Swinton
Manchester
M27 8LP
Tel: 0161 727 1000
(ceramic tiles)

Dennis Ruabon
Hafod Tileries
Ruabon
Clwyd
LL14 6ET
Tel: 01978 842283
(quarry and terracotta tiles)

Tarkett Ltd
Poyle House
PO Box 173
Blackthorne Road
Colnbrook
Slough
Berks
SL3 OAZ
Tel: 01753 684533
(cork)

Vigers Flooring
Beachfield Walk
Sewardstone Road
Waltham Abbey
Essex
EN9 1AG
Tel: 01992 711133
(wood flooring)

Wicanders (GB) Ltd
Stoner House
Kilnmead
Crawley
West Sussex
RH13 8RA
Tel: 01403 710001
(wood flooring)

World's End Tiles
The British Rail Yard
Silverthorne Road
London SW8 3HE
Tel: 0171 819 2100
(marble, quarry and
terracotta tiles)

The York Handmade Brick
Company
Forest lane
Alne
North Yorks
TO6 2LU
Tel: 01347 838881
(brick flooring)

Natural fibre flooring
The Carpet Library
(see Carpets, above)

Crucial Trading
PO Box 11
Duke Place
Kidderminster
DY10 2JR
Tel: 01562 825200

Jaymart
Woodlands Trading Estate
Eden Vale Road
Westbury
Wiltshire
BA13 3QS
Tel: 01373 864926

Semi-hard flooring
Altro Ltd
Works Road
Letchworth
Herts
SG6 1NW
Tel: 01462 480480
(vinyl)

Armstrong World Industries
Teeside Industrial Estate
Thornaby
Cleveland
TS17 9JT
Tel: 01642 763224
(vinyl)

Dalsouple
PO Box 140
Bridgewater
TA5 1HJ
Tel: 01984 667551
(rubber)

First Floor
174 Wandsworth Bridge
Road
London SW6
Tel: 0171 736 1123
(rubber, vinyl and linoleum)

Forbo-Nairn
PO Box 1
Kirkcaldy
Fife
Scotland
KY1 2SB
Tel: 01592 643111
(linoleum and vinyl)

Gerland
43 Crawford Street
London W1H 2AP
Tel: 0171 723 6601
(vinyl)

Marley Floors
Dickley Lane
Lenham
Maidstone
Kent
ME17 DE
Tel: 01622 858877
(vinyl)

Siesta Cork Tiles
Unit 21
Tait Road
Gloucester Road
Croydon
CRO 2DP
Tel: 0181 683 4055

Tarkett Ltd
(vinyl: see Hard flooring for
details)

Wicanders (GB) Ltd
(cork: see Hard flooring for
details)

KITCHEN APPLIANCES

AEG
Cornwall House
55-57 High Street
Slough, Berkshire
SL1 1BZ
Tel: 01635 572700

Belling Appliances Ltd
Talbot Road
Mexborough
South Yorkshire
S64 8AJ
Tel: 01709 579900

Candy
New Chester Road
Bromborough
Wirral
L62 3PE
Tel: 0151 334 2781

Creda Ltd
Creda Works
Blythe Bridge
Stoke-on-Trent
Staffs
ST11 9LJ
Tel: 01782 388388

Electrolux
55-77 High Street
Slough
Berks
SL1 1DL
Tel: 0990 146 146

Hotpoint
Celta Road
Peterborough
PE2 9JB
Tel: 01733 568 9890

Indesit
Merloni House
3 Cowley Business Park
High Street
Cowley
Uxbridge
UB8 2AD
Tel: 01895 858200

Miele Company Ltd
Fairacres
Marcham Road
Abingdon
Oxon
OX14 1TN
Tel: 01235 554488

Neff UK Ltd
Grand Union House
Old Wolverton Road
Old Wolverton
Milton Keynes
MK12 5TP
Tel: 01908 328300

Servis Groupd Ltd
Darlaston Road
Kings Hill
Wednesbury
West Midlans
WS10 7TJ
Tel: 0121 526 3199

Siemens Domestic
Appliances Ltd
(see Neff, above)

Smeg UK Ltd
Corinthian Court
80 Milton Park
Abingdon
Oxon
OX14 4RY
Tel: 01235 861090

Viking
Kenn Road
Clevedon
Bristol
BBS21 6LH
Tel: 01275 343000

Whirlpool UK Ltd
PO Box 45
209 Purley Way
Croydon
CR9 4RY
Tel: 0181 649 5000

Zanussi
(see Electrolux, above)

KITCHEN WORKSURFACES

Laminates
Formica
Coast Rd
North Shields
Tyne & Wear
NE29 8RD
Tel: 0191 259 3000

Orama
Azalea Close
Clover Nook Industrial
Estate
Summercoats
Derbyshire
DE55 4RF
Tel: 01773 524014

Solid surfaces
Formica (Surrel)
(see Laminates, above)

Dupont UK Ltd (Corian)
MCD Marketing
Hemel Hempstead
Hertfordshire
HP2 7DP
Tel: 0800 962116
Stainless Steel

Blanco
Oxgate Lane
Cricklewood
London NW2 7JN
Tel: 0181 450 9100

Stone
Pyrolave
Windfallwood
Windfallwood Common
Hazlemere
Surrey
GU27 3BX
Tel: 01438 871047

Wood
Junckers
(see Hard flooring, above)

LIGHTING

BHS
Tel: 0171 262 3288 for
nearest retail outlet

B&Q
Tel: 0181 466 4166 for
nearest retail outlet

Habitat
Tel: 0645 334433 for
nearest retail outlet

Ikea
Tel: 0181 208 5607 for
nearest retail outlet

John Lewis
Tel: 0171 629 7711 for
nearest retail outlet

Mazda
Tel: 0181 626 8500 for
brochure

Philips
Tel: 0181 689 2166 for
brochure

PAINTS

Blackfriar paints
Blackfriars Rd
Nailsea
Bristol
BS48 4DJ
Tel: 01275 854911

Crown Decorative Products
Ltd
PO Box 37
Crown House
Hollins Road
Darwen
Lancs
BB3 0BG
Tel: 01254 704951
Crown technical advice:
Tel: 01254 704951

Dulux
Wexham Road
Slough
SL2 5DS
Tel: 01753 550000

Farrow and Ball
Uddens Estate
Wimborne
Dorset
BH21 7NL
Tel: 01202 876141

Hammerite Products
Prudhoe
Northumberland
NE42 6LP
Tel: 01661 830000

Fired Earth
(see Hard flooring, above)

International Paints
24-30 Canute Road
Southampton
Hants
SO9 3AS
Tel: 01703 226722

Nutshell Natural paints
Hamlyn House
Mardle Way
Buckfastleigh
Devon
PQ11 ONR
Tel: 01364 642892

SOFT FURNISHINGS

Custom-made soft furnishings
Montgomery Tomlinson Ltd
Broughton Mill Road
Bretton
Chester
CH4 0BY
Tel: 01244 661363

Blinds and tiebacks
Sunflex
15/16 Bellsize Close
Norton Canes
Cannock
Staffs
WS11 3TQ
Tel: 01543 271421

Artisan Curtain Rails
4a Union Court
20 Union Road
London SW4 6JP
Tel: 0171 498 6974

Copes and Timmins Ltd
(see Curtain tracks and poles, above)

Habitat
Tel: 0645 334433 for nearest retail outlet

Ikea
Tel: 0181 208 5607 for nearest retail outlet

John Lewis
Tel: 0171 629 7711 for nearest retail outlet

Bedroom furnishings
Allerayde
Queens head Court
42 Kirk Gate
Newark
Notts
NG24 1AB
Tel: 01636 613444
(non-allergenic bedding)

Alprotec
Advanced Allergy technologies
Royd House
224 Hale Road
Altringham
WA15 8EB
Tel: 0161 903 9293
(non-allergenic bedding)

Banamite Anti-Allergy Bedding
Medivac
Bollin House
Riverside Works
Manchester Road
Wilmslow
SK9 1BJ
01625-539401
(non-allergenic bedding)

Brinkhaus/Yves Delorme
The French Linen Company
Unit 7 and 8
The Vale Industrial Centre
Southern Road
Aylesbury
Buckinghamshire
HP19 3EW
Tel: 01296 394980
(bedding and non-allergenic bedding)

Descamps
197 Sloane St
London SW1X 9QX
Tel: 0171 235 6957

Dorma
PO Box 7
Lees Street
Swinton
Manchester
M27 6DB
Tel: 0161 251 4400

Dreamland
Dreamland Appliances Ltd
Middleton Rd
Royton
Oldham
OL2 5LN
Tel: 0800 525089
(electric blankets)

Earlys of Witney
Witney Mill
Burford Road
Witney
Oxon
OX8 5ED
Tel: 01993 703131

The Eiderdown Studio
Tel: 01395-271147
(cleans, resizes, refills and re-covers duvets, eiderdowns and pillows and rejuvenates duvet fillings)

Habitat
Tel: 0645 334433 for nearest retail outlet

Ikea
Tel: 0181 208 5607 for nearest retail outlet

Imetec UK
Herald Drive
Crew
Cheshire
CW1 6EQ
Tel: 01270 252123
(electric blankets)

The Iron Bed Co
584 Fulham Rd
London SW6
Tel: 0171 610 9903

Keys of Clacton
132 Old Rd
Clacton-on-Sea
Essex
CO15 3AJ
Tel: 01255 432518
(non-standard size sheets, valances, quilts, bedspreads and recovers eiderdowns and duvets)

John Lewis
Tel: 0171 629 7711 for nearest retail outlet

Laura Ashley
Tel: 01686 622116 for nearest retail outlet

Marks and Spencer
Tel: 0171 935 4422 for nearest retail outlet

Medibed Ltd
Burnley Wood Mill
Parliament Street
Burnley
BB11 3JT
Tel: 01282 839700
(non-allergenic bedding)

Louis Moreau
The Quilters
Units 11-12
Harpers Yard
Ruskin Rd
Tottenham
London N17 8QQ
Tel: 0181 808 1337
(quilt your own fabric to make all types of bedspreads and quilts)

Sketchley Cleaners
Tel: 01455 238133 for nearest shop
(launders duvets and pillows and re-covers and converts eiderdowns to duvets)

Winterwarm Ltd
Portland St
Birmingham
B6 5RX
Tel: 0121 322 2377
(electric blankets)

Fabrics and trimmings
Artisan Curtain Rails
4a Union Court
20 Union Road
London SW4 6JP
Tel: 0171 498 6974

Jane Churchill
19/23 Grosvenor Hill
London W1X 9HG
Tel: 0171 493 2231

Copes and Timmins
(curtain jewellery: see Curtain tracks and poles, above)

Designers Guild
Tel: 0171 243 7300 for
nearest retail outlet

Habitat
Tel: 0645 334433 for
nearest retail outlet

Ikea
Tel: 0181 208 5607 for
nearest retail outlet

John Lewis
Tel: 0171 629 7711 for
nearest retail outlet

Osborne and Little Plc
49 Temperley Road
London
SW12 8QE
Tel: 0181 675 2255

VV Rouleaux
54 Cliveden Place
London
SW1W 8AX
Tel: 0171 730 3125

STORAGE

Aero
96 Westbourne Grove
London W2 5RT
Tel: 0171 221 1950

Chelsea Trading Company
Bemco Building
Wandsworth Bridge South
London
SW18 1TN
Tel: 0181 877 9635

Cube Store
Charlwood Rd
East Grinstead
West Sussex
RH19 2HP
Tel: 01342 310033

Habitat
Tel: 0645 334433 for
nearest retail outlet

The Holding Company
241-245 Kings Rd
Chelsea
London
W3 5EL
Tel: 0171 610 9160 for mail
order catalogue

Ikea
Tel: 0181 208 5607 for
nearest retail outlet

Lakeland Ltd
Alexandra Buildings
Windermere
Cumbria
LA23 1BQ
Tel: 01539 488100

The London Wall Bed
Company
263 The Vale
Acton
London
W3 7QA
Tel: 0181 743 1174

McCord design by Mail
Tel: 01793 435553 for copy
of brochure

Mugi Stores Direct
Tel: 0171 323 2208 for
nearest retail outlet in
London and Manchester

The Pier
Tel: 0171 814 5020 for
nearest retail outlet and
mail order catalogue

WALLPAPER

Coloroll
Riverside Mills
Crawford Street
Nelson
Lancs
BB9 7QT
Tel: 01282 727000

Crown Decorative Products
Ltd
(see Paints, above)

Designers Guild
Tel: 0171 243 7300 for
nearest retail outlet

John Lewis
Tel: 0171 629 7711 for
nearest retail outlet

Osborne and Little Plc
(see Fabrics, above)

Vymura
PO Box 15
Talbot Road
Hyde
Cheshire
SK14 4EJ
Tel: 0161 368 4000

WALL TILES

Carol Sinclair Ceramics
Unit 3
Albion Business Centre
78 Albion Road
Edinburgh
EH7 5QZ
Tel: 0131 652 0490

Fired Earth
(see Hard flooring, above)

Marlborough Tiles
(see Hard flooring, above)

Paris Ceramics
(see Hard flooring, above)

The Reject Tile Shop
Tel: 0171 731 6098 for
nearest retail outlet

Wellington Tiles
Tonedale Ind Est
Milverton Road
Wellington
Somerset
TA21 0AZ
Tel: 01823 667242

USEFUL ASSOCIATIONS

The British Bathroom
Association
Tel: 01782 844006

The British Oriental Rug
Dealers Association
Tel: 01727 841046 for
advice on UK dealers

Council for Registered Gas
Installers (CORGI)
Tel: 01256 372200

The Decorative Gas Fire
Manufacturers Association
Tel: 01703 631593

The National Fireplace
Association
Tel: 0121 200 1310

National Institute of Carpet
and Floor Layer
Tel: 0115 9583077

INDEX

ACKNOWLEDGMENTS

The publisher thanks the photographers and organisations for their kind permission to reproduce the following photographs in this book. All photographs are the copyright property of the National Magazine Company unless otherwise stated:

3 Polly Wreford; 4 top Debbie Patterson; 4 middle Polly Wreford; 4 bottom Peter Aprahamian; 7 Polly Wreford; 8 Polly Wreford; 10 Simon Brown; 11 Simon Brown; 13 Peter Aprahamian; 15 Peter Aprahamian; 16-17 Polly Wreford; 18 Marianne Majerus; 19 Simon Brown; 20-21 Mark Luscombe-Whyte; 22 Polly Wreford; 23 Peter Aprahamian; 24-25 Nadia Mackenzie; 26 Polly Wreford; 27 Debbie Patterson; 28-29 all Polly Wreford; 30 Polly Wreford; 31 top Caroline Arber; 31 bottom left Caroline Arber; 31 bottom right Pia Tryde; 33 Peter Aprahamian; 34 Peter Aprahamian; 35 Peter Aprahamian; 36 left Ebury Press/Michael Newton; 36 black and white Peter Aprahamian; 37 Ebury Press/Michael Newton; 38 Simon Brown; 39 Simon Brown; 40 Polly Wreford; 41 Peter Aprahamian; 42 Debbie Patterson; 43 Polly Wreford; 44-45 Simon Brown; 46 Polly Wreford; 47 Simon Brown; 48 left Polly Wreford; 48 right Debbie Patterson; 49 left Christopher Drake; 49 right Jennifer Cawley

50 left Polly Wreford; 50 right Simon Brown; 51 top Simon Brown; 51 bottom Peter Aprahamian; 52 courtesy of Moyra Fraser; 53 Ebury Press/Laurence Dutton; 54-55 Ebury Press/Laurence Dutton; 56 left Ebury Press/Michael Newton; 56 black and white Ebury Press/Laurence Dutton; 57 Ebury Press/Michael Newton; 58 Elizabeth Zeschin; 59 Polly Wreford; 61 Elizabeth Zeschin; 62 Trevor Richards; 63 Mark Lusombe-Whyte; 64 Harry Cory Wright; 65 Elizabeth Zeschin; 66 ieft Elizabeth Zeschin; 66 right Pia Tryde; 67 top Pia Tryde; 67 bottom Elizabeth Zeschin; 68 left Simon Brown; 68 right Debbie Patterson; 69 left Debbie Patterson; 69 right Simon Brown; 70 Trevor Richards; 71 Steve Dalton; 72 courtesy of Dulux plc; 73 courtesy of Dulux plc; 74 Simon Brown; 76 top Simon Brown; 76 bottom Debbie Patterson; 77 Marianne Majerus; 78 Simon Brown; 79 top Nadia Mackenzie; 79 bottom left Peter Aprahamian; 79 bottom right Simon Brown; 80 Mark Luscombe-Whyte; 81 Polly Wreford; 82-3 Marianne Majerus; 84 Debbie Patterson; 85 Simon Brown; 87 Peter Aprahamian; 88-9 Jan Baldwin; 90 top Polly Wreford; 90 bottom Pia Tryde; 91 left Simon Brown; 91 right Polly Wreford; 92 left Simon Brown; 92 right Simon Brown; 93 top Harry Cory-Wright; 93 bottom Debbie Patterson; 94 Ebury Press/Laurence Dutton; 95 Ebury Press/Laurence Dutton; 96 Ebury Press/Laurence Dutton; 97 Ebury Press/Laurence Dutton; 98 left Ebury Press/Michael Newton; 98 black and white Ebury Press/Laurence Dutton; 99 top Ebury Press/Michael Newton; 99 bottom courtesy of Ikea; 100 Brian Harrison; 101 Simon Brown; 102 Simon Brown; 103 Trevor Richards; 104 Simon Brown; 106-107 Elizabeth Zeschia; 108 David Montgomery; 109 Polly Wreford

110 Polly Wreford; 111 top Debbie Patterson; 111 bottom left Jennifer Cawley; 111 bottom right Debbie Patterson; 112 top left Polly Wreford; 112 top right Polly Wreford; 112 bottom Polly Wreford; 113 David Montgomery; 114 courtesy of Kimberley Watson; 115 Ebury Press/Laurence Dutton; 116 top left Jennifer Crawley; 116 bottom left Ebury Press/Laurence Dutton; 116 right Ebury Press/Laurence Dutton; 117 Ebury Press/Laurence Dutton; 118 left Ebury Press/Michael Newton; 118 black and white Ebury Press/Laurence Dutton; 119 Ebury Press/Michael Newton; 120 Simon Brown; 121 Simon Brown; 122 Simon Brown; 123 Elizabeth Zeschin; 124 David Montgomery; 125 Nick Pope; 126-127 courtesy of Dulux plc; 128 left Polly Wreford; 128 right Polly Wreford; 129 left Polly Wreford; 129 right Polly Wreford; 130 Ebury Press/Laurence Dutton; 131 Ebury Press/Laurence Dutton; 132-133 Ebury Press/Laurence Dutton; 134 left Ebury Press/Michael Newton; 134 black and white Ebury Press/Laurence Dutton; 135 Ebury Press/Michael Newton; 136 David Brittain; 137 Polly Wreford; 138-139 Tevor Richards; 140-141 Polly Wreford; 142 Polly Wreford; 143 Polly Wreford; 144 courtesy of Ikea; 145 bottom Polly Wreford; 145 top Polly Wreford; 145 right Polly Wreford; 146 courtesy of Ikea; 147 top Polly Wreford; 147 right Polly Wreford; 147 bottom courtesy of Ikea

147-151 Ebury Press/Debbie Patterson; 152 Ebury Press/Michael Newton; 152 black and white Ebury Press/Debbie Patterson; 153 Ebury Press/Michael Newton; 154 Spike Powell; 155 Peter Aprahamian; 156 courtesy of Appeal Blinds; 157 Harry Cory-Wright; 158-159 Debbie Patterson; 160 left Pia Tryde; 160 right Polly Wreford; 161 left Pia Tryde; 161 right Pia Tryde; 162-163 Simon Brown; 165 Polly Wreford; 166 Ebury Press/Michael Newton; 167 Marianne Majerus; 168 Ebury Press/Michael Newton; 169 courtesy of Laura Ashley; 170 Ebury Press/Michael Newton; 171 Mark Bolton; 172 Ebury Press/Michael Newton; 174 Ebury Press/Michael Newton; 175 Mark Luscombe-Whyte; 176 Ebury Press/Michael Newton; 177 Debi Treloar; 179 Polly Wreford; 180 Ebury Press/Michael Newton; 181 Simon Brown; 182 Ebury Press/Michael Newton; 184 Ebury Press/Michael Newton; 185 Simon Brown; 186 Ebury Press/Michael Newton; 187 Polly Wreford; 188 Ebury Press/Michael Newton; 189 Polly Wreford; 190 Ebury Press/Michael Newton; 191 courtesy of Smeg (UK) Ltd; 192 Ebury Press/Michael Newton; 193 Christopher Drake; 194

Ebury Press/Michael Newton; 196 Ebury Press/Michael Newton; 197 Polly Wreford; 198 courtesy of CP Hart; 199 Simon Brown

200 Ebury Press/Michael Newton; 201 Brian Harrison; 203 Simon Brown; 204 Ebury Press/Michael Newton; 205 Polly Wreford; 206 courtesy of Laura Ashley plc; 207 Simon Brown; 208 Simon Brown; 209 Simon Brown; 210 Ebury Press/Michael Newton; 211 Simon Brown; 212 courtesy of Laura Ashley plc; 213 Simon Brown; 214 Ebury Press/Michael Newton; 215 courtesy of Harlequin; 216 Simon Brown; 217 Simon Brown; 218 Simon Brown; 219 Polly Wreford; 220 Ebury Press/Michael Newton; 221 Rosemary Weller; 222 Peter Aprahamian; 223 Polly Wreford; 224 Pia Tryde; 225 courtesy of Ikea; 226 courtesy of The Iron Bed Co; 227 Simon Brown; 228-229 courtesy of Elgin & Hall; 231 Debbie Patterson; 232 courtesy of Coloroll; 234 Nadia MacKenzie; 236 courtesy of Elgin & Hall; 239 Peter Aprahamian; 240 courtesy of Elgin & Hall; 242 Simon Brown; 244 Mark Bolton; 247 Trevor Richards; 249 Ebury Press/Laurence Dutton

250 Ebury Press/Michael Newton; 251 courtesy of Laura Ashley plc; 253 Ebury Press/Michael Newton; 254 courtesy of World's End Tile Co; 258 Simon Brown; 259 Simon Brown; 261 Polly Wreford; 262 Polly Wreford; 267 Pia Tryde; 268 Peter Aprahamian; 273 courtesy of Jane Churchill; 274 Peter Aprahamian.

The publisher also thanks the following companies for supplying accessories for the special photography: Artisan, The Carpet Library, First Floor, The Holding Company, Philips Lighting, VV Rouleaux and World's End Tiles.

The Good Housekeeping Institute

The Good Housekeeping Institute was created in 1924 to provide readers of Good Housekeeping magazine with expert consumer advice and delicious, classic and contemporary easy-to-follow recipes. These ideals still hold true today. The Institute team are all experienced cooks, home economists and consumer researchers. They test the latest products in purpose-built, modern kitchens, where every recipe published in the magazine and its range of best-selling cookery books is developed and rigorously tested so that you can cook any GH recipe with confidence. When any new ingredient appears on supermarket shelves, you can be sure that GH has tried and tasted it way ahead and interpreted a food trend into a workable, stylish recipe.

Television crews and radio broadcast units are regular visitors to the renowned Institute kitchens, which have become a popular location for leading food and consumer programmes.

Good Housekeeping magazine's authority and experience go well beyond the kitchen and cooking. The Institute can also tell you the best buys in anything from wine to computers and luxury lingerie. The Good Housekeeping Institute is synonymous with quality and impartial advice, offering good value for the consumer. You can trust the authority